HARVARD EAST ASIAN MONOGRAPHS

106

Studies in the Modernization of
The Republic of Korea: 1945–1975

Financial Development in Korea, 1945–1978

North Korea

KYŎNGGI

Kŭmhwa

Sokch'o

East Sea

38°

38°

Ch'unch'ŏn

KANGWŎN

Kangnŭng

Ŭijŏngbu

Mukho
Pukp'yŏng

Samch'ŏk

Inch'ŏn

Seoul

Wŏnju

Chŏngsŏn

Yŏju

Suwŏn

37°

37°

Ansŏng

Ch'ungju

NORTH
CH'UNGCH'ŎNG

Ch'ŏnan

Ch'ŏngju

Ŭmsŏng

NORTH KYŎNGSANG

SOUTH
CH'UNGCH'ŎNG

Taejŏn

Yŏnmu

Changhang

Kimch'ŏn

P'ohang

36°

36°

Kunsan

I-ri

Okku

Chŏnju

Taegu

Kyŏngju

Yellow Sea

NORTH CHŎLLA

SOUTH KYŎNGSANG

Pŏpsŏngp'o

Chinju

Chinhae

Kwangju

Samch'ŏnp'o

Pusan

35°

35°

SOUTH CHŎLLA

Changsŭngp'o

Sunch'ŏn

Yosu

Mijo-ri

Mokp'o

Sin'gŭm-ni

34°

128°

129°

THE REPUBLIC OF KOREA

CHEJU ISLAND

Cheju

0 20 40 60 80 100 120 140 160
KILOMETERS

Sŏgwip'o

0   20   40   60   80   100
MILES

126°

127°

Studies in the Modernization of
The Republic of Korea: 1945–1975

Financial Development in Korea
1945-1978

DAVID C. COLE

AND

YUNG CHUL PARK

PUBLISHED BY
COUNCIL ON EAST ASIAN STUDIES
HARVARD UNIVERSITY

Distributed by
Harvard University Press
Cambridge, Massachusetts and London, England
1983

© Copyright 1983 by
The President and Fellows of
Harvard College

The Council on East Asian Studies at Harvard University publishes a monograph series
and, through the Fairbank Center for East Asian Research and the Japan Institute,
administers research projects designed to further scholarly understanding of
China, Japan, Korea, Vietnam, Inner Asia, and adjacent areas.

The Harvard Institute for International Development
is Harvard University's center for interdisciplinary research, teaching, and
technical assistance on the problems of modernization in less developed countries.

The Korea Development Institute
is an economic research center, supported in part by the Korean government,
that undertakes studies of the crucial development issues and prospects of Korea.

Library of Congress Cataloging in Publication Data

Cole, David Chamberlin, 1928–
Financial development in Korea, 1945–1978.

(Harvard East Asian monographs ; 106) (Studies in
the modernization of the Republic of Korea, 1945–1975)
Bibliography: p.
Includes index.
1. Finance—Korea (South)—History. 2. Korea (South)
—Economic conditions. I. Park, Yung Chul. II. Title.
III. Series. IV. Series: Studies in the modernization
of the Republic of Korea, 1945–1975.
HG187.K62C64 1983   332.1'09519'5   82-23267
ISBN 0-674-30147-1

Foreword

This is one of the studies on the economic and social modernization of Korea undertaken jointly by the Harvard Institute
for International Development and the Korea Development
Institute. The undertaking has twin objectives; to examine the
elements underlying the remarkable growth of the Korean
economy and the distribution of the fruits of that growth,
together with the associated changes in society and government;
and to evaluate the importance of foreign economic assistance,
particularly American assistance, in promoting these changes.
The rapid rate of growth of the Korean economy, matched in
the less developed world (apart from the oil exporters) only by
similar rates of growth in the neighboring East Asian economies
of Taiwan, Hong Kong, and Singapore, has not escaped the
notice of economists and other observers. Indeed there has been
fairly extensive analysis of the Korean case. This analysis, has

been mainly limited to macroeconomic phenomena; to the behavior of monetary, fiscal, and foreign-exchange magnitudes and to the underlying policies affecting these magnitudes. But there are elements other than these that need to be taken into account to explain what has happened. The development of Korean entrepreneurship has been remarkable; Korea has an industrious and disciplined labor force; the contribution of agricultural development both to overall growth and to the distribution of income requires assessment; the level of literacy and the expansion of secondary and higher education have made their mark; and the combination and interdependence of government and private initiative and administration have been remarkably productive. These aspects together with the growth of urban areas, changes in the mortality and fertility of the population and in public health, are the primary objects of study. It is hoped that they will provide the building blocks from which an overall assessment of modernization in Korea can be constructed.

Economic assistance from the United States and, to a lesser extent, from other countries, has made a sizable but as yet unevaluated contribution to Korean development. A desire to have an assessment undertaken of this contribution, with whatever successes or failures have accompanied the U.S. involvement, was one of the motives for these studies, which have been financed in part by the U.S. Agency for International Development and, in part, by the Korea Development Institute. From 1945 to date, U.S. AID has contributed more than $6 billion to the Korean economy. There has also been a substantial fallout from the $7 billion of U.S. military assistance. Most of the economic assistance was contributed during the period before 1965, and most of it was in the form of grants. In later years the amount of economic assistance has declined rapidly and most of it, though concessional, has been in the form of loans. Currently, except for a minor trickle, U.S. economic assistance has ceased. The period of rapid economic growth in Korea has been since 1963, and in Korea, as well as in other countries receiving foreign assistance, it is a commonplace that it is the receiving country that is overwhelmingly responsible for what growth, or absence of growth, takes place. Nevertheless, economic assistance to Korea was exceptionally large, and whatever contribution was in fact made by outsiders needs to be assessed. One of the studies, *The Developmental Role of the Foreign Sector and Aid,* deals with foreign assistance in macroeconomic terms. The contribution of economic assistance to particular sectors is considered in the other studies.

All the studies in this series have involved American and Korean collaboration. For some studies the collaboration has been close; for others less so. All the American participants have spent some time in Korea in the course of their research, and a number of Korean participants have visited the United States. Only a few of the American participants have been able to read and speak Korean and, in consequence, the collaboration of their colleagues in making Korean materials available has been invaluable. This has truly been a joint enterprise.

The printed volumes in this series will include studies on the growth and structural transformation of the Korean economy, the foreign sector and aid, urbanization, rural development, the role of entrepreneurship, population policy and demographic transition, and education. Studies focusing on several other topics—the financial system, the fiscal system, labor economics and industrial relations, health and social development—will eventually be available either in printed or mimeographed form. The project will culminate in a final summary volume on the economic and social development of Korea.

Edward S. Mason

Edward S. Mason
Harvard Institute
for International Development

Mahn Je Kim

Mahn Je Kim
President,
Korea Development Institute

A Note on Romanization

In romanizing Korean, we have used the McCune-Reischauer system and have generally followed the stylistic guidelines set forth by the Library of Congress. In romanizing the names of Koreans in the McCune-Reischauer system, we have put a hyphen between the two personal names, the second of which has not been capitalized. For the names of historical or political figures, well-known place names, and the trade names of companies, we have tried to follow the most widely used romanization. For works written in Korean, the author's name appears in McCune-Reischauer romanization, sometimes followed by the author's preferred romanization if he or she has published in English. For works by Korean authors in English, the author's name is written as it appears in the original publication, sometimes followed by the author's name in McCune-Reischauer romanization, especially if the author has published in Korean also. In ordering the elements of persons' names, we have adopted a Western sequence—family name first in all alphabetized lists, but last elsewhere. This is a sequence used by some, but by no means all, Koreans who write in English. To avoid confusion, however, we have imposed an arbitrary consistency upon varying practices. Two notable exceptions occur in references to President Park Chung Hee, and Chang Myon, for whom the use of the family name first seems to be established by custom and preference. Commonly recurring Korean words such as si (city) have not been italicized. Korean words in the plural are not followed by the letter "s." Finally, complete information on authors' names or companies' trade names was not always available; in these cases we have simply tried to be as accurate as possible.

Contents

Contents

Tables

Figures

Abbreviations

BOK	Bank of Korea
CD	certificate of deposit
CFFC	Central Federation of Fisheries Cooperatives
CNB	Citizens' National Bank
CPI	consumer price index
DMB	deposit money bank
EIB	Export-Import Bank of Korea
EPB	Economic Planning Board
FSP	Financial Stabilization Program
GNP	gross national product
IFC	investment and finance company
IMF	International Monetary Fund
KDB	Korea Development Bank
KDFC	Korea Development Finance Corporation
KEB	Korea Exchange Bank
KRB	Korea Reconstruction Bank
L/C	letter of credit
LDC	less-developed country
M_1	narrow money supply (currency plus demand deposits of the deposit money banks)
M_2	broad money supply (M_1 plus time and savings deposits at the deposit money banks)
MIB	Medium Industry Bank
MCI	Ministry of Commerce and Industry
MOF	Ministry of Finance
MPC	military payment certificate
MSFC	mutual savings and finance company
NACF	National Agricultural Cooperatives Federation

NIF	National Investment Fund
OFM	official financial market
PF	private finance companies
PL 480	Public Law 480
RFI	regulated financial institution
RFM	regulated financial market
RFS	regulated financial system
UFI	unregulated financial institution
UFM	unregulated financial market
UMM	unregulated money market
VAT	value-added tax
WPI	wholesale price index

Preface

This study has taken longer to ripen than most of the companion volumes in the series on Korea's modernization. At its inception, we thought we were in basic agreement as to both our conception of financial development and our perceptions of what had transpired in Korea. In the elaboration of the study, however, we discovered some minor differences, and it has taken time to work these out over such long distances. One factor contributing to our differences was that our periods of intense involvement in Korea's financial affairs were dissimilar, and this gave us divergent perspectives on what happened. One of us (Cole) was on the scene in the early 1950s and again in the 1960s, while the other (Park) has been a "participant observer" in the 1970s. While this has ultimately enriched the comprehensiveness and detail of our collective coverage of Korean history, we have each had to overcome the tendency to view Korean experience in terms of the problems and policies of "our decade." And the one thing that is clear in Korea's recent history is that there has been dramatic change, not only in the standard of living and the physical infrastructure, but also in the level of organizational and analytical capacity to deal with the problems of a modern economy. Similarly, the problems and the orientation of economic policy have changed, although the policy instruments and methods of implementation based upon direct intervention and strong suggestion have been more constant. But, because that policy framework operates so much through interpersonal contact rather than formal rules, ratios, and regulations, and departs so substantially from textbook notions of financial policy, it has been possible to gain a realistic understanding of the way the Korean financial system operates only after extensive study and involvement in it. We believe we have made some headway in achieving that kind of understanding, partly because we are now more aware of what we don't know. We have a sense of where the lacunae are in the statistics, and in some obscure markets we can guess who the main actors are, what the main motivations are for their action, and, in very rough terms, what the orders of magnitude of their activities are. For two authors of disparate background to reach such common understanding takes time.

In seeking to record the development of Korea's financial system and the contribution of that system to Korea's economic development, we have marshaled a considerable array of statistics and institutional description as background for the analysis. We hope that those who are looking for details on particular aspects of the Korean financial system will find what they seek. Those who are more interested in the analytical aspects may wish to skim over Chapters 2, 3, and 4 and parts of Chapter 8.

So much for explanation and apology. We also wish to express our appreciation to the many persons who have contributed to our learning and our research. To Hugh Patrick, Jack Gurley, and Edward Shaw, who played such active roles in conceptualizing the financial reforms in 1965. To Mahn Je Kim and Kwang Suk Kim, who worked with Gurley, Patrick, and Shaw fifteen years ago and have continued to take an active interest in financial research and financial policy over the years. To Kim Yong-hwan, Nam Duck-woo and Lee Seung-Yun, all Ministers of Finance, who have been both students of monetary policy and then forceful implementers of it. To Sang Wu Nam for his contribution to the discussion of capital markets in Chapter 3. To Il Sa-Kong and Leroy Jones, whose discussion and companion volume, *Government, Business, and Entrepreneurship in Economic Development,* has contributed to our understanding. To Don Lessard for his valuable comments on an earlier draft of this manuscript. To Millard Long for his always insightful comments on finance and development, and to Ron McKinnon for providing a foil on which to test and sharpen our divergent views. And, finally, to Edward Mason and Dwight Perkins for their questions, encouragement, and patience.

ONE

Theories of Financial Development
and the Relevance of Korean Experience

The financial sector of an economy consists of those entities that specialize in the buying and selling of financial claims. Primitive economies have very limited and simple financial systems, consisting only of some rudimentary form of money, such as beads or metal, and unwritten interpersonal claims. Modern, developed countries have highly complicated and differentiated financial structures, consisting of thousands of different types of financial instruments and institutions, with complex patterns of ownership and regulation of both institutions and markets.

Financial development has been described by Edward Shaw as a process of financial deepening in which "stocks of financial assets . . . grow relative to income . . . and their range of qualities widens. There is a lengthening of maturities, and a wider variety of debtor gains access to the financial markets."[1] In contrast to this emphasis on the growth and diversity of financial instruments, markets, and participants, other writers have focused on the emergence of modern types of financial institutions, such as central and development banks, securities, and money markets, as the harbingers of financial development.[2] While there is clear evidence that both financial instruments and institutions tend to grow and diversify in the process of economic development, there is little agreement on many questions of causality and of desirability. What are the best measures of the size and structure of the financial system and of financial development? What causes financial development? Does financial development contribute to economic development, or does a lagging financial sector impede economic development? Does inflation undermine financial development and diminish national savings? Is there some optimal level and structure of financial development? What are the determinants of optimality? Is it possible to have freely competitive financial markets, or are market imperfections and regulations inevitable? Does the pattern of ownership and control of the financial system affect the efficiency of the system, its contribution to economic development and to income distribution? How do the ownership and regulatory patterns of the financial system relate to the broader politico-economic structure of the country?

These are some of the critical questions about financial development and the structure of financial systems that have been receiving increased attention in the development literature. After years of neglect, a number of authors have recently attempted to devise improved measures of financial development to test whether variations in the size, structure, and organization of the financial system do make a difference.[3] A number of case studies have been undertaken that attempt to describe in detail the evolution of the financial systems of individual countries to see what evidence these cases offer on the theoretical issues.[4]

This volume is one more in the series of case studies. We have not tried to compare Korean experience with that of other countries to any great extent, leaving that to others. Rather, we have sought to describe in some detail the financial development, financial policy, and institutional arrangements in Korea and thereby to clarify some of the ambiguous interpretations of that history.

FUNCTIONS OF THE FINANCIAL SYSTEM

There are four generally agreed upon functions of a financial system. The first is to provide a medium of exchange and a store of value. As simple economies move beyond self-production and barter to increasing specialization and exchange, there is need for some means of payment that can be transmitted across space and time. In the early stages of development, some form of currency will usually suffice to meet this need, but, as transactions become larger and payments must be made over longer distances, in an increasingly complex and interdependent economy, there is a growing need for transferable deposits.

There have always been some alternative means for performing this payments function, such as the village store that supplies goods to farmers over the year in exchange for repayment at harvest time.[5] Recently, the use of credit cards has greatly reduced reliance on both currency and demand deposits for transactions purposes in developed countries. And, in some countries, when the domestic currency has become an unstable or unreliable medium of exchange or short-term store of value, foreign monies or precious metals have been used as substitutes.

The second major function of the financial system is to mobilize the savings of surplus units and make those savings available to investors—to intermediate between savers and investors.[6] This role also grows with economic development, as the needs for investment expand and the lumpiness of investment units increases. Also, as incomes rise, there is a tendency in most countries to increase the proportion saved and to reduce the proportion directly invested in own-capital.

Here, too, there are alternative mechanisms—or in Gurley-Shaw terminology—alternative technologies, for mobilizing and allocating savings. One way is through the fiscal process of taxation and government spending. Another is through self-financing by enterprises out of current surplus. A third is through inflationary means that allocate resources to investors and force involuntary savings indiscriminately from consumers. A fourth is through reliance on foreign aid or foreign intermediaries, which has its counterpart in some countries, such as Switzerland and Singapore, that specialize in international intermediation and whose financial systems are very large by international standards.

The third function of the financial system is the transformation and distribution of risk.[7] Different financial assets have differing degrees of risk, and financial institutions specialize in analyzing risk and combining assets in packages that offer savers varying combinations of risk and return to satisfy savers' preferences. As economies become more complex, it is increasingly difficult for savers to obtain sufficient information and make accurate assessments of the degree of risk involved in different financial claims. Accordingly they tend to rely increasingly on the financial intermediaries to make those assessments for them. This reduces the risk for both savers and borrowers and thus leads to both more savings and greater willingness to invest.

Much of the regulation and intervention by government in the financial sector is intended to reduce the risk to savers. Deposit insurance schemes, restrictions on types of assets that can be held by different kinds of financial insitutions, requirements for full disclosure of information by corporations issuing financial claims are all indicative of government efforts to reduce risk. When these fail, many governments either bail out or take over the faltering institutions. On the other hand, there have been instances when governments have acted to increase the riskiness of claims on institutions they did not favor, as a way of discouraging savers from holding these claims.

A fourth function of the financial system is to affect the overall level of prices and output. The financial sector, by providing a numeraire (a unit of account), in which the prices of other goods are measured, also makes it possible for the prices of other goods to fluctuate relative to the numeraire. The way in which the financial system is managed thus affects the stability of the overall price level in the short run and the secular trend of prices over the longer run. Expansion of the supply of money more rapidly than the rise in the demand for it leads to a bidding up of the price of other goods and a decline in the value of money, which in turn tends to reduce the demand for money. Short-run fluctuations in the price level are generally viewed as undesirable in that they increase uncertainty, reduce investment and the level of output. There is more controversy about whether the longer-run trend of prices should be gently rising, constant, or even declining. Some have argued that a moderately rising price trend helps transfer resources from lagging to leading sectors and is an inherent feature of structural change.[8] Others have argued that a rising trend results in a permanent depressant on the financial system because of resistance by financial institutions, especially the monetary institutions, to paying an inflation premium to depositors.[9] Probably the worst situation is to have frequent shifting of targets between some positive price trend and a constant trend, because this in itself creates instability.[10]

There are other means for stabilizing output and price trends than sole reliance on the financial system. Fiscal instruments, balance of payments instruments, and direct controls are the major alternatives. In the years of the Great Depression, in developed countries there was a strong belief that financial measures were ineffective in dealing with the problem. In more recent times, when inflation has been the dominant problem, some have argued that finance should be the primary instrument. But there are others who maintain that a combination of fiscal, financial, and direct controls is needed to deal with the recent combination of rising prices, declining output, and exceptional pressures from the balance of payments. This combination is a relatively novel experience for most developed countries but has been a frequent problem in less-developed countries.[11]

In the following chapters, we shall attempt to assess how well the Korean financial system has fulfilled these four basic functions.

THE RELEVANCE OF KOREAN EXPERIENCE

A thorough review of Korea's financial development is useful on several counts. First, the country's experience with modernization of the financial system is both lengthy and well documented. The first modern bank was established over one hundred years ago, and financial statistics have been available since 1910. Second, the nature of Korean financial experience has been highly varied, with strains of Chinese, Japanese, and American influence. Also, there have been periods of rapid financial growth and periods of decline. Many different financial policies have been tried over the years; some have succeeded, some have failed. And many new institutions have been launched, with mixed results.

An overriding consideration, however, is the fact that Korean experience has been cited in many recent writings on financial development as support for one or another of the new theories about the relationship between finance and development.[12] Just as frequently, the Korean evidence has been challenged or has been used to support an opposing theory.[13] Thus, it seems important to look at the evidence to see whether it is being misinterpreted, or simply drawn from different time periods. In the process, we shall try to present a more accurate set of lessons from the Korean experience.

One example of the ambiguity of Korean experience was Arthur Bloomfield's proposals for institutional reform as a way of rescuing the Korean financial system from the condition of near collapse he perceived it to be in 1949–1950.[14] Bloomfield recommended the establishment of a strong autonomous central

bank and the transfer of commercial banks to private ownership to promote competition and efficiency. His principal policy recommendation was for strict control over the money
supply to stop inflation. Implementation of his recommendations was interrupted by the Korean War, but, when they were
finally all put into effect from 1957 to 1960, prices were stabilized and the financial system did grow moderately, but the
economy practically stopped growing. Nevertheless, Bloomfield's
institutional and policy recommendations have been reiterated
down through the years and at times seriously debated within
the government.[15] The question to be investigated is whether
the institutional reforms of the 1950s were really effective or
largely cosmetic, and whether they have had any real impact on
financial or economic growth. More generally, is this type of institutional reform, calling for diffusion of economic power,
compatible with, or feasible under, an authoritarian political
system?

Another kind of institutional reform issue has been confronted in Korea over the years in connection with the so-called
unorganized money markets. U Tun Wai, writing in the mid-
1950s, said, "In underdeveloped countries . . . unorganized
money markets also play a very important role, and any study
of credit conditions in these countries that is to be adequate
must be extended to cover the unorganized as well as the organized markets."[16] He went on to describe the unorganized
markets as very imperfect, non-competitive, having limited information or interaction within the unorganized markets or
with the organized markets, charging exhorbitant interest rates,
and exploiting the poorer members of the society. He also saw
them as undermining the effectiveness of monetary policy.
Given all these negative features, it is not surprising that he recommended a number of measures for curtailing the unorganized
markets and replacing them with services from the organized
sector.

The nature of the so-called unorganized sector in Korea appears to be quite different from this stereotype. It has been

characterized as relatively competitive, efficient, and quick to respond to changing circumstances; also as serving large as well as small borrowers, capable of amassing large quantities of money on short notice, and closely tied into the modern parts of the financial system.[17] On the other hand, it does seem to conform to U Tun Wai's description in having been large relative to the organized sector and possibly neutralizing some of the impact of monetary policy.

The Korean government carried out two major assaults on what we prefer to call the informal or unregulated money markets, first in 1961 and again in 1972. Both assaults disrupted the markets for a period of time but failed to impair them permanently. The markets soon resumed their roles as important intermediaries between a broad spectrum of savers and borrowers. While they may, in one sense, have counteracted the influence of monetary policy by facilitating offsetting changes in the velocity of money, they nevertheless seem to have helped the economy absorb rather abrupt changes in policy without precipitating financial crises. Thus, we agree ultimately with U Tun Wai on the point that the role of the informal institutions needs to be assessed very carefully to determine whether they have been a positive or negative factor in Korean financial and economic development.

A third example of financial development measures tested in Korea and differently assessed were the attempts to "get the financial prices right" in the mid-1960s and thereby to promote financial deepening. Adoption of a floating exchange rate and positive real interest rates on bank deposits in 1965 has been cited by Gilbert Brown, Edward Shaw, and Ronald McKinnon as a leading example of financial liberalization that brought about high growth of the financial system, a rise in the savings rate, and more efficient allocation of investment.[18] On the other hand, Homer Jones, writing about the same period, said, "The single greatest cause of financial failure (in Korea) has been unwillingness to permit freedom of interest rate determination. . . . The managed interest rates have promoted inflation while the inflation has made still more unrealistic the managed interest rates."[19] A third interpretation of this experience was that the financial reform of 1965 mainly resulted in a transfer of savings from the informal financial institutions and from abroad into increased holdings of commercial bank time deposits, so that the recorded rapid increases in the size of the financial system and private domestic savings were largely statistical fiction. Had there been better statistics on the unregulated financial markets and on foreign asset holdings, these shifts would have been perceived for what they were.

We shall need to look carefully at the various measures of the size of the financial sector including, where possible, the informal sector; and then to assess the rate of growth of the financial system over time as well as the determinants of that growth.

Many writers have said that inflation is inimical, not only to financial growth, but, more important, to economic growth, and Korean officials have been told repeatedly over the years by "experts" from many sources that they couldn't hope to achieve a high rate of economic growth if they didn't control their inflation.[20] Despite these dire warnings, the Korean economy has grown at very rapid rates for fifteen years (1963-1978), during which the rate of inflation, as measured by the wholesale price index, has ranged from 6.4 to 42.1 percent and averaged 14.4 percent. We shall review this experience to try to determine whether there has in fact been any relation between the rates of inflation and overall economic growth.

A similar warning has been expressed over the years to the effect that extensive government involvement in decisions concerning the allocation of credit by the financial system would inevitably lead to corruption, misallocation, and inefficiency.[21] Despite these warnings and periodic expressions of intent to disengage, the Korean government has remained deeply involved in the credit allocation process for the past thirty years. Also, the interest rates on most types of loans from the government-owned or dominated financial institutions have been low in nominal terms and negative in real terms, so that they have not been an effective instrument for rationing credit to the more efficient borrowers. What have been the consequences for corruption and resource allocation?

Shaw defines financial developments as a widening of the range of financial instruments and a growing involvement in financial markets.[22] Clearly, Korean businesses have been heavily dependent on external finance for funding much of their investment as well as current production. The Korean government has been encouraged to broaden the range of financial instruments, to develop capital markets, and to encourage investment in primary securities.[23] These measures have been implemented with considerable energy, and the results have been viewed by some as quite successful, by others as disappointing.[24] Which view is more accurate?

Finally, there is the question of whether the financial structure has been consistent with the structure of the economy and of the political system. Gurley and Shaw have suggested that there is such a thing as an optimal mix of savings-investment technologies that changes over time and is conditioned by both economic and political criteria.[25] Ranis sees the financial structure as depending mainly on the basic development strategy or stage of development of the country.[26]

He suggested that, as developing countries move out of colonial agrarianism into a primary-import-substitution phase, the overriding policy objective becomes the creation and expansion of the industrial sector, and of the services and overhead required to facilitate that expansion. This, in turn, necessitates a shift of domestic as well as foreign financial resources to the industrial sector. Financial institutions and interest rates can be utilized as important instruments in the government's effort to achieve this objective. The banking system contributes to this process by assuming a submissive-partner role to the government effort to force some saving through inflation and to shift the functional distribution of income in favor of profits. The interest rates in the organized or regulated financial sector are likely to be kept below an equilibrium level in an effort to encourage investment while the limited credit available is channeled into the new industries. Thus, during the primary-import-substitution period, the financial sector is characterized by a continued state of repression and disequilibrium.

When the primary-import-substitution phase runs its course, the developing countries are faced with the decision of moving either on to an export-substitution phase (that is, substitution of manufactured exports for primary exports), as Taiwan and Korea did in the 1950s and 1960s and Japan during the Meiji period, or to a secondary-import-substitution phase of intermediate and capital goods, consumer durables, and processing industries, as India, the Philippines, and Brazil did.

According to Ranis, it is preferable for the labor-surplus developing countries to follow the path of export substitution. These economies are, by the end of the primary-import-substitution stage, ready to expose themselves to competition in the international markets for industrial consumer goods. They are then able to shift from traditional land-based to non-traditional labor-based exports, and to a substantial increase in the level of material interaction between agriculture and non-agriculture.

The direction of the general policy package to bring about this change in the production and trade pattern is gradual liberalization of a number of markets previously controlled by government. One would thus expect a monetary reform designed to raise interest rates to realistic levels and to reduce subsidies and the role of credit rationing in investment decisions.

As the economy becomes more export-oriented and efficiency-oriented, there is an increasing need for expansion and specialization of the financial intermediaries to meet the financial requirements of differentiated industrial activities and the portfolio preferences of increasingly sophisticated savers. So, during the export-orientation phase, all the ratios of financial assets to GNP are expected to rise, reflecting substantial financial growth.

Finally, according to Ranis, although an export-oriented strategy appears to be more suitable for many of the developing countries, most have nevertheless continued to pursue import substitution in the capital-intensive intermediate and capital-goods industries. In such economies, the financial system generally retains the repressive characteristics of the primary-import-substitution period and fails to provide incentives for savings, although the need to generate and channel savings to the new industries is even greater than before. As a result, the economic authorities are likely to continue to resort to inflationary financing and to foreign borrowing. Inflation together with the low interest rates then constricts financial growth, which, in turn, impedes industrialization. Frequently, international lenders from the developed countries have been willing to provide financing for such investments, despite the developing countries' growing foreign indebtedness and limited prospects for repayment.

This model of financial development is obviously drawn with Korean experience in mind, but is it a relevant standard for assessing how well the Korean financial structure has fit the needs of the times?

These are the kinds of questions we shall be trying to address in the remainder of this study.

TWO

The Financial System: Size, Structure, and Patterns of Intermediation

The modern financial system in Korea has gone through two cycles of growth and diversification—the first under the Japanese from 1910 to 1940, and the second beginning in the mid-1960s. In between these two growth periods were two decades of disruption, inflation, and repression when the modern financial system shrank back down to the level that existed at the beginning of the colonial era. Between 1965 and 1970, the system grew rapidly in overall size and, since 1970, although growth has slowed, it has achieved a more diversified structure than it had under the Japanese. Where before it was basically an appendage of the Japanese system and served mainly the interests of Japanese business, it is now an independent national system with linkages to the capital and money markets of the world. These long cycles of financial expansion and contraction were roughly concurrent with periods of growth and decline or stagnation in the real economy, as described in the companion volume by Kim and Roemer.[1]

In this chapter, we shall present several perspectives on the size and structure of the Korean financial system in accounting terms, and show how it has intermediated between savers and investors in recent years. In the following chapters we shall take up the institutional evolution and structure of the system.

MEASURES OF SIZE AND STRUCTURE

There are a number of ways to measure the size of a financial system. One is to look at the liability side of the balance sheet of the financial institutions; another is to look at the asset side. Since total assets are supposed to equal total liabilities plus net worth, the difference should be equal to net worth, usually a rather small item relative to total liabilities for most financial institutions. The bulk of the liabilities of financial institutions consists of funds borrowed from others, either in the form of deposits or in exchange for other types of claims. The assets, on the other hand, consist mainly of loans or other types of financial claims, with fixed assets making up a rather small portion of total assets. Thus, in using the asset statistics, it is necessary to distinguish between financial and fixed assets, whereas, for the liability side, the distinction between liabilities and net worth is important. In either case, the financial assets and liabilities are the dominant elements.

Another problem that arises in trying to measure the total size of a financial system is the double counting due to claims of one financial institution on another. In general, the financial statistics for most countries do a better job of eliminating the double counting on the liability side than on the asset side. As Goldsmith has indicated in his study of financial development comparing the experience of thirty-five countries, clearing up the duplication in the asset accounts is a major undertaking.[2] Gurley's studies have generally used the liability statistics.[3] In this analysis of the Korean system we shall use both assets and liabilities because they reveal somewhat different pictures of the role and size of the system.

The third and most critical problem in measuring the size of the financial system arises because part of the system is invisible. At least it is not recorded in the official financial statistics and, therefore, is commonly ignored completely or, at best, mentioned in a qualifying footnote. We are, of course, referring to the unregulated or informal financial institutions that, as mentioned in the previous chapter, often play such a critical role in developing countries. The lack of consistent and comprehensive information on these unregulated institutions leaves a serious hole in the financial statistics; the problem is compounded by the fact that, for most countries, there is no basis for estimating the size of the hole, that is, there are no aggregative data on either the assets or liabilities of these informal institutions at any point in time, much less for changes over time. Fortunately, from the analytical perspective of this study, there was a required recording of the financial assets of the unregulated financial institutions in Korea in 1972 and, as described in Chapter 4, this provides a peg on which to hang some estimates of the overall size of the Korean informal financial sector as well as changes over time. These are admittedly shaky, imprecise estimates, but they are incorporated at some points in the analysis of this chapter to give an approximation of the size and structure of the total financial system.

HISTORICAL GROWTH OF BANK LIABILITIES

A first approximation of financial development, as measured by the financial liabilities of the modern banking institutions, is given in Table 1. It shows the currency in circulation and the total deposits of all banking institutions located within the whole of Korea at five-year intervals from 1910 to 1935 and then within South Korea from 1955 to 1978. Comparable statistics for 1940, 1945, and 1950 are either distorted or not available, due to the wartime conditions in those years. To give

TABLE 1 Relation of Financial Institution Liabilities to Output, Korea 1910–1978

	Commodity Output	Currency in Circulation	Demand Deposits	Other Deposits	Total Deposits
All Korea (million wŏn)					
1911	339	32	15	5	20
1915	400	43	28	8	36
1920	1,331	98	104	47	151
1925	1,297	84	100	139	239
1930	846	99	107	227	334
1935	1,469	127	201	437	638
South Korea (billion wŏn)					
1955	65	6	3	0	3
1960	128	14	9	9	18
1965	463	32	34	46	80
1970	1,308	134	174	636	800
1975	5,050	507	675	2,135	2,798
1977	8,424	953	1,219	3,927	5,418
1978	10,988	1,364	1,349	6,361	7,710

TABLE 1 (continued)

| | | Ratios to Commodity Output | | | | |
	Currency	Demand Deposits	Other Deposits	Narrow Money	Total Deposits	Broad Money
All Korea						
1911	.09	.04	.01	.14	.06	.12
1915	.11	.07	.02	.18	.09	.20
1920	.07	.08	.04	.15	.12	.19
1925	.07	.08	.11	.14	.18	.25
1930	.12	.13	.27	.25	.39	.51
1935	.09	.14	.30	.22	.44	.52
South Korea						
1955	.09	.05	.00	.13	.05	.13
1960	.11	.07	.07	.18	.14	.25
1965	.07	.07	.10	.14	.17	.24
1970	.10	.13	.49	.24	.61	.71
1975	.10	.13	.42	.23	.55	.65
1977	.11	.14	.47	.26	.64	.75
1978	.12	.12	.58	.25	.70	.83

Sources: Currency in Circulation, 1910–1940, BOK, *Annual Economic Review*, 1949. Deposit data for 1910–1940 are from the Government General of Korea, *Korea Statistics Yearbook*. Commodity output is the value added in agriculture, forestry, fisheries, mining and manufacturing. From 1910–1940 from Sang-Chul Suh. From 1955–1978, BOK *Economic Statistics Yearbooks*.

a measure of the relative size of these financial liabilities, we have used the statistics on total commodity output as estimated by Sang-Chul Suh for the Japanese period,[4] and as derived from the national product accounts for the post-war years. The ratio of commodity output to total GNP has remained fairly constant throughout these later years, averaging about 55 percent, so there appears to be no significant distortion from using commodity output as a surrogate for GNP.

As shown in Table 1, currency in circulation has ranged from 7 to 12 percent, but has remained close to 10 percent of the value of commodity output (or 5 percent of GNP) throughout the whole period from 1910 to 1978. (This was not the case between 1940 and 1945, when both currency and demand deposits rose to relatively high levels, as the Japanese used credit expansion to finance the war effort against China and imposed price controls and forced savings campaigns to restrain the resulting inflationary pressures.) Demand deposits exhibited some interesting parallels in the Japanese and post-war periods. From 1910 through 1925 the ratio of demand deposits to commodity output rose gradually from 4 to 8 percent. It was at the same level from 1955 to 1965. In the 1930s and again in the 1970s, the ratio was 13–14 percent.

Other bank deposits, which are mainly time deposits, experienced substantial and fairly steady growth throughout the Japanese period and then disappeared almost completely during the two war-induced inflations. They recovered somewhat in 1960–1965 and then jumped to very high levels after 1965.

Viewed in broad terms, these ratios of modern banking sector liabilities to output exhibited the following features:

1) In the early years of both the Japanese period and post-war independence, the modern financial system was functioning at a low level. Money supply, narrowly defined, was roughly 15 percent of commodity output (or 7 percent of GNP) and evolved from about two-thirds currency and one-third demand deposits to half and half. Other deposits were inconsequential to start

with in both periods, but grew to 10 percent of commodity output near the end of these low-level phases.

2) There were two periods of rapid expansion after 1925 and 1965, in which time deposits jumped dramatically and demand deposits also increased significantly. The size of this part of the financial system in the 1970s was substantially greater than that of the 1930s—ratios of 70–80 percent as opposed to 50 percent.

Another perspective on the relative size of the formal financial system—as measured from the liability side—is to compare it with that of other countries. As Gurley has shown, per capita income is a significant variable in explaining the ratio of M_2 (money broadly defined) to GNP. Our own investigations have shown that there are regional differences in this pattern and that the less-developed countries of Asia, North Africa, and Europe have a substantially higher ratio than do those of Latin America and the rest of Africa. Using a regression based on twenty-nine less-developed countries of Asia, North Africa, and Europe, Table 2 shows that the M_2/GNP ratio for post-war Korea was well below the norm for its per capita income level from 1955 to 1965. Between 1965 and 1969, the Korean ratio rose sharply and was slightly above the norm through 1973, but then it dropped back below the norm by 1975 and continued that way through 1978. Thus, the size of Korea's modern financial system, at least as measured in terms of bank liabilities, has tended to be below the average of other countries at comparable levels of development as measured by per capita GNP.

GROWTH OF FINANCIAL ASSETS

Turning to the asset side of the financial institution balance sheet brings us to a somewhat broader perspective, because the several sources of financial statistics—business financial statements, flow of funds accounts—give a more comprehensive picture of the available sources of finance. Unfortunately, these

TABLE 2 Comparison of Korean M_2/GNP Ratio to Norm for Sample of Asian and African Countries

	Actual Korea (%)	Norm[a] (%)	Per Capita GNP[b]
1955	8.8	23.3	98
1960	10.4	24.1	103
1965	12.1	27.4	131
1969	32.7	31.8	179
1973	38.6	36.4	249
1975	32.3	37.5	269
1978	34.8	41.7	364

Source: International Monetary Fund, International Financial Statistics.

Notes: [a]Norm based on regression of 75 observations on 29 low to middle income countries in Asia, North Africa, and Europe.

$$\frac{M_2}{GNP} = \underset{(-3.73)}{-.4115} + \underset{(6.90)}{.1406} \log y \qquad R^2 = .38$$

(Numbers in parentheses are t statistics.)

[b]Per capita income of Korea in U.S. dollars of 1967 purchasing power ($= y$).

more extensive statistical sources are available only for the post-war years. For the Japanese period, the data cover only the regulated financial institutions. For reasons that will be discussed in Chapter 3, the banks probably occupied a much more dominant position during the colonial era than in recent years.

An overview of the size and structure of financial assets of both the regulated financial institutions (RFIs) and unregulated financial institutions (UFIs) is provided in Table 3. As with the liability measures, the estimates of commodity output are used as a denominator for comparing the Japanese and recent periods. The main types of financial assets included in the table are the regular bank loans of all banks, the bank guarantees of repayment of foreign loans, which are a measure of the level of borrowings from abroad (see Chapter 3 for a discussion of the guarantee system), and the loans of the unregulated financial institutions which are based on the estimates presented in

Chapter 4. Loans of other financial institutions include insurance companies, savings institutions, private finance companies, and investment banking institutions. The loans from the Bank of Korea to other banks and to the government are excluded.

The growth of bank loans generally paralleled the growth of bank liabilities, as presented in Table 1. The levels were modest in the early years of both the colonial and the post-war periods, and then rose rapidly after 1925 and again after 1965. The major difference in the post-war period has been the loans in foreign currencies and bank guarantee of foreign loans, which shot up from practically nothing in 1960 to exceed the level of bank loans by 1970. Other regulated financial institutions, especially finance companies, dealing in short-term bills, have taken over some of the role of the UFIs. Also, in recent years, securities have become increasingly important, but the figures on their activities have not been included in Table 3.

Looking at the total of all kinds of loans by financial institutions relative to commodity output, we see that the levels of 1970–1978 were more than twice those of 1930–1940. The main difference is in the foreign-currency loans and foreign-loan guarantees. In the earlier period, loans to Korea from Japanese sources were mainly channeled through the banks, so the bank loan figures undoubtedly include substantial amounts of external financing, and are therefore roughly comparable to the more recent figures for loans plus guarantees. Thus, it appears that the financial institutions provided, or facilitated through guarantees, a significantly higher level of financing relative to output in recent years than they did under the Japanese.

STOCKS OF FINANCIAL ASSETS AND LIABILITIES

A third perspective on the size and structure of the regulated financial system is derived from the flow of funds and financial asset-and-liability accounts, which are available since 1962.

TABLE 3 Relation of Loans and Loan Guarantees of All Financial Institutions to Commodity Output, 1910–1975

	Commodity Output	Domestic Bank Loans[a]		Loans in Foreign Currency and Bank Guarantees of Foreign Loans		UFI Loans		Loans of Other Financial Institutions		Total Loans as % of Output
	Amount	Amount	%	Amount	%	Amount	%	Amount	%	
(million wŏn)										
1910	238	38.7	16.3							16.3
1915	400	61.7	15.4							15.4
1920	1,331	280.9	21.1							21.1
1925	1,297	449.0	34.6							34.6
1930	846	644.6	76.2							76.2
1935	1,469	960.2	65.4							65.4
1940	2,919	2,411.0	82.6							82.6
(billion wŏn)										
1955	64.6	6.9	10.7							10.7
1960	128.1	40.2	31.4	0.6	0.5	10.0[b]	7.8			40.0
1965	463.3	108.9	23.5	75.3	16.3	43.8	9.5	10.0	2.2	51.4
1970	1,308.3	851.5	65.1	1,198.4	91.6	250.0	19.1	109.1	8.3	184.1

TABLE 3 (continued)

	Commodity Output	Domestic Bank Loans[a]		Loans in Foreign Currency and Bank Guarantees of Foreign Loans		UFI Loans		Loans of Other Financial Institutions		Total Loans as % of Output
	Amount	Amount	%	Amount	%	Amount	%	Amount	%	
1975	5,050.4	3,483.4	69.0	4,198.9	83.1	500[b]	9.9	1,194.2	23.6	185.6
1978	10,987.7	8,052.5	73.3	11,562.0	105.2	1,000.0[b]	9.1	3,680.5	33.5	221.1

Sources: Commodity output is the value added in agriculture, forestry, fisheries, mining, and manufacturing. From 1910–1940 from Sang-Chul Suh. From 1955–1975, BOK, Economic Statistics Yearbooks, BOK, Monthly Economic Statistics, 1979, 1–3. Loan data for 1910–1940 are from the Government General of Korea, Korea Statistics Yearbook, thereafter from the BOK; UFI loans are from Chapter 4.

Notes: [a]Excludes loans of the Korea Development Bank.
[b]Estimates

These accounts are prepared by the Bank of Korea and give information on both the types of financial claims and institutions issuing or holding such claims. Tables 4 and 5 give the nominal values of financial assets and their ratio to GNP for the recent seventeen-year period of rapid financial and economic growth. It should be kept in mind that these statistics generally exclude the UFIs.

Table 5, the most informative for analytical purposes, highlights a number of aspects of Korea's recent financial development. The ratio of total financial assets to GNP reached a low of 0.82 in 1964, increased by more than 150 percent to 2.12 in 1972, then leveled off over the next six years. In the early years, domestic financial assets accounted for the lion's share of total financial assets, but foreign assets (that is, foreign-held claims on Korean enterprises) grew steadily and reached levels of over 45 percent of GNP and 20 percent of total financial assets in 1975. Of the domestic financial assets, the proportion held by financial institutions has increased relative to that of non-financial institutions (that is, government, corporations, and households). The financial asset holdings of both financial institutions and non-financial institutions more than doubled as a share of GNP between 1965 and 1972 and then leveled off. The increased financial asset holdings of the non-financial institutions, which were mainly the liabilities of financial institutions, made possible the increased holdings of assets by the financial institutions.

Two key categories of financial assets are also shown in the table: M_2, or broad money, and stocks and bonds. The M_2 ratio has oscillated over time, rising from 1960 to 1962 in what turned out to be an excessive monetary expansion that then led to inflation and a decline in the ratio over the next two years. Thereafter came five years of rapid growth in the M_2 ratio, mainly in the form of increased time deposits. The ratio peaked at 0.39 in 1973 and declined thereafter in the face of renewed inflation. The stock and bond ratio has also been somewhat cyclical. It doubled between the low point of 0.12 in 1966 and

0.12 in 1966 and 0.25 in 1972, then declined for two years and rose again after 1975. Two of the Korean government's major programs for financial development, to be discussed in later chapters, have been to stimulate the demand for time deposits (from 1965 through 1969) and, subsequently, the demand for corporate securities.

These financial ratios can also be compared with the evidence from other countries to get a sense of whether Korea has a relatively large or small financial system. Goldsmith has calculated the ratios of *the assets of financial institutions* to GNP for thirty-four countries in 1963, as shown in Table 6.[5] He finds an average ratio for developed countries of 1.56 and for less-developed countries of 0.64. This would compare with a Korean ratio of 0.33 in 1963 and 0.80 in recent years. Goldsmith's less-developed countries are mostly on the upper levels of that category as can be seen from Table 6. This suggests that, in recent years, the Korean ratios are somewhat above the norm. Also, there is a question in the Korean case as to whether the foreign financial assets should be added to the domestic financial assets of financial institutions. These foreign assets are mainly loans of foreign financial institutions that are guaranteed by the domestic financial institutions and therefore represent a source of financing provided through the domestic institutions. If these foreign financial assets are included, they raise the ratio of total assets of financial institutions to GNP to 1.2, quite high by comparison with other developing countries but still well below the Japanese level of 2.2 in 1963.

Gurley suggests that ratios of *total financial assets* to GNP in the range of 3 or 4 to 1 are characteristic of developed countries, the difference depending mainly on the degree of separation between savers and investors. The Korean ratio of 2:2 is still well below this level but not abnormally so, given Korea's level of per capita income.[6]

While these several comparisons are quite crude, they do indicate that the level of financial development in Korea in the 1970s was moderately high relative to countries at comparable

TABLE 4 The Financial Structure of Korea: Nominal Financial Assets, 1960–1978
(billion wŏn)

	(I) Total Financial Assets	(II) Domestic Financial Assets (II=I-VIII)	(III) Assets of Financial Institutions	(IV) Assets of Non-Financial Institutions (IV=II-III)	(V) Money (M₂)	(VI) Indirect Securities[a]	(VII) Stocks & Bonds	(VIII) Foreign Claims
1960					25.70			
1961					41.25			
1962	374.90	362.88	150.90	211.98	51.63	73.35	56.29	12.02
1963	452.84	426.84	163.60	263.24	55.38	78.17	84.69	26.00
1964	585.84	527.97	204.72	323.25	63.63	93.34	106.88	57.87
1965	720.37	654.13	251.15	402.98	97.11	137.36	116.00	66.25
1966	996.65	876.38	344.18	532.20	156.95	208.83	127.00	120.27
1967	1,569.61	1,376.63	538.64	837.99	253.15	328.17	156.38	201.98
1968	2,371.43	2,027.14	801.86	1,225.28	436.63	539.06	247.80	344.30
1969	3,629.53	3,038.80	1,212.28	1,826.52	704.58	834.91	392.00	590.73
1970	4,814.76	3,983.98	1,624.17	2,359.81	897.79	1,054.25	537.22	830.78
1971	6,421.41	5,144.86	2,104.00	3,040.86	1,084.91	1,293.31	637.62	1,276.55
1972	8,493.53	6,906.26	2,841.40	4,064.86	1,451.78	1,755.48	992.15	1,587.28
1973	11,029.74	9,154.98	3,726.91	5,428.07	1,973.58	2,442.04	1,302.09	1,874.76
1974	15,402.24	12,202.35	5,241.07	6,961.28	2,435.28	3,114.21	1,640.87	3,199.89

TABLE 4 (continued)

	(I) Total Financial Assets	(II) Domestic Financial Assets (II=I−VIII)	(III) Assets of Financial Institutions	(IV) Assets of Non-Financial Institutions (IV=II−III)	(V) Money (M_2)	(VI) Indirect Securities[a]	(VII) Stocks & Bonds	(VIII) Foreign Claims
1975	20,865.61	16,371.34	7,062.63	9,308.71	3,116.90	4,060.26	2,153.27	4,494.27
1976	28,146.41	22,550.25	9,638.57	12,911.68	4,132.40	5,558.19	3,172.07	5,596.31
1977	37,593.84	30,923.88	13,330.54	17,593.34	5,754.80	7,806.58	4,504.32	6,669.96
1978	49,039.04	41,415.08	18,149.64	23,265.44	7,751.00	10,694.48	6,692.82	7,623.96

Source: BOK, *Flow of Funds Accounts in Korea* (1978).

Note: [a]Include money, deposits with the Bank of Korea, time and savings deposits at DMBs and other financial institutions, money in trust, insurance, and investment and finance company deposits.

TABLE 5 Ratios of Financial Assets to GNP, 1960–1978[a]

	Nominal GNP (in billion wŏn)	(I) Total Financial Assets	(II) Domestic Financial Assets	(III) Assets of Financial Institutions	(IV) Assets of Non-Financial Institutions	(V) Money (M_2)	(VI) Indirect Securities	(VII) Stocks & Bonds	(VIII) Foreign Claims
1960	244.93					0.10			
1961	294.18					0.14			
1962	355.54	1.05	1.02	0.42	0.60	0.15	0.21	0.16	0.03
1963	502.90	0.90	0.85	0.33	0.52	0.11	0.16	0.17	0.05
1964	716.31	0.82	0.74	0.29	0.45	0.09	0.13	0.15	0.08
1965	805.72	0.89	0.81	0.31	0.50	0.12	0.17	0.14	0.08
1966	1,037.04	0.96	0.85	0.33	0.51	0.15	0.20	0.12	0.12
1967	1,281.23	1.23	1.07	0.42	0.65	0.20	0.26	0.12	0.16
1968	1,652.93	1.43	1.23	0.49	0.74	0.26	0.33	0.15	0.21
1969	2,155.27	1.68	1.41	0.53	0.85	0.33	0.39	0.18	0.27
1970	2,675.40	1.80	1.49	0.61	0.88	0.34	0.39	0.20	0.31
1971	3,276.24	1.96	1.57	0.64	0.93	0.33	0.39	0.19	0.39
1972	4,002.19	2.12	1.73	0.71	1.02	0.36	0.44	0.25	0.40
1973	5,119.12	2.15	1.79	0.73	1.06	0.39	0.48	0.25	0.37
1974	7,279.57	2.12	1.68	0.72	0.96	0.33	0.43	0.23	0.44
1975	9,644.24	2.16	1.70	0.73	0.97	0.32	0.42	0.22	0.47
1976	13,051.25	2.16	1.73	0.74	0.99	0.32	0.43	0.24	0.43
1977	16,652.35	2.26	1.86	0.80	1.05	0.35	0.47	0.27	0.40
1978	22,255.73	2.20	1.86	0.82	1.04	0.35	0.48	0.30	0.34

Sources: BOK, *Flow of Funds Accounts in Korea*, (1978); BOK, *Economic Statistics Yearbook*, various issues.

Note: [a]These ratios are obtained by dividing financial assets (I to VIII) in Table 4 by GNP.

TABLE 6 Asset/GNP Ratios of Financial Institutions in Individual Countries in 1963

Argentina	0.52
Brazil	0.55
Egypt	1.11
Greece	0.83
India	0.53
Israel	1.38
Jamaica	0.50
Mexico	0.56
Nigeria	0.20
Pakistan	0.37
Philippines	0.60
Spain	1.05
Thailand	0.47
Trinidad	0.33
Venezuela	0.66
Average	0.64

Source: Goldsmith, *Financial Structure and Development,* p. 209.

levels of development, especially when the guaranteed foreign loans are included, but that the ratios would still be expected to rise substantially as economic expansion continues.

FINANCIAL INTERMEDIATION

A fourth perspective on financial development in Korea is in terms of the intermediation between savers and investors. As pointed out in Chapter 1, the extent and form of such inter-mediation is a major determinant of the size of the financial system. Financial intermediation is best recorded through the flow-of-funds accounts which, unfortunately, are only available since 1963. Furthermore, the system of classification is less than fully revealing because unincorporated businesses are lumped with households. This was a reasonable consolidation when farm households were the dominant unincorporated enterprise, but, since farm households have diminished to 30 percent of all households (in 1978) and small-scale service and industrial enterprises have assumed greater importance in the unincorporated enterprise group, the consolidation has become more arbitrary and fails to distinguish between important economic groups. Nevertheless, households are the predominant savers, or financial-surplus units, and corporations are the predominant borrowers, so that the intermediation between these units is an important function of the financial system. The statistics in Tables 7 and 8 show how this intermediation has grown and changed in structure between 1963 and 1978.

At the beginning of the period, Korean corporations relied on internally generated funds (depreciation plus retained earnings) for about half their financing. External financing came from a mixture of bank loans, non-bank loans, foreign loans, and securities, in roughly equal proportions.

After the interest-rate reform of 1965 and the opening up of foreign-loan guarantees, the balance shifted markedly. Internally generated funds dropped to one-fourth and external financing increased to three-fourths of total financing through 1970. Also, bank loans and foreign loans became the dominant forms of external financing.

In the 1970s, as the growth of the banking system slowed down, corporations raised their reliance on internal funds to approximately one-third and used external sources to cover two-thirds of their financial needs. Bank loans were the predominant source of external funds in all years except 1975 and 1976, when foreign loans were at a peak. Securities and non-bank loans rose steadily through the 1970s and, taken together, exceeded either bank loans or foreign loans after 1975.

Households and unincorporated enterprises made complementary shifts in their asset-holding patterns between the early 1960s, the latter half of the 1960s, and the 1970s as shown in

TABLE 7 Sources and Uses of Finance by Korean Corporations, Public and Private, 1963–1978 (billion wŏn)

	1963		1964		1965		1966		1967		1968	
	Amount	%	Amount	%	Amount	%	Amount	%	Amount	%	Amount	%
Financing	53.9	100.0	46.3	100.0	97.8	100.0	153.5	100.0	263.7	100.0	367.1	100.0
Internal	24.2	44.9	27.1	58.5	39.7	40.5	48.9	31.9	63.8	24.2	89.7	24.4
External	29.7	55.1	19.2	41.5	58.1	59.5	104.6	68.1	199.9	75.8	277.4	75.6
Bank Loans	9.2		5.6		21.4		16.4		63.6		115.6	
Loans from non-bank financial institutions[a]	7.6		7.0		7.8		20.9		31.7		33.2	
Securities	8.0		5.4		9.1		12.5		9.1		23.6	
Foreign Loans	8.3		2.7		4.7		48.8		64.6		108.7	
Others[b]	-3.4		-1.5		15.1		6.0		30.9		19.9	
Investment												
Real	49.6	92.0	46.9	101.3	82.2	84.0	131.1	85.4	185.2	70.2	257.5	70.1
Fixed	34.1		44.3		65.3		125.2		160.8		226.8	
Inventory	15.5		2.6		16.9		5.9		24.4		30.7	
Financial	4.3	08.0	-0.6	-01.3	15.6	16.0	22.4	14.6	78.5	29.8	109.6	29.9

(continued)

TABLE 7 (continued)

	1969		1970		1971		1972		1973		1974	
	Amount	%	Amount	%	Amount	%	Amount	%	Amount	%	Amount	%
Financing	517.7	100.0	470.3	100.0	565.4	100.0	809.4	100.0	1,111.8	100.0	1,805.2	100.0
Internal	107.9	20.8	126.1	26.8	161.9	28.6	246.4	30.4	431.2	38.8	599.1	33.2
External	409.8	79.2	344.2	73.2	403.5	71.4	563.0	69.6	680.6	61.2	1,206.1	66.8
Bank Loans	130.6		142.3		182.8	32.3	156.2	19.3	307.4	38.5	625.5	53.2
Loans from non-bank financial institutions[a]	67.8		69.1		69.7	12.3	93.9	11.6	135.8	17.0	159.3	
Securities	59.5		70.3		85.6	15.1	157.8	19.5	172.1	21.5	148.9	
Foreign Loans	124.1		146.3		137.1	24.2	102.8	12.7	184.1	23.0	246.3	
Others[b]	27.8		-83.8		-71.7		52.3		-118.8		26.1	
Investment												
Real	308.9	59.7	373.3	79.5	476.1	84.2	490.3	60.6	774.4	69.7	1,394.6	77.3
Fixed	291.0		339.1		393.1		455.7		733.6		1,071.5	
Inventory	17.9		34.7		83.0		34.6		40.8		323.1	
Financial	208.8	40.3	96.5	20.5	89.3	15.8	319.1	39.4	337.4	30.3	410.6	22.7

TABLE 7 (continued)

	1975		1976		1977		1978	
	Amount	%	Amount	%	Amount	%	Amount	%
Financing	2,427.7	100.0	3,123.2	100.0	4,069.8	100.0	5,856.2	100.0
Internal	792.8	32.7	984.1	31.4	1,254.9	30.8	1,715.6	29.3
External	1,634.9	67.3	2,139.1	68.6	2,814.9	69.2	4,140.6	70.7
Bank Loans	523.6		554.0		757.2		1,826.6	40.9
Loans from non-bank financial institutions[a]	234.9		376.2		604.6		988.7	22.2
Securities	295.5		498.4		719.9		1,373.8	30.8
Foreign Loans	793.3		621.9		573.7		273.4	6.1
Others[b]	-212.4		88.6		159.5		-321.9	
Investment								
Real	1,650.0	68.0	1,861.4	60.0	2,508.9	61.6	3,792.8	64.8
Fixed	1,427.6		1,778.7		2,483.5		—	
Inventory	222.4		82.7		25.4		—	
Financial	777.7	32.0	1,261.8	40.0	1,560.9	38.4	2,063.4	35.1

Source: BOK, Flow of Funds Accounts in Korea (1978).

Notes: [a]Include private loans.
[b]Include trade credit, government loans, equities other than stocks, and miscellaneous and adjustment items. Negative figures reflect net repayments in excess of new sources of financing.

Table 8. At the beginning of the period, they were investing nearly two-thirds of their asset accumulation in fixed assets and only one-third in financial assets. This changed dramatically in 1965 when financial assets absorbed 85 percent of their asset accumulation and then continued thereafter at roughly two-thirds financial assets and one-third real assets through 1973. From 1974 through 1978, the split was nearer 60:40 as between financial and real asset accumulation.

The composition of financial assets being accumulated also changed after the interest rate reform of 1965 and again in the 1970s. Time and savings deposits jumped from inconsequential levels before 1965 to about half of financial asset accumulation from 1965 to 1970 and then dropped to about 40 percent between 1971 and 1978. Money (currency plus demand deposits) was a major form of accumulation (over 40 percent) in 1964 and 1965 but declined thereafter and averaged about 20 percent through the 1970s.

Private loans to business, which may reflect loans to unregulated financial institutions, averaged about 15 percent of financial asset accumulation through the 1960s and are recorded as having dropped to inconsequential levels in the 1970s. On the other hand, securities, an insignificant form of asset accumulation in most years of the 1960s, accounted for one-fourth of financial asset accumulation from 1970 through 1978.

Putting the two parts together, we see that financial intermediation increased substantially after 1965. Corporations raised their reliance on external financing, while households and unincorporated enterprises expanded the portion of their investment in financial assets and curtailed investment in real assets. Initially the corporations relied most heavily on bank loans and foreign loans (most of which were guaranted by the domestic banks), but they were making increasing use of securities by the end of the period. Households and unincorporated enterprises initially put much of their expanded financial asset holdings into time and savings deposits with the banks, but they too were increasing the share of security holdings throughout the

1970s. While the increased reliance on securities represented, in many cases, direct investment by households in corporations, it depended upon the existence of new types of financial institutions to arrange the new issues and make the markets for those securities.

It is also important to note that there was approximately a 10-fold increase in the nominal value of corporate financing between 1963 and 1971 and another 10-fold increase between 1971 and 1978. There was only one 10-fold increase in the price level between 1963 and 1978, so that the real increase in corporate financing was still about 10-fold. Throughout this period, the corporate sector was investing heavily, accounting for roughly 60 percent of gross capital formation or 15 percent of GNP. Two-thirds of the financing for this investment came from external funds either directly through the modern financial institutions or through channels, such as foreign loans and securities, in which the modern financial system played a role. That the financial system was able to handle and make possible these rates of financial and economic growth was, in itself, a substantial achievement.

Summing up the main trends over nearly seventy years from 1910 through 1978, we can see that the Korean financial system experienced two periods of accelerated development (1930–1940 and 1965–1978) that were associated with rapid economic growth. There was an intervening decade of chaos and collapse (roughly 1945 to 1955) and a decade of consolidation 1955–1965, similar in some respects to the earlier consolidation phase under the Japanese.

Bank deposits and loans have been important elements of the total financing system in both the 1930s and the recent period of growth, and their levels relative to output of the economy have been remarkably similar. The main difference in the recent period has been the influx of foreign loans, guaranteed by the domestic banks, which has pushed external financing and business investment up to very high levels, that is, nearly 20 percent

TABLE 8 Sources and Uses of Finance by Households and Unincorporated Businesses, 1963–1978 (billion wŏn)

	1963	1964	1965	1966	1967	1968	1969	1970
Total Financing	34.4	44.8	43.9	105.1	149.6	240.3	396.3	346.6
Internal (savings)	28.7	41.1	24.1	72.4	55.2	91.4	207.6	189.0
External	5.7	3.7	19.8	32.7	94.4	148.9	188.7	157.6
Asset Accumulation								
Real assets	21.4	28.7	6.4	41.1	28.9	54.6	131.2	153.9
(investment)	(62.2)[b]	(64.1)	(14.6)	(39.1)	(19.3)	(22.7)	(33.1)	(44.4)
Financial assets	13.0	16.1	37.5	64.0	120.7	185.7	265.1	192.7
	(37.8)[b]	(35.9)	(85.4)	(60.9)	(80.7)	(77.3)	(66.9)	(55.6)
Money	2.1	7.8	14.1	17.9	32.4	47.5	57.7	24.1
	(16.2)[c]	(48.4)	(37.6)	(28.0)	(26.8)	(25.6)	(21.8)	(12.5)
Time and savings deposits	0.6	1.5	15.7	35.3	46.4	90.9	141.0	98.6
	(4.6)	(9.3)	(41.9)	(55.2)	(38.4)	(48.9)	(53.2)	(51.2)
Deposits at non-bank financial institutions	3.1	1.4	3.4	8.5	15.5	24.1	20.8	13.3
	(23.8)	(8.7)	(9.1)	(13.3)	(12.8)	(13.0)	(7.8)	(6.9)
Securities	3.9	-1.1	1.5	4.5	-0.1	6.5	25.2	35.2
	(30.0)	(-6.8)	(4.0)	(7.0)	(-0.1)	(3.5)	(9.5)	(18.3)
Private loans to businesses	2.1	3.3	2.3	9.6	23.2	13.1	21.8	25.3
	(16.2)	(20.5)	(6.1)	(15.0)	(19.2)	(7.1)	(8.2)	(13.1)
Others[a]	1.2	3.3	0.4	-11.8	3.2	3.6	-1.3	-3.8
	(9.2)	(20.5)	(1.1)	(-18.4)	(2.7)	(1.9)	(-0.5)	(-2.0)

TABLE 8 (continued)

	1971	1972	1973	1974	1975	1976	1977	1978
Total Financing	459.6	419.4	918.3	1,056.6	1,274.6	1,997.0	2,883.4	4,441.5
Internal (savings)	203.2	301.9	653.8	819.0	716.8	1,289.7	2,091.9	3,157.4
External	256.4	117.5	264.5	237.6	557.8	707.3	791.5	1,284.1
Asset Accumulation								
Real assets (investment)	145.7 (31.7)[b]	155.6 (37.1)	283.7 (30.9)	555.0 (52.5)	551.6 (43.3)	786.4 (41.7)	1,044.1 (36.2)	1,850.5 (41.7)
Financial assets	313.9 (68.3)[b]	263.8 (62.9)	634.6 (69.1)	501.6 (47.5)	723.0 (56.7)	1,210.6 (58.3)	1,839.3 (63.8)	2,591.0 (58.3)
Money	40.8 (13.0)[c]	77.9 (29.5)	138.3 (21.8)	119.4 (23.8)	144.1 (19.9)	224.1 (18.5)	205.1 (22.0)	229.9 (9.3)
Time and savings deposits	93.2 (29.7)	140.7 (53.3)	225.1 (35.5)	200.5 (40.0)	347.0 (48.0)	440.4 (33.1)	648.2 (35.2)	1,081.4 (41.7)
Deposits at non-bank financial institutions	45.4 (14.5)	25.7 (9.7)	72.7 (11.5)	84.3 (16.8)	77.0 (10.7)	177.8 (14.7)	213.3 (11.6)	230.9 (8.9)
Securities	57.3 (18.3)	86.2 (32.7)	130.9 (20.6)	123.6 (24.6)	178.9 (24.7)	370.1 (30.6)	440.1 (23.9)	886.1 (34.2)
Private loans to businesses	24.4 (7.8)	−24.2 (−9.2)	0.4 (0.1)	−23.2 (−4.6)	8.5 (1.2)	−5.8 (−0.5)	45.5 (2.5)	101.8 (3.9)
Others[a]	52.9 (16.9)	−42.59 (−16.1)	67.2 (10.6)	−3.1 (−0.6)	−32.4 (−4.5)	43.9 (3.6)	87.1 (4.7)	50.9 (2.0)

Sources: BOK, *Flow of Funds Accounts in Korea* (1978); *Monthly Economic Statistics.*

Notes: [a]Include equities other than stocks and miscellaneous. [b]Percentage of total financing. [c]Percentage of financial assets.

of GNP. In this respect, the modern financial system has made a critical contribution to high growth.

The unregulated financial institutions have, according to our available estimates, been relatively small in absolute size, and, in recent years, have lost ground to some of the newly established types of regulated financial institutions and increasing use of direct securities. As we shall explain in subsequent chapters, however, the unregulated financial institutions have played an important role during certain periods in the past when the regulated institutions were functioning poorly. But, with the combined growth of the regulated financial sectors and government efforts to eliminate the unregulated institutions, the latter are being pushed into a subsidiary position, and the short- and long-term capital markets seem destined to play a growing role.

THREE

Korea's Regulated Financial Institutions

Korea, like many developing countries, has a dualistic financial structure: one part traditional, diverse, relatively competitive, largely unregulated, and relatively unknown; the other part modern, more clearly structured, regulated, and statistically recorded. These two systems have existed side by side for the past century, with the modern sector expanding its scope but never totally supplanting the traditional institutions; at times, when the modern sector has experienced crises or periods of decline, the traditional sector has filled in and helped keep the economy functioning. In this chapter, we shall describe the two financial sectors and how they have evolved over time, with major emphasis on the regulated sector. In Chapter 4, the traditional institutions are discussed in greater detail and in Chapter 5, the recent pattern of interaction between the two sectors is analyzed.

As can be seen in Figure 1, Korea in 1978 had a rather elaborate regulated financial system with a variety of modern and

FIGURE 1 Financial Institutions in Korea

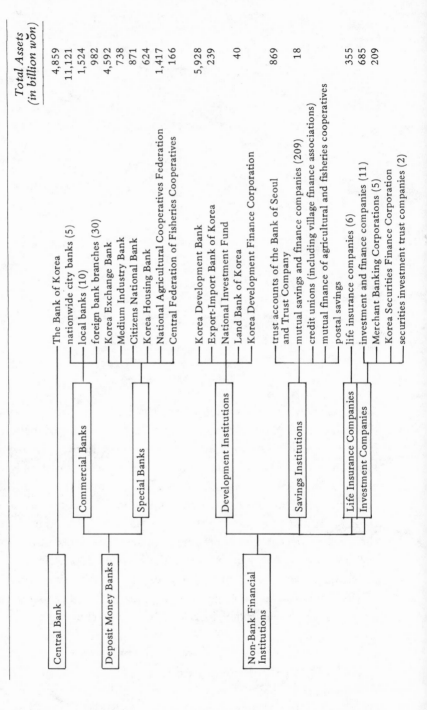

	Total Assets (in billion wŏn)
The Bank of Korea	4,859
nationwide city banks (5)	11,121
local banks (10)	1,524
foreign bank branches (30)	982
Korea Exchange Bank	4,592
Medium Industry Bank	738
Citizens National Bank	871
Korea Housing Bank	624
National Agricultural Cooperatives Federation	1,417
Central Federation of Fisheries Cooperatives	166
Korea Development Bank	5,928
Export-Import Bank of Korea	239
National Investment Fund	
Land Bank of Korea	40
Korea Development Finance Corporation	
trust accounts of the Bank of Seoul and Trust Company	869
mutual savings and finance companies (209)	18
credit unions (including village finance associations)	
mutual finance of agricultural and fisheries cooperatives	
postal savings	
life insurance companies (6)	355
investment and finance companies (11)	685
Merchant Banking Corporations (5)	209
Korea Securities Finance Corporation	
securities investment trust companies (2)	

Central Bank

Deposit Money Banks
— Commercial Banks
— Special Banks

Non-Bank Financial Institutions
— Development Institutions
— Savings Institutions
— Life Insurance Companies
— Investment Companies

FIGURE 1 (continued)

	Total Assets (in billion wŏn)
Quasi-Financial Institutions	Korea Credit Guarantee Fund
	leasing companies
Securities Market	Securities Supervisory Board
	Korea Stock Exchange
	securities companies (27) 667

Source: BOK, Financial System in Korea (December, 1978), p. 3.

Note: Figures in parentheses represent the number of institutions at the end of 1978.

specialized financial institutions. These financial institutions are divided into monetary institutions and non-bank financial intermediaries. Monetary institutions include the Bank of Korea (BOK), which is the central bank, and deposit money banks (DMBs), which consist of commercial and special banks. Nonbank financial institutions are classified into four categories of intermediaries—development institutions, savings institutions, life insurance companies, and investment companies. In addition, two types of institutions, the Korea Credit Guarantee Fund and leasing companies, though not defined as financial institutions, are engaged in financial activities in a broad sense. They may be regarded as quasi-financial institutions.

THE SITUATION BEFORE 1945

THE TRADITIONAL SYSTEM

A recent study by James B. Palais[1] provides some interesting insights into Korean financial history and the nature of the traditional financial institutions. Korea for centuries relied upon two commodities—grain and cloth—as the means of exchange, and grain loans as the main form of credit. Some grain loans were provided by the government, but there were also voluntary private associations, called *kye,* which pooled resources to give loans to members who might use them to pay taxes and repay grain loans from government.[2] Both metallic and paper money were used intermittently from the tenth century onward but were viewed as contrary to Confucian tradition, so they were frequently banned, or their use discouraged. By the nineteenth century, copper cash was in common use and provided the basis for two unfortunate monetary ventures by the government in the 1860s and 1870s.

In 1867, the government began minting a new coin—called, appropriately, 100 cash, nominally worth 100 units of regular cash but with only five to six times the intrinsic metallic value of regular cash.[3] The new coin was minted for only five months, but many counterfeits appeared, and the rapid rise in the supply of money caused a 5- to 6-fold increase in rice prices.[4] Older coins disappeared from circulation, and the government sought by exhortation and edict to force use of both currencies, but to no avail. After two years, the government acknowledged that the new currency was a failure and withdrew it from circulation.

But, faced with a continuing deficiency of revenues, the government turned to a new source of debased currency—the cash of China. According to Palais, the Korean government probably purchased Chinese copper coins because they were cheaper in China than in Korea by one third ". . . due to trade and exchange barriers between the two countries."[5] The Chinese coins were used by the Korean government for expenditures within Korea, and, in time, they too drove the traditional currency out of circulation. After six years of expansion of the money supply and resulting inflation, King Kojong, in January 1872, suddenly prohibited circulation of the Chinese coins, only to discover that his treasuries were the major repositories of them. The result was a financial crisis. All levels of government were without funds and unable to collect taxes. Commodity prices continued to rise as people demanded goods rather than the uncertain currencies. And the government was left holding large amounts of Chinese cash which could not be used domestically and were not worth transporting back to China.

This pattern of excessive expansion of multiple currencies leading to inflation and then to sudden and arbitrary demonetization of part of the currency has been repeated several times in the twentieth century.

THE JAPANESE INVASION

Because of Korea's special relation to China as a vassal state, the flow of trade and money between the two countries was considered a normal practice, but relations with Japan were a different matter. Korea—the "hermit kingdom"—managed to resist Japanese incursions until the Japanese finally landed troops and forced the Kanghwa Agreement in 1876, by which they obtained rights to trade and to establish businesses within Korea. Inevitably, with this came demands for modern banking facilities;

the first branch of a Japanese bank, the Daiichi Ginkō, was opened in Pusan in 1876. This bank extended its activities to Wŏnsan, Inch'ŏn, and Seoul over the next twelve years and was followed by several other banks over the next two decades. Concurrently, there were attempts by a number of Koreans to establish modern banks, but all but three had failed by 1910.

In 1905, the Korean government promulgated a currency law, which gave the currency issued by the Daiichi Ginkō legal status within Korea and thus established the first unified currency system within the country. The same bank also became a major source of credit for the Korean government and rapidly assumed the functions of a central bank. In 1909, these functions were transferred to a newly established Bank of Korea, but, in 1911, that bank was renamed the Bank of Chōsen, which continued to function as the central bank of Korea until 1945. It also carried on normal commercial operations. Three other important institutions were established in the years immediately prior to formal Japanese annexation of Korea. One was the Agriculture-Industry Bank, a government-owned and supported institution, destined to become a major source of financing for Japanese investment.[6] Another was the Oriental Development Company, which worked together with the Agriculture-Industry Bank to develop new enterprises and investments. The third new institution comprised the local financial associations, mainly oriented to agricultural financing authorized by regulations issued in 1909.

The formal annexation of Korea by Japan in 1910 accelerated the process of Japanese penetration into, and modernization of, the Korean economic and financial systems. It also precipitated a period of sustained expansion of the financial system, as shown in terms of financial ratios in Table 2.

Another perspective on the financial growth during the colonial period is presented in Table 9, which shows the number of head offices and branches of various types of institutions. The Bank of Chōsen (actually the Bank of Korea until 1911) was already well established in 1910 with twelve branches, a number

TABLE 9 Financial Institutions During the Japanese Occupation

	Bank of Chōsen (Branches)	Korean Agriculture-Industry Bank (Main Offices)	(Branches)	Commercial Banks (Main Offices)	(Branches)	Federation of Financial Associations (Main Offices)	(Branches)	Financial Associations	Korea Savings Bank (Branches)
1910	12	6	27	4	20			120	
1915	12	6	37	11	29			240	
1920	10	1	52	21	59	13		400	
1925	10	1	52	16	74	13		517	
1930	10	1	57	13	92	13		644	
1935	12	1	60	7	110	1	13	698	5
1940	14	1	66	6	121	1	13	723	13
1945	16	1	74	2	136	1	13	912	21

Sources: 1910-1940—Government General of Korea, Korea Statistics Yearbook (1943); MOF, Uri nara kŭmyung chedo mit chŏngch'aek kaegwan (August 1966), p. 18.

that did not change much over the next three decades. Similarly, the Agriculture-Industry Bank had relatively extensive facilities in 1910. It was particularly the commercial banks and the financial associations that expanded their number of branches roughly 6-fold between 1910 and 1940. Another interesting indicator is that the number of commercial banks proliferated from four in 1910 to twenty-one in 1920 and then was reduced steadily to only six by 1940. Clearly, from 1920 on, there were both growth and increasing concentration within the commercial banking sector.

A third perspective on the colonial financial system involves the growth and composition of the loans and deposits of the different types of institutions, as shown in Table 10. Several interesting features emerge from these statistics. One is the dominant role of the Agriculture-Industry Bank on the lending side and the ever-increasing gap between its deposits and loans. In 1929, the Savings Bank was established to serve as an accumulator of deposits for the Agriculture-Industry Bank, but the other banks, including the Bank of Chōsen, channeled funds into the Agriculture-Industry Bank. The commercial banks maintained approximate balance between loans and deposits until the latter part of the 1930s, when they began to build up a sizable deposit surplus. The financial associations had outstanding loans well in excess of deposits, until they too made a shift to a surplus of deposits in the late 1930s. These are clear indicators of the Japanese government's efforts to mobilize savings and channel them through the Agriculture-Industry Bank into the war effort after 1937.

During the colonial period, the financial system in Korea was owned and controlled by the Japanese and was used to channel savings initially into Japanese industrial and commercial expansion and finally into the Japanese war effort. Koreans did have some access to the modern financial institutions, particularly the financial associations, but by and large they relied on their traditional institutions both as depositories for their savings and sources for their borrowings.

TABLE 10 Deposits and Loans of Financial Institutions During the Japanese Occupation (million yen)

	Bank of Chōsen		Korean Agriculture-Industry Bank		Commercial Banks		Korean Federation of Financial Associations		Financial Associations		Korea Savings Bank	
	Deposits	Loans	Deposits	Loans	Deposits	Loans	Deposits	Loans	Deposits	Loans	Deposits	Loans
1910	5.5	20.3	3.2	6.3	9.7	11.3				.8		
1915	15.8	30.2	6.5	11.5	13.4	18.9				1.1		
1920	46.9	77.2	38.0	86.0	54.4	67.5	1.5	18.8	10.1	31.4		
1925	21.4	57.4	59.2	197.1	90.6	97.5	20.7	30.6	47.3	66.4		
1930	30.2	48.3	52.6	298.5	109.4	104.4	35.9	63.6	80.1	123.4	24.5	6.4
1935	73.6	105.4	127.8	412.3	159.3	157.6	80.6	86.1	153.4	179.3	43.7	19.5
1940	231.6	531.6	333.6	948.3	446.8	391.6	210.4	129.8	432.1	364.1	127.9	45.6

Source: Government General of Korea, *Korea Statistics Yearbook* (1943).

The colonial government gave some support and encouragement to one category of private financial institution, the *mujin*,
a kind of savings and loan brokerage like the *kye*, but incorporated and subject to government supervision.[7] Thus the *mujin*
stood halfway between the regulated and unregulated financial
sectors. Subsequently, under the Korean government, the *mujin*
was transformed into a government entity, the Citizens' Bank,
and became a part of the regulated financial sector, which led to
a decline in its relative importance.

1945 TO 1960

THE INTER-WAR PERIOD

At the end of World War II, Korea had the shell of a modern financial system—and a modern economy—but lacked sufficient
people experienced in running it. Japanese had held most of the
middle and top positions in the banks, in industry, and in government.[8] Inevitably, it would have taken time and experience
to get the institutions back to efficient operation. But division
of the country, the collapse of the Japanese economy, rampant
inflation as wartime controls disappeared, the imposition of
first a U.S. Military Government in 1945 and then a new Korean
government in 1948, which were both ill-equipped to run the
Korean economy, and ultimately the war with North Korea all
contributed to the complexity of Korea's problems and the
severe decline of its modern financial institutions.

This chaotic period and its effects on the financial system have
been described at some length by Bloomfield and Jensen in their
1950 report and proposals on banking reform in South Korea.[9]
They emphasize the disappearance of customary Japanese
sources and users of funds and the eroding effects of inflation as
the major factors leading to financial decline after 1945. The financial institutions in Korea could no longer float debentures in
Japan or hold deposits of Japanese enterprises, and the level of
operation of the enterprises within Korea was not such as to

generate or require significant cash holdings. Furthermore, in the face of rapid inflation, businesses and individuals were reluctant to hold financial assets, so the sources of bank funds were severely limited. On the lending side, also, the viability of most businesses in Korea was sufficiently suspect to discourage much bank financing. The ownership of all former Japanese enterprises, including the banks, had been taken over initially by the U.S. Military Government and then was transferred to the Korean government in 1948, so the banks were faced with having to make loans to government-owned enterprises, from which it was difficult to obtain repayment. Furthermore, interest rates on bank loans were sufficiently below the prevailing rates of inflation and the even higher private lending rates that those who held bank loans were loath to pay them back.

The financial structure in South Korea in early 1950 was characterized as follows by Bloomfield and Jensen:

> The specialization of functions which was a significant feature of Korean financial institutions before the liberation has now almost entirely disappeared. All the existing banking institutions are engaging predominantly in a regular commercial banking business consisting essentially of accepting demand deposits and of making short-term loans and advances to primary producers, to businessmen and to Government Agencies. The Industrial Bank is still granting some intermediate and long-term credits for capital development, though on a greatly reduced scale relative to its commercial banking and in large part on the basis of long-term borrowing from the central bank. About 25 per cent of its total loans at the end of 1949 had maturities of from 2 to 15 years, and 20 per cent of its total loans consisted of loans of from 10 to 15 years for irrigation works. Formally, the medium-term and long-term loans of other banking institutions are very small or non-existent, but an apparently substantial fraction of their total loans is in effect of that nature in view of frequent renewals of ostensibly short-term credits. The specialized pre-liberation functions of the Trust Bank, the Mutual Aid Bank and the Savings Bank have declined greatly in importance. The trust business of the Trust Bank has been almost entirely stagnant since 1945 in view of the inflation, the redistribution of Japanese land holdings to peasant farmers, the breakup or vesting of other Japanese estates, and the

decline in the volume of securities in the hands of the public. A comparison of the trust account of the Trust Bank on the eve of liberation and at the end of 1949 shows very little change in any of the major liabilities and assets. The Mujin business of the Mutual Aid Bank has sunk to only an insignificant fraction of its total business; in fact, the lottery business appears to have been increasingly assumed by a number of separate lottery companies established under special law since the liberation. So far as the Savings Bank is concerned, its savings business has been hard hit by the inflation, although apparently about 20 per cent of its total deposit liabilities still consists of genuine savings deposits. The Commercial Bank and the Choheung Bank have continued to engage exclusively in commercial banking. The volume of financial operations performed by the Post Office has shown no expansion since the liberation, nor has any genuine progress been recorded in the insurance (and especially the life insurance) business, despite the establishment of a number of new companies; this state of affairs has been largely attributable to the continuing inflation. Korea is still, after four years, without stock exchange or formal underwriting facilities, in large part because the bulk of the country's industrial shares is owned by the Government, because the stock of private companies is usually held closely by a relatively few people, because few new large companies have been established since the liberation, and because of the absence, until very recently, of any Government bonds. A few attempts have been made to establish such facilities, but these attempts have met with little success.[10]

Faced with the kind of financial system just described, it is not surprising that the Korean and U.S. governments agreed to work together on the rebuilding of the system, and it was for this reason that Bloomfield and Jensen visited Korea in the spring of 1950. In close collaboration with officials from the Ministry of Finance and the Bank of Chosun, they worked out a reform program calling for:

1) Transforming the Bank of Chosun into a strong, autonomous central bank, divested of its commercial banking activities, and concentrating primarily on the management of monetary policy and supervision of the commercial banks;

2) Creation of a Monetary Board to set monetary policy and oversee the functioning of the monetary system;

3) Strengthening the controls over the commercial banks and transferring them as rapidly as possible from government to private ownership;

4) Implementation of forceful anti-inflationary policies, thereby achieving sufficient stability to create conditions favorable for financial growth and further institutional reform.

Unfortunately, shortly after this program was agreed upon, the Korean War began, and most elements of the program had to be abandoned or severely compromised in the interests of financing the war. The transformation of the Bank of Chosun into the Bank of Korea was carried out in June of 1950, but the new General Banking Act was not implemented until 1954. The Ministry of Finance found it necessary to borrow heavily from the Bank of Korea and thereby exercised dominant control over monetary policy. The Bank of Korea was unable to take effective steps to curtail inflation, which was inevitably exacerbated by the wartime disruptions (see Chapter 8).

Perhaps the best that can be said for the Korean financial system during the Korean War period is that it continued to function, but at a very low level. To a considerable extent, the formal financial insitutions were supplanted by the unregulated money markets which dealt primarily in U.S. military payment certificates (MPCs) and "greenbacks." The Bank of Korea continuously expanded the note issue of Korean currency to cover loans and advances to the Korean and U.S. governments. But the public was generally unwilling to hold any significant amounts of these rapidly depreciating notes, so they exchanged them for dollars, or MPCs, or commodities, as protection against inflation. The role of the commercial banks was minimal, since both their loans and their deposits equaled only about one-fourth of the money supply (narrowly defined) which, in turn, was less than 10 percent of GNP.

POST-KOREAN WAR DEVELOPMENT

With the end of the Korean War, attention turned to the reconstruction of the war-devastated economy. Foreign aid flows increased, and their composition shifted from mainly consumer goods to a mix of consumer, intermediate, and capital goods. The financial system also underwent some transformation to give better support to the reconstruction effort. In 1954, the Korea Development Bank (KDB, initially called Korea Reconstruction Bank) was established with the primary objective of granting medium- and long-term loans to industry. The KDB took over some of the assets, liabilities, and facilities of the Industrial Bank, which, in turn, was an outgrowth of the Agriculture-Industry Bank of the Japanese era. The original Japanese bank had done a mixture of long- and short-term lending, but with emphasis on the long term. The Industrial Bank had shifted the emphasis to short-term financing during the inter-war and Korean War periods, and the KDB represented a shift back in the other direction, as it was to be exclusively involved in term lending.[11]

The KDB was placed directly under the authority of the Ministry of Finance and thereby independent of any control by the Bank of Korea. This set the pattern for a number of subsequent special banks that were able to operate largely outside central-bank controls. Ironically, the KDB proved to be heavily dependent upon the Bank of Korea for funds because, in the face of inflationary conditions, very limited private savings, and ceilings on interest rates, it was unable to sell long-term debt instruments to the general public. To carry out the ambitious financing programs the government set for it—which contributed further to the inflation—the KDB ended up borrowing heavily from the BOK. By the end of 1955, after only twenty-one months of operations, the KDB accounted for over 40 percent of total bank lending. Roughly one-third of its loans were supported by aid counterpart funds, while the remaining two-thirds came from the Bank of Korea.

A second institution established by the government during this period was the Korea Agriculture Bank, which represented an attempt to set up a pure banking institution to deal with the

farmers associations and thus separate the banking and marketing activities of the former Federation of Financial Associations.
Like the KDB, the Agriculture Bank experienced difficulty in
raising funds from sources other than the government or the
central bank.

At the same time the government was creating these new
government-owned institutions to support its programs for reconstruction of industry and agriculture, it was moving to reduce
its direct authority over the commercial banks. In August 1954,
the General Banking Act, originally approved in 1950, was actually implemented. The main effect of this was to give the
Monetary Board greater authority over the licensing and regulation of the commercial banks. Also in 1954, the government
initiated action to divest itself of its holdings of shares in the
commercial banks that it had acquired via the U.S. Military
Government from the former Japanese owners. One commercial
bank, the Cho-Heung Bank, had been largely Korean-owned, so
it had not passed through this process. The shares of the other
three banks were not finally disposed of until 1957, after several unsuccessful auction attempts. They were purchased by a
relatively small number of large stockholders, mainly wealthy
businessmen who were prospering from high profits on government-controlled import licenses.

The case for private ownership of the commercial banks had
been presented with considerable fervor by Bloomfield and Jensen:

> The fact that the Government holds the controlling interest in the
> majority of Korean Banks has had at least two major disadvantages.
> Firstly, it has subjected these institutions to objectionable political
> pressures and arbitrary and shortsighted interferences of a sort that
> have not been conducive to sound and healthy banking policies. Sec-
> ondly, with Government control, bankers have had far less incentive,
> and have been subject to far less inducement, to pursue such policies
> than if the controlling shares were in the hands of private stock-
> holders with a personal financial interest in the banks concerned. It
> is our firm opinion that one of the major requirements of banking

reform in South Korea must be to get most of the banks as rapidly as possible out of Government hands into the hands of private owners.[12]

The importance for Korean economic and financial welfare of getting the ownership and control of these banks into private hands is so great, and so out of proportion to the small amount of money involved, that it is to be hoped that special efforts will be made by those in charge of vested property disposal to seek out responsible private interests who would be willing to purchase these shares. With sounder banking policies and better management, moreover, such as should follow from private ownership, there is no good reason why bank shares should not begin, especially at a time of inflation, to yield very high returns on capital.[13]

It is perhaps unnecessary to record that all the benefits claimed for private ownership did not, in fact, materialize, but there were some improvements. It appears that the monetary authorities found it easier to restrict the expansion of commercial bank credit when those banks were privately owned rather than government-owned. As shown in Table 11, the share of commercial bank loans in total loans dropped from 45 percent in 1955 to 29 percent in 1960. Most of this change occurred in 1957, the year in which ownership was transferred from government to private hands. The KDB share of total loans, after expanding dramatically in 1954 and 1955, declined slightly during the 1955-1960 period, so the main expansion in the relative share of the special banks was attributable to the Agriculture Bank— the only institution classified as a special bank at that time.

Thus, during the brief period from 1954 to 1958, the KDB was created and assumed a dominant position in the allocation of credit. The Agriculture Bank took over responsibility for the financing of agriculture and also moved into a commanding position. The three government-owned commercial banks were transferred to private ownership, and the relative position of the four commercial banks in terms of their share of total credit outstanding declined substantially. There were no further institutional changes of major significance until after the takeover of the military government in 1961.

TABLE 11 Shares of Total Bank Lending of Main Types of Banks, 1955–1960

	Commercial		Special		KDB		Total	
	Amount (billion wŏn)	%	Amount (billion wŏn)	%	Amount (billion wŏn)	%	Amount (billion wŏn)	%
1955	3.1	45	1.0	15	2.8	40	6.9	100
1956	5.5	43	1.8	14	5.4	43	12.6	100
1957	5.9	30	5.0	25	9.2	45	20.1	100
1958	7.6	29	8.3	31	10.5	40	26.4	100
1959	9.3	29	9.0	28	14.1	43	32.4	100
1960	11.5	29	12.8	32	15.9	39	40.2	100

Source: BOK, *Economic Statistics Yearbook,* various issues.

1961 TO 1978

REFORMS UNDER THE MILITARY GOVERNMENT

The advent of the Military Government in May 1961 led to a number of "reforms" in the financial domain. The new government was committed to a "mixed" economy encompassing "powerful government programs" aimed at overcoming the country's economic underdevelopment.[14] Within three months, the government reorganized the agricultural financing and marketing institutions by combining the agricultural cooperatives and the Agriculture Bank into one entity known as the National Agricultural Cooperatives Federation (NACF), responsible for providing credit to farmers, supplying them with agricultural inputs, and marketing their output, including purchasing grain on government account to help stabilize grain prices and assure supplies for government needs. One of the first activities of the new NACF was to refinance a sizable amount of the existing debts of farmers to private moneylenders. This was an attempt to reduce the dependence of farmers on the unregulated financial institutions and thereby reduce the importance of those institutions.[15] Many farmers saw the refinancing as a gift from the government, and the default rate on the NACF loans was high. Over time the NACF did become the major source of credit for the farmers, but, in its early years, because of the poor repayment record, it did not have the financial resources to meet the demand for rural credit.

The second major innovation of the Military Government was the Medium Industry Bank (MIB), also established in August 1961, for the purpose of providing loans to medium and small enterprises. Its functions were and are similar to those of commercial banks in that it accepts deposits and makes mainly short-term loans, but its loans must go only to enterprises with fewer than a prescribed number of employees and amount of total assets.

Both these initial ventures, the NACF and the MIB, were manifestations of the government's desire and commitment to improve the lot of the small farmer and small business man. The rapid expansion of loans through these institutions in 1961 resulted in a significant shift in the allocation of credit. The share of these two banks in total bank credit jumped from 32 to 38 percent during 1961, largely at the expense of the commercial bank share, which dropped from 29 to 24 percent.

In October 1961, the government repossessed the shares of the commercial banks held by large stockholders on the grounds that they were illegally hoarded properties.[16] The government was responding to concerns that the privately owned banks would contribute to concentration of economic power along the lines experienced in Japan.[17] The return of the commercial banks to government ownership in late 1961 was followed by a big increase in loans by the commercial banks in 1962, bringing their share of total loans back up to 30 percent.

The next step in the financial reform program of the Military Government was revision of the KDB's charter to increase its capital, to authorize it to borrow funds from abroad and to guarantee foreign loans obtained by Korean enterprises. This guarantee procedure was subsequently extended to the other commercial and special banks and proved to be a major factor in the inducement of foreign capital.[18]

The culmination of these institutional changes came in May 1962, when the Bank of Korea law was revised so as to bring the central bank unequivocally under the control of the Minister of Finance. As we have suggested previously, the Minister of Finance had de facto authority over the Bank of Korea from its inception, in part because of the needs for financing the war and post-war reconstruction. But there was a continuing debate from 1950 to 1962 between those who supported the autonomy of the central bank, as provided for in its charter, and those who believed that monetary policy should be one of several coordinated elements of economic policy with the Minister of Finance, as Chairman of the Monetary Board, providing the focal point of that coordination.[19]

The legislative changes of 1962 were largely a recognition of reality, but they were also a manifestation of the orientation of the new government towards a centrally managed and powerful set of institutions and instruments for carrying out the government's policies. Both the principles espoused by Bloomfield and Jensen, of an autonomous central bank and privately owned commercial banks as the key elements of a democratic, capitalistic financial system, as well as the Japanese model of a partnership between big business and government, were repudiated by the military leaders, who moved towards greater government ownership and control of the financial institutions.

Each of the institutional innovations in 1961 and 1962 seemed to lead to a significant expansion of bank lending, first by the NACF and MIB in 1961, then by the KDB and the government-owned commercial banks in 1962. This caused a build-up of inflationary pressure by mid-1962, which the government sought to deal with in an arbitrary, authoritarian manner, symbolic of its new control over monetary policy. In June 1962, the government carried out a currency reform, described by one observer as "ill-conceived, ill-prepared, ill-timed and therefore ill-fated."[20]

There had been a substantial increase (nearly 50 percent) in the money supply during the twelve months prior to the currency reform, and, although there had been no significant effects on prices, the government feared that such effects would materialize in the near future. Also, the government apparently thought money was being hoarded by large speculators who would soon act in ways that would disturb the stability of the economy. The currency reform consisted of changing the denomination of the currency, making 10 old hwan equal to one new wŏn, limiting conversion to 500 new wŏn (equal to less than $4.00) to meet current living expenses, requiring registration of all cash, checks, and money orders, and finally trying to force all "surplus" funds into a new "Industrial Development Corporation" that would finance new industrial activities.

The immediate effect of these measures was to bring economic activity nearly to a standstill because of lack of funds. The large hoards of idle money proved nonexistent, not surprising in view of the fact that the money supply amounted to only about 12 percent of GNP. The larger money balances that did exist were being used relatively efficiently by businesses to carry out current production, and, when these funds were shut off, businesses could not meet current payments. The working cash balances of the unregulated financial institutions were similarly blocked, so they had no means for meeting the immediate cash needs of business. Within one week, the monetary authorities began to undo the reform, and this proceeded in stages until, after five weeks, "on July 13, all the blocked deposits were allowed to be withdrawn freely and thus all the currency reform measures were scratched out completely."[21]

This experience, which parallels the arbitrary demonetization of Chinese cash by King Kojong ninety years before, helped the new government learn that, while it could control the financial institutions, it could also bring the economy to a standstill by trying to enforce policies that conflicted strongly with the interests and needs of the private sector. In subsequent years, the Korean government carried out a number of similarly audacious moves, particularly in the area of finance, but they were better conceived and prepared so that, while disruptive and often painful for some elements of the economy, they were beneficial to, and gained the support of, other elements and were therefore more successful. The ultimate effect of the currency reform of 1962 was to undermine confidence in the currency and the financial institutions, to precipitate a shift from holding money to holding goods, which stimulated the inflationary behavior that the government had originally been trying to prevent.

Over the next several years, the government's attention was largely taken up with curtailing inflation and inducing a greater inflow of foreign capital, rather than further institutional change in the domestic financial arena. In late 1962, the government did consolidate a number of small mutual financing companies into the Citizens' National Bank, which was to concentrate on small loans to business and households. Also in 1962, a Central Federation of Fisheries Cooperatives (CFFC) was created to provide credit and marketing services to the fishing industry comparable to those NACF provided to agriculture.

GUARANTEEING REPAYMENT OF FOREIGN LOANS— A NEW ROLE FOR KOREAN BANKS

While clamping a lid on domestic credit creation in 1963 and 1964, largely in response to strong pressure from the United States government, the Korean government opened up new channels for increased foreign financing. The impetus for this appears to have come mainly from the prospective normalization of relations with Japan, which, in turn, was expected to lead to a sizable inflow of financing from Japan. The Korean government preferred to have this capital inflow in the form of loans rather than equity so as to minimize Japanese ownership and control of Korean businesses.[22]

The main instrument devised for this purpose was the system of bank guarantees for the repayment of foreign loans. Korean enterprises wishing to borrow abroad first had to obtain the approval of the Economic Planning Board, which, in turn, sought approval of the National Assembly for the issuance of guarantees covering repayment of the foreign borrowings. While this often led to acrimonious debates in the National Assembly, involving charges of corruption and influence, few proposals were ever rejected as a result of Assembly pressure. Once the guarantee had been authorized, the Bank of Korea (and subsequently the Korea Exchange Bank) issued a guarantee to the foreign lender, while the Korea Development Bank (and subsequently the commercial banks) issued guarantees to the Bank of Korea. The ultimate borrower was committed to repay the loan, and bear any exchange risk, but he had the backing of both the KDB and the BOK that, in the event of his default, the loan would be repaid. United States assistance to, and support of, Korea undoubtedly gave further assurance that Korea's external financial commitments would be met. In addition to all of this, the U.S. and Japanese governments granted various types of investment guarantees to their nationals who made loans to, or invested in, Korea. Thus, the risk of default for the lender was practically negligible, while the Korean borrower had assurances of support, not only from the domestic banking institutions, but also the central bank and the Economic Planning Board.

The foreign-loan-guarantee operations became significant in 1963 when, as shown in Table 12, KDB acceptances went up from 2.2 billion to 18.1 billion wŏn. Over the next two years, the total guarantees increased by over 25 billion wŏn each year, and then jumped by nearly 70 billion wŏn in 1966, by which time they were nearly equal to the total of outstanding bank loans. Also in 1966, the commercial banks assumed a significant role in the guarantee activity, accounting for nearly 30 billion of the 70 billion increase in that year. Thus, the Korean banking system, while not actually intermediating between the foreign lenders and domestic borrowers, was definitely facilitating such lending activity, and, from 1963 to 1966, this was the major source of new financing for Korean businesses.

The banks played a very limited role in the decision-making process regarding these loans. Arrangements were worked out directly between the borrower and lender, then approved by the government. The banks basically issued the guarantees on instruction from the government and took little responsibility for evaluating either the economic or financial feasibility of the project. Eventually, when some of the projects proved unsound, the government had little basis for holding the banks accountable, and therefore had to take extraordinary measures to relieve the banks of the bad debts. But, from the institutional point of view, the banking system became involved in a major new activity after 1963, without committing much of its own financial or human resources. The domestic banks were facilitators and guarantors of external finance, but not intermediaries. The commercial banks did not try to develop skills in term lending, and both they and the KDB responded mainly to government directives.

TABLE 12 Amounts and Shares of Deposits, Loans, and Foreign-Loan Guarantees of the Main Types of Banks, 1960–1978
(billion wŏn)

	Commercial Banks						Special Banks					
	Deposits		Loans		Guarantees		Deposits		Loans		Guarantees	
	Amount	%	Amount	%	Amount	%	Amount	%	Amount	%	Amount	%
1960	14.1	79.2	11.5	28.6	0.4	66.7	3.0	16.9	12.8	31.8		
1961	19.3	73.1	12.8	24.4	1.4	87.5	5.4	20.5	19.2	36.7		
1962	29.0	69.4	20.9	31.0	2.8	56.0	10.1	24.2	22.3	33.0		
1963	26.3	64.8	22.8	29.8	3.7	17.0	12.7	31.3	26.2	34.2		
1964	28.2	63.7	23.1	27.3	9.9	20.5	14.9	33.6	29.9	35.3		
1965	55.3	69.0	37.5	34.4	11.8	15.7	23.2	28.8	34.6	31.8	1.4	1.8
1966	82.5	66.9	57.9	38.8	40.2	27.8	38.4	31.1	44.8	30.0	1.4	1.0
1967	137.0	66.0	105.6	45.8	50.3	25.7	68.9	32.8	72.4	31.4	2.7	1.4
1968	249.5	66.0	210.0	52.8	126.1	41.4	123.6	32.6	121.2	30.5	3.3	1.1
1969	410.1	65.6	359.3	54.5	225.1	42.5	209.0	33.7	203.7	30.9	4.0	0.8
1970	505.4	63.3	441.8	51.9	319.3	42.6	284.2	35.3	280.7	33.0	6.0	0.8
1971	635.7	64.5	568.4	52.8	435.5	41.5	341.9	34.6	351.1	32.6	13.2	1.2
1972	892.4	66.4	742.5	51.7	422.0	40.4	431.5	32.1	455.5	31.7	11.1	1.1
1973	1,179.2	66.8	987.5	51.8	585.3	42.4	574.4	32.5	600.0	31.5	9.0	0.6
1974	1,408.2	66.5	1,543.9	54.1	788.9	37.2	699.3	33.0	883.8	31.0	18.3	0.9
1975	1,923.3	68.7	1,877.9	53.9	1,448.4	48.8	855.9	30.6	1,027.7	29.5	38.0	1.3
1976	2,495.4	67.0	2,411.3	54.0	2,165.3	46.0	1,192.7	32.0	1,313.6	29.4	34.6	0.7
1977	3,474.1	64.1	3,001.7	52.5	3,140.6	48.6	1,862.2	34.4	1,707.3	29.9	48.7	0.8
1978	4,840.6	62.9	4,242.9	52.7	4,565.7	52.9	2,764.8	35.9	2,366.1	29.4	159.9	1.9

Source: BOK, *Economic Statistics Yearbook.*

Note: Acceptances of the special banks omit those of the Foreign Exchange Bank, which are secondary guarantees of acceptances of the other banks.

TABLE 12 (continued)

| | Korea Development Bank | | | | | | Totals | | |
| | Deposits | | Loans | | Guarantees | | | | |
	Amount	%	Amount	%	Amount	%	Deposits	Loans	Guarantees
1960	0.7	3.9	15.9	39.6	0.2	33.3	17.8	40.2	0.6
1961	1.7	6.4	20.3	38.8	0.2	12.5	26.4	52.3	1.6
1962	2.7	6.4	24.3	36.0	2.2	44.0	41.8	67.5	5.0
1963	1.6	3.9	27.6	36.0	18.1	83.0	40.6	76.6	21.8
1964	1.2	2.7	31.7	37.4	38.3	79.5	44.3	84.7	48.2
1965	1.7	2.2	36.8	33.8	62.1	82.5	80.2	108.9	75.3
1966	2.4	2.0	46.6	31.2	103.0	71.2	123.3	149.3	144.6
1967	2.5	1.2	52.4	22.7	143.0	73.0	208.4	230.4	196.0
1968	5.3	1.4	66.4	16.7	175.0	57.5	378.4	397.6	304.4
1969	4.1	0.7	96.1	14.6	300.0	56.7	623.2	659.1	529.1
1970	10.9	1.4	129.0	15.1	424.0	56.6	800.5	851.5	749.3
1971	9.1	0.9	157.5	14.6	600.0	57.2	986.7	1,077.0	1,048.7
1972	10.6	0.8	239.1	16.6	611.0	58.5	1,334.5	1,437.1	1,044.1
1973	12.4	0.7	318.5	16.7	787.0	57.0	1,766.0	1,906.0	1,381.3
1974	11.3	0.5	425.7	14.9	1,311.0	61.9	2,118.8	2,853.4	2,118.2
1975	28.8	0.7	577.8	16.6	1,480.0	49.9	2,808.0	3,483.4	2,966.4
1976	37.8	1.0	739.9	16.6	2,511.7	53.3	3,725.9	4,464.8	4,711.6
1977	81.7	1.5	1,007.9	17.6	3,278.8	50.6	5,418.0	5,716.9	6,468.1
1978	95.6	1.2	1,443.5	17.9	3,898.3	45.2	7,701.0	8,052.5	8,623.9

THE INSTITUTIONAL EFFECTS
OF FINANCIAL REFORM

The interest-rate reform of September 1965, while sometimes viewed as a revamping of the whole interest-rate structure, was essentially a major increase in the interest rate paid on time deposits. There were some increases in the rates charged on loans, but these had little impact on the volume of lending or lending practices, because the new rates were still not high enough to affect the demand for loans significantly. The increase in the time deposit rate from 15 to 30 percent per year, however, did result in a quantum jump in the financial resources of the commercial and special banks and substantially changed their institutional role. All the banks, except the KDB, which did not raise its deposit rate, became important mobilizers of financial savings and, for the first time, began to give some attention to this role. They were also relieved to a degree from the tight leash of dependence on central bank credit or government budgetary allocations of aid counterpart funds as primary sources for their lending.

Over the four years from 1965 through 1969, total bank deposits rose from 10 percent to nearly 30 percent of GNP (see Table 13).[23] During this period, real GNP increased by 57 percent and nominal GNP by 158 percent, while total deposits rose by nearly 700 percent. The relative shares of the different banks in total deposits did not change very much, but the national commercial banks lost some ground to the new local commercial banks and the Korea Exchange Bank, after their establishment in 1967. The deposits of the Korea Development Bank dropped below 1 percent of the total.

Total bank loans increased by an amount almost exactly equal to the increase of deposits between 1965 and 1969. A substantial excess of deposits over loans in the commercial banks, and to a lesser degree in the special banks, was offset by a loan surplus at the KDB.

In spite of the monumental increases in both deposits and loans of the Korean banking system, in the latter half of the

1960s there was a similar explosion in the guarantees of foreign loans, and the commercial banks took over the dominant role in the granting of such guarantees. Thus, the total available financing either directly from the banks, or from external sources and guaranteed by the banks, played a key role in financing the high 12 percent real growth of the Korean economy that occurred during this period. As shown in Chapter 2, the increase in total bank loans and foreign-loan guarantees financed a large part of the corporate capital formation that occurred from 1966 through 1969.

Clearly, the role of the banking system had undergone a dramatic change from the early 1960s, when it was mainly engaged in rationing a limited supply of credit. Although the banks had not acquired any greater degree of independence in decision-making as to the allocation of credit, since decisions on all the guarantees and many of the larger loans were made by the government, they did at least have a greatly expanded managerial role over a system that exerted a major influence on the allocation of resources.

NEW BANKING INSTITUTIONS IN THE LATE 1960s

A number of new government banking institutions were established in 1967, and the doors were opened to creation of new private banking ventures. The Korea Exchange Bank (KEB) was constituted as a separate entity out of the personnel, facilities, and financial resources of the foreign-exchange and foreign-operations departments of the Bank of Korea. The KEB's stock was wholly owned by the Bank of Korea, and it has functioned largely as an extension of the BOK since its inception. Thus, the change was mainly one of form rather than substance.

Much the same can be said for the Korea Trust Bank, which represented a consolidation in 1967 of the trust departments of the five national commercial banks. Trust accounts in Korea are fairly close substitutes for time deposits. The Korea Trust Bank held substantial amounts of demand deposits from its inception. Thus, it functioned much like a commercial bank and was treated as such by both the central bank and the financial authorities before it was merged with the Seoul Bank in 1976 to become the Bank of Seoul and Trust Company.

The Korea Housing Bank was also created in 1967 "to finance housing funds for low-income families."[24] It was to extend loans for construction and purchase of houses, and to firms producing housing construction materials. The Housing Bank has raised roughly a third of its funds through the sale of debentures and 55 percent of its funds through demand and time deposits. Depositors receive preferential treatment in the granting of loans, which provides an incentive in addition to the interest rate for holding its deposits. Still, the Housing Bank's share of total bank deposits has not risen above 4 percent.

Of greater significance was the government's action in 1967 authorizing the chartering of "local banks" to conduct commercial banking business, principally in the provinces. One objective of the government was to achieve greater dispersion of banking services and see that the banks would concentrate on meeting the needs of local enterprises. The local banks engage in branch banking, with their head offices in the provincial capitals and branches in the same province. Initially they were prohibited from engaging in foreign-exchange operations, but, as they became better established, this prohibition was relaxed. Also the local banks were authorized to charge interest rates on loans up to 2.5 percentage points higher than the national commercial banks, and to pay higher interest rates on time deposits. These banks are privately owned and less closely regulated and controlled than the government-owned banks. They are examples of the kind of banks that Bloomfield and Jensen and subsequent foreign advisors, such as Edward Shaw and Homer Jones, advocated for Korea.[25] While they have grown quite rapidly, their share of total bank deposits had reached only 10 percent by 1978 (see Table 13). The remaining 90 percent of deposits, and an even higher percentage of total loans, were still administered by government-owned or -controlled banks.

A final institutional innovation of 1967 was the granting of permission to a limited number of foreign banks to open branch offices in Korea. In the first year, five banks—three American and two Japanese— established branches, and, by the end of 1974, four more were permitted. Since then, the number of foreign bank branches has risen rapidly, reflecting a growing volume of external transactions. At the end of 1978, there were thirty branches and fifteen foreign bank representative offices.[26] The kinds of activities in which these branches can participate are quite circumscribed, and their share of total bank deposits reached only 1.1 percent by 1978. They rely mainly on funds borrowed from their head offices to make loans in foreign currency, especially to importers.

RELATIVE GROWTH OF BANKING ACTIVITIES, 1970–1978

As discussed previously, the deposits, loans and guarantees of the banking institutions expanded dramatically in nominal terms, in real terms, and as a share of GNP between 1965 and 1969 (see Tables 12 and 13). Thereafter, the growth of deposits slowed down, and the ratio of deposits to GNP actually declined from 33.7 percent in 1973 to 27.8 percent in 1976—a period of rapid inflation—and moved up again to the 1973 level in 1978. Loans and guarantees of foreign loans moved in quite erratic patterns between 1970 and 1978, and so did the relative roles of different types of banks as sources of finance.

Guarantees of foreign loans doubled between the end of 1969 and the end of 1971, and grew by 100 billion wŏn or 25 percent more than bank credit. The KDB was responsible for 60 percent of the guarantees and the commercial banks for the rest. This expansion of guarantees was a major factor in the financial difficulties of 1972, when devaluation and a slowdown of exports forced many large enterprises to default on their foreign-loan payments, thus making it necessary for the guaranteeing banks to bail them out. The volume of outstanding guarantees actually declined in 1972, as very few new ones were issued.

TABLE 13 Amounts and Shares of Total Deposits of Various Types of Banks 1965–1978 (billion wŏn)

	1965		1966		1967		1968		1969	
	Amount	*%*	*Amount*	*%*	*Amount*	*%*	*Amount*	*%*	*Amount*	*%*
GNP at current market prices	805.7		1,037.0		1,281.2		1,652.9		2,155.3	
Total bank deposits as % of GNP		9.7		11.7		16.0		22.5		28.7
Bank deposits, total	78.4	100.0	120.9	100.0	205.1	100.0	371.6	100.0	618.8	100.0
Commerical banks	55.3	70.5	82.5	68.2	137.0	66.8	248.8	67.0	480.6	66.0
National	55.3	70.5	82.5	68.2	135.5	66.1	240.0	64.6	388.1	62.7
Local					0.9	0.4	6.8	1.8	16.9	2.7
Foreign banks					0.6	0.5	2.0	0.5	3.6	0.6
Specialized banks	23.1	29.5	38.4	31.8	68.2	33.3	122.8	33.0	210.2	34.0
MIB	5.8	7.4	9.3	7.7	15.4	7.5	25.4	6.8	39.8	6.4
CNB	7.6	9.7	13.5	11.2	21.7	10.6	36.1	9.7	60.3	9.7
KEB					3.2	1.6	11.2	3.0	21.3	3.4
KMB					0.7	0.5	3.3	0.9	10.7	1.7
Agriculture coops	9.6	12.2	15.2	12.9	27.2	13.3	46.7	12.6	75.9	12.3
Fisheries coops							0.2	0.1	2.2	0.4

Source: BOK, *General Review on Savings in Korea* (1978).

TABLE 13 (continued)

	1970		1971		1972		1973		1974	
	Amount	*%*	*Amount*	*%*	*Amount*	*%*	*Amount*	*%*	*Amount*	*%*
GNP at current market prices	2,675.44		3,276.2		4,002.2	33.1	5,199.1	33.7	7,279.6	28.9
Total bank deposits as % of GNP		29.5		29.8						
Bank deposits, total	788.1	100.0	976.9	100.0	1,323.8	100.0	1,753.5	100.0	2,107.5	100.0
Commercial banks	505.4	64.1	635.7	65.1	892.4	67.4	1,179.2	67.2	1,408.1	66.8
National	467.1	59.3	574.8	58.8	787.2	59.5	1,018.0	58.1	1,192.8	56.6
Local	32.8	4.2	54.4	5.6	93.3	7.0	144.2	8.2	197.8	9.4
Foreign banks	5.5	0.7	6.5	0.7	11.9	0.9	17.0	1.0	17.5	0.8
Specialized banks	282.7	35.9	341.2	24.9	431.4	32.6	574.4	32.8	699.4	33.2
MIB	58.3	7.4	70.8	7.2	88.2	6.7	113.8	6.5	130.4	6.2
CNB	80.1	10.2	100.7	10.3	127.8	9.7	166.8	9.5	199.1	9.4
KEB	28.3	3.6	32.5	3.3	44.4	3.4	72.3	4.1	84.0	4.0
KMB	16.2	2.1	23.1	2.4	31.3	2.4	43.1	2.5	53.3	2.5
Agriculture coops	95.6	12.1	4.9	0.5	6.6	0.5	9.7	0.6	15.0	0.7
Fisheries coops	4.2	0.5	109.2	11.2	133.2	10.1	168.7	9.6	217.4	10.3

TABLE 13 (continued)

	1975		1976		1977		1978	
	Amount	%	Amount	%	Amount	%	Amount	%
GNP at current market prices	9,644.2		13,051.3		16,652.4		22,255.7	
Total bank deposits as % of GNP		28.8		27.8		31.6		33.7
Bank deposits, total	2,779.1	100.0	3,688.1	100.0	1,237.8	100.0	7,589.0	100.0
Commercial banks	1,923.3	69.2	2,495.4	67.7	3,474.1	65.1	4,840.6	63.7
National	1,610.2	57.9	2,054.9	55.9	2,865.0	53.7	4,003.8	52.8
Local	283.5	10.2	397.5	10.8	550.6	10.3	745.1	9.8
Foreign banks	29.5	1.1	43.0	1.2	58.5	1.1	9.7	1.2
Specialized banks	855.9	30.8	1,192.7	32.3	1,863.7	34.9	2,748.4	36.2
MIB	158.4	5.7	203.9	5.5	310.8	5.8	481.7	6.3
CNB	239.0	8.6	341.4	9.3	544.2	10.2	795.9	10.5
KEB	109.9	4.0	161.2	4.4	287.9	5.4	402.9	5.3
KMB	66.2	2.4	95.8	2.6	193.8	3.6	313.9	4.1
Agriculture coops	260.3	10.4	356.7	9.7	474.5	8.9	675.3	8.9
Fisheries coops	22.1	0.8	34.7	0.9	52.5	1.0	78.7	1.0

As Chapter 5 will show, the government shifted most of the burden of adjustment to this financial crisis onto the unregulated financial institutions by forcing a stretching out of the repayment period and reduction of interest rates on all UFI loans. Thus, the commercial banks and the KDB were able to hold down their refinancing of the foreign debts and got back into the issuance of new guarantees in a big way in 1973. The KDB issued 524 billion wŏn worth of guarantees in 1974, and the commercial banks took the lead in 1975 with 660 billion wŏn, by which time the level of outstanding guarantees, (2,966 billion wŏn) exceeded total bank deposits (2,798 billion wŏn). The commercial banks and the KDB held about equal amounts of guarantees, while those held by the special banks continued to be negligible.

Bank loans grew at a higher rate than bank deposits—28.5 percent versus 25.1 percent per year—between 1969 and 1978. In part, this was due to a substantial amount of direct borrowing abroad by the commercial banks towards the end of the period. The relative shares of the three types of banks in total lending remained fairly constant over the period, with the commercial banks accounting for slightly more than half, the special banks nearly one-third, and the KDB one-sixth. On the deposit side, the commercial banks had two-thirds and the special banks one-third, with negligible amounts in the KDB.

DEVELOPMENT OF NON-BANK FINANCIAL INSTITUTIONS

Banking institutions and unregulated financial institutions accounted for most of the financial intermediation during the two post-war decades. Life insurance, postal savings, and money in trust accounted for a commanding share of the non-banking financial sector, although money in trust was actually time and savings deposits at the DMBs with longer maturities. Since the early 1970s, however, the government has made numerous attempts to encourage new types of non-bank financial institutions and, in the process, to undermine and eventually eliminate the unregulated institutions.

Owing to these efforts, a variety of new non-banking institutions have come into existence, and their assets and liabilities have grown rapidly in the 1970s. Given the nature of their operations, it also seems that some of these, such as the IFCs and MSFCs, have been instrumental in attracting private savings from the unregulated to the regulated financial institutions.

In the latter part of the 1960s, the volume of indirect securities issued by the non-banking financial institutions was no more than 15 percent of M_2. Within less than a decade, however, the volume had risen to 2,138.5 billion wŏn, equivalent to 30 percent of M_2. Among the non-banking institutions, the IFCs have registered the highest rate of growth, followed by mutual savings of primary cooperatives of the NACF and CFFC. At the end of 1977, the IFCs accounted for 31.5 percent of the non-banking finance (see Table 14). Life insurance companies and trust businesses, which once dominated the non-bank financial sector, have gradually lost their market shares. Their combined share declined from 84 percent in 1965 to 31 percent in 1977.

DEVELOPMENT INSTITUTIONS

Development institutions in the category of the non-bank financial intermediaries include the KDB, the Export-Import Bank of Korea (EIB), the National Investment Fund, the Land Bank of Korea, and the Korea Development Finance Corporation. These institutions supply long-term industrial credit with the funds raised by borrowing from the government, international financial institutions, and foreign banks, and by issuing debentures. They differ from the deposit money banks (DMBs) in that they are not permitted to accept deposits from the general public except from specific customers.

The KDB, previously treated as a special bank, was placed in the non-bank category when a functional reclassification of financial institutions was made in 1973. The bank is allowed to receive time deposits from the public, but demand deposits only from those to whom the bank has extended loans or other financial services. Thus, unlike the DMBs, the KDB does not depend upon deposits for loanable funds. At the end of 1978, deposits accounted for less than 1 percent of its total liabilities and net worth.

In 1967, the Korea Development Finance Corporation (KDFC) was organized with help from the World Bank "to assist in the development and creation of private enterprises by providing medium- and long-term industrial financing and equity participation, as well as technical and managerial consulting services."[27] One of the major roles of the KDFC was to be the sponsoring and underwriting agency of equity shares and debentures. Opportunities for entering into this range of activities were enhanced by the passage of a series of laws regulating speculative holdings in real estate (1967), fostering the capital market (1968), giving tax preference for publicly held corporations (1968 and 1972), suppressing the curb-market loans (1972), and encouraging business firms to go public (1974). All these measures were intended to force closely held family corporations to broaden their ownership and to develop long-term capital markets as alternatives to the prevailing dependence on bank loans, foreign loans, and the curb market.

The establishment of the Land Bank of Korea is a case in point. Real estate has long been one of the most attractive assets as a hedge against inflation in Korea. Understandably, businesses have held land and other real properties in excess of their actual needs for speculation as well as for collateral for bank loans. In an effort to reduce business holdings in land and to reallocate the land to residential sites and other productive uses, a bank specialized in land financing was created in 1975. The bank buys and sells land and makes loans for the purchase of land for industrial uses. The bank was set up as a temporary institution and was expected to become a land development corporation in 1979.

TABLE 14 Amounts and Shares of Total Deposits of Various Types of Non-Bank Financial Institutions, 1965–1977 (billion wŏn)

	1965		1966		1967		1968		1969	
	Amount	*%*	*Amount*	*%*	*Amount*	*%*	*Amount*	*%*	*Amount*	*%*
Total	14.8	100.0	27.2	100.0	49.2	100.0	81.9	100.0	113.6	100.0
Money in trust	7.6	51.4	15.5	57.0	30.0	61.0	51.5	62.9	67.2	59.2
Life insurance premiums	4.8	32.4	7.4	27.2	12.1	24.6	17.7	21.6	28.7	25.3
Sales of notes of Investment and Finance Co.	—	—	—	—	—	—	—	—	—	—
Postal savings	2.0	13.5	3.5	12.9	5.7	11.6	8.4	10.3	12.3	10.8
National savings associations trust in National Investment Fund	—	—	—	—	—	—	—	—	—	—
Mutual savings of Agricultural and Fisheries Coop	—	—	—	—	—	—	—	—	3.5	3.0
Installment deposits at Mutual Savings and Finance Co.	—	—	—	—	—	—	—	—	—	—
Contributions to and deposits at credit unions	—	—	—	—	—	—	—	—	—	—
Investment trust beneficiary certificates	—	—	—	—	—	—	—	—	—	—
Time and savings deposits at the Korea Development Bank	0.4	2.7	0.7	2.6	1.4	2.8	4.3	5.3	1.8	1.6

Source: BOK, *General Review on Savings in Korea* (1978).

TABLE 14 (continued)

	1970		1971		1972		1973		1974	
	Amount	%	Amount	%	Amount	%	Amount	%	Amount	%
Total	145.0	100.0	209.0	100.0	288.9	100.0	478.6	100.0	687.6	100.0
Money in trust	79.2	54.6	124.8	60.0	158.2	54.8	182.5	38.1	190.2	27.7
Life insurance premiums	39.9	27.5	51.0	24.4	67.9	23.5	91.4	19.1	124.2	18.1
Sales of notes of Investment and Finance Co.	—	—	—	—	3.9	1.3	67.2	14.0	162.2	23.6
Postal savings	15.1	10.4	16.1	7.7	27.2	9.4	34.6	7.2	41.5	6.0
National savings associations trust in National Investment Fund	—	—	—	—	—	—	—	—	4.1	0.6
Mutual savings of Agricultural and Fisheries Coop	7.0	4.8	13.6	6.5	24.5	8.5	43.7	9.1	83.9	12.2
Installment deposits at Mutual Savings and Finance Co.	—	—	—	—	—	—	36.9	7.7	48.3	7.0
Contributions to and deposits at credit unions	—	—	—	—	—	—	14.1	2.9	22.9	3.3
Investment trust beneficiary certificates	0.1	0.1	0.0	—	0.4	0.1	1.7	0.4	5.3	0.8
Time and savings deposits at the Korea Development Bank	3.7	2.6	3.4	1.6	6.8	2.4	6.5	1.4	5.0	0.7

TABLE 14 (continued)

	1975		1976		1977	
	Amount	%	Amount	%	Amount	%
Total	905.3	100.0	1,363.2	100.0	2,089.0	100.0
Money in Trust	186.5	20.6	251.0	18.4	354.8	17.0
Life insurance premiums	162.6	18.0	211.0	15.5	294.4	14.1
Sales of notes of Investment and Finance Co.	254.2	28.1	438.1	32.1	658.7	31.5
Postal savings	47.6	5.3	59.0	4.3	29.6	1.4
National savings associations trust in National Investment Fund	9.4	0.0	16.0	1.2	24.0	1.1
Mutual savings of Agricultural and Fisheries Coop	125.2	13.8	203.6	14.9	340.1	16.3
Installment deposits at Mutual Savings and Finance Co.	43.4	4.8	55.1	4.0	84.9	4.1
Contributions to and deposits at credit unions	38.3	4.2	66.7	4.9	148.7	7.1
Investment trust beneficiary certificates	14.8	1.6	42.1	3.1	124.4	6.0
Time and savings deposits at the Korea Development Bank	23.3	2.6	20.5	1.5	29.7	1.4

As discussed earlier, the KDB played a dominant role as the long-term credit bank in the 1950s and 1960s, though other special banks had increased in importance as suppliers of long-term funds in the 1960s. In the early 1970s, when the Third Five-Year Development Plan was prepared, it was clear that the DMBs and the KDB could hardly be expected to provide sufficient financing for the development of heavy and chemical industries, one of the major objectives of the Third Plan. Out of the need for augmenting the flow of domestic savings to the investment in heavy and chemical industries, a new financing channel, the National Investment Fund (NIF), was established in 1974.

The major sources of the NIF loanable funds consist of (1) the proceeds from the sales of NIF bonds, (2) contributions in the form of deposits made by the DMBs (exclusive of foreign bank branches and fisheries cooperatives), the members of the National Savings Association, money in trust, insurance premiums of non-life insurance companies, and various public funds managed by the central and local governments and other public entities, and (3) transfers (or deposits) from the various government budgetary accounts. As for the contributions, the DMBs are, for instance, required to deposit at the NIF 15 percent of the increase in their savings deposits, and non-life insurance companies 50 percent of their insurance premiums and other revenues. Despite these compulsory contributions, the NIF held only 1.1 percent of the deposits of non-bank financial institutions by 1977.

The MOF is responsible for the administration of the Fund, but its actual management has been entrusted to the BOK. The NIF makes loans for both fixed investment and working capital to the heavy, chemical, and other major industries with the DMBs, KDB, and EIB acting as intermediaries.

At the end of 1978, interest rates on NIF deposits ranged from 6 percent per annum (for three-month deposits) to 18.6 percent (for one-year-and-over deposits and NIF bonds), whereas the lending rates varied from 6 percent for export suppliers' credit to 16 percent for the loans to the heavy and chemical industry with three- to eight-year maturities. The losses resulting from the negative margin between the deposit and lending rates were fully compensated by the government. The deposits and holdings of NIF bonds by the DMBs accounted for 45 percent of the NIF's total financial resources; about 65 percent of the Fund resources were loaned out to the heavy and chemical industries.

The Export-Import Bank is another institution created for the promotion of exports of heavy and chemical products. The bank was legally established in 1969, but its operations were handled by the KEB for the next seven years. Since becoming a separate entity in 1976, the size of its loan portfolio has increased markedly. The bank provides medium- and long-term credit for foreign trade and overseas investment with its own resources and funds borrowed from the government and NIF.

SAVINGS INSTITUTIONS

In 1972, three laws were enacted authorizing investment and finance companies (IFCs), mutual savings and finance companies (MSFCs), and credit unions. These three new types of regulated financial institutions were intended to take up the short-term financing activities of the unregulated financial institutions.

The MSFCs were established by consolidating *mujin* and popular funds, two private credit institutions that stood midway between the unregulated and the regulated institutions. The MSFCs serve as the organizer of mutual-credit *kye,* accept mutual installment savings deposits, extend unsecured loans to and discount the bills of their members.

There were 299 such companies registered in 1972, but, by mid-1975, their number had declined to 221 and fell further to 209 at the end of 1978, due to mergers and bankruptcies. Despite the decline in number, their total deposits rose markedly between 1975 and 1978. The growth may have been associated with the takeover of some of the MSFCs by large business groups. It is alleged that the business groups channel some of their idle funds through the MSFCs to take advantage of MSFCs' close ties with the unregulated money markets and their relatively high deposit rates. At the end of 1978, MSFCs' total deposits stood at 138.5 billion, more than four times the figure of six years before, and 5 percent of total non-bank financial institution deposits.

Credit unions were first organized in the early 1960s in businesses, government agencies, and other public and private organizations to encourage employees to save and to provide them with an opportunity to borrow cheaply. Until 1972, establishment and management of credit unions were left to the unions themselves. With the enactment of the Credit Union Act in that year, however, they have been placed under government guidance and supervision. At the end of 1977, contributions to and installment deposits at credit unions amounted to 148.7 billion wŏn, about 7 percent of the total indirect securities issued by non-bank financial intermediaries (see Table 14). The Credit Union Act also applies to mutual savings and finance operations of primary cooperatives of the NACF and CFFC and to village finance associations.

Agricultural and fisheries cooperatives are the basic units of the pyramid of cooperative institutions for agricultural and fishery finance which have the NACF and CFFC at their apex and the regional cooperatives in the middle tier. Credit activities of the NACF and CFFC and their regional cooperatives are treated as those of a special bank (see Figure 2).

Primary cooperatives of the NACF (since 1969) and CFFC (since 1974) have been engaged in mutual savings and finance operations. Financial resources of these cooperatives consist of equity subscriptions and various deposits by their members. Deposits at the cooperative include: (1) temporary deposits, similar to pass-book deposits at the DMBs; (2) fixed-term deposits; and (3) mutual installment deposits. A fixed percentage (about 10 percent) of these deposits is held at the NACF and CFFC as reserves, the remainder loaned out to cooperative members or redeposited at banking institutions.

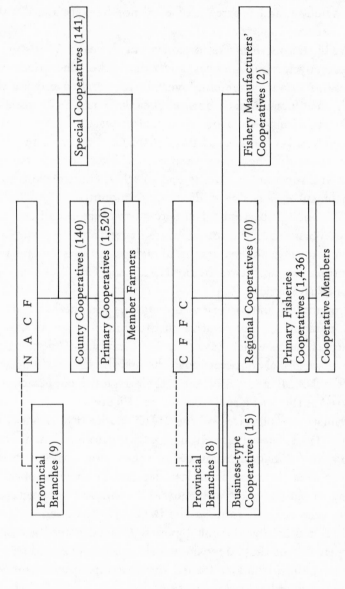

FIGURE 2 Organization of Agricultural and Fisheries Cooperatives

Source: BOK, *Financial System in Korea* (1978), pp. 34–36.
Note: Figures in parentheses represent the number of cooperatives at the end of 1978.

The interest rates on the deposits are higher than those on similar deposits at the DMBs. Partly for this reason and mostly because of marked increases in farm-household incomes, deposits at the primary cooperatives have grown by more than ten times since the start of operation in 1969. Primary and regional cooperatives of the NACF and CFFC also took over postal savings deposits in 1977.

The village finance associations are a form of credit union whose members usually consist of the residents of a rural village or a *dong,* the smallest administrative unit in urban areas. These associations were first established in 1964 as part of the rural development movement. The latest figure available (July 1978) shows that the total of equity subscriptions and deposits at the associations amounted to 171.7 billion wŏn.

INVESTMENT COMPANIES

Investment companies comprise four types of non-banking institutions: investment and finance companies (IFCs), merchant banking corporations, securities investment trust companies, and the Korea Securities Finance Corporation. Among the three non-bank institutions established in 1972, the IFCs have been the most successful. Their main activity is dealing in commercial paper, primarily that which they issue themselves; but they also buy, sell, accept, and guarantee the paper of other business enterprises. Their interest rates are supposedly market-determined, but in reality controlled by the Ministry of Finance.

In addition, they may act as investment bankers and issue and place securities for business enterprises. The amount of outstanding bills of the IFCs—equivalent to deposit liabilities of the banking institutions—has risen rapidly, as shown in Table 15.

For purposes of comparison, total DMB deposits at the end of 1978 were 7.7 trillion wŏn, so the bills were nearly 7 percent of total deposits. Thus, it appears that the finance companies are proving to be an effective substitute for the unregulated short-term lending institutions. The fact that interest rates on the finance company bills are flexible and substantially higher than

TABLE 15 Outstanding Bills of Investment and Finance
Companies
(million wŏn)

End of Year	
1972	1,130
1973	47,661
1974	118,846
1975	180,505
1976	289,524
1977	386,357
1978	542,498

Source: BOK, *Economic Statistics Yearbook* (1978).

bank lending or deposit rates is undoubtedly a significant factor
affecting their viability and competitiveness.

Merchant banking corporations were introduced in 1976 because of the desire to diversify the channel of borrowing from
abroad after a serious foreign-exchange shortage caused by the
oil crisis during 1973–1974. At the end of 1978, there were five
such corporations, all joint ventures with foreign investors who
held an equity share less than 50 percent.

These corporations carry out a wide range of financial services
that include: (1) brokerage of foreign loans and making loans in
foreign currencies; (2) the discount, acceptance, and guarantee
of commercial paper; and (3) investment banking activities. Although the corporations were patterned after British multi-
faceted private financial institutions, their operations have been
limited to discounting commercial paper and securities investment trusts.

Securities investment trust companies raise funds by selling
beneficiary certificates to public investors. These funds are then
transfered to the Bank of Seoul and Trust Company which acts
as the trust company to establish a trust fund. Each fund is put
in the custody of the trust company (the Bank of Seoul and

Trust Company) and managed by the securities investment trust companies.

The Korea Securities Finance Corporation was established in 1955 as the principal organization for securities financing. With funds borrowed mostly from banks, the corporation channels funds necessary for clearing brokers' trading on margin and extends loans to underwriters and registered members of the Korea Stock Exchange.

DEVELOPMENT OF THE CAPITAL MARKET

The Korean securities market has evolved over time from the initial Chosun Securities Exchange, created in 1943 by the Japanese, mainly for the purpose of selling public debentures to finance the war. The market was closed in early 1946, following independence, and, for ten years thereafter, debentures were traded among securities companies in an unorganized manner and sold over the counter to individuals.

In March 1956, the Korea Stock Exchange was established, with equity participation by banks, insurance companies, and securities companies. The Exchange, however, remained merely a market for government bonds without an institutional structure able to facilitate the issuance or circulation of new stocks or corporate bonds.

In the early 1960s, with the launching of the First Five-Year Economic Development Plan, the government decided to foster the capital market as a means of domestic savings. The Securities and Exchange Law was enacted in 1962 whereby the Korea Stock Exchange was reorganized as a corporation, a step closer to a stock market and away from a government bond market. At the same time, some government enterprises also revalued their real assets to reflect past inflation and started to pay dividends, thereby creating a demand for their stock. The market was too shallow and unprepared however, to take advantage of the growing interest in stocks. Two stocks, those of the Korea Stock Exchange and the Korea Securities Finance Corporation, dominated the market. Furthermore, since transactions were typically settled at the end of each month, investors could earn capital gains with only a small down payment by concluding the opposite transactions before the date of settlement. This mode of transaction and settlement encouraged speculation and manipulation of stock prices to such an extent that prices rose to a level far in excess of the intrinsic value of the stocks. This at last resulted in a massive collapse in stock prices towards the end of 1962 and a shutdown of the market for three months in early 1963.[28]

The Korea Stock Exchange was reopened again in May 1963, this time with equity participation and heavy control by the government, which hoped to restore public confidence in the market. Nevertheless, there was little prospect of the market playing a significant role in the mobilization of domestic savings. First of all, few high-quality securities were offered in the market, because most business firms were typically closely held and run by families. The owners had no incentive to go public and thereby incur not only a possible loss of control over the corporation, but also obligations to issue public financial reports and to pay dividends, and in some cases a financial loss which resulted from the fact that the appreciation of non-operating real estate was not allowed once the corporation became publicly owned.

Furthermore, the public image of large corporations was unfavorable. Corporate management was dominated by government and could not be trusted to report honestly or deal fairly with minority shareholders. Other profitable investment opportunities were available elsewhere, especially in the real-estate and unorganized money markets. For these reasons, the capital market remained dormant for the next five years after the reopening of the Korea Stock Exchange in 1963.

In the meantime, however, it became evident that heavy reliance on bank loans and foreign loans to meet the financial requirements for the rapid growth target set in the Second Five-Year Development Plan (1967–1971) was leading to high debt-equity ratios dominated by short-term debt for many businesses. With this realization and the government's desire for greater diffusion of corporate ownership and diversification of business financing sources, the government renewed its efforts to develop a modern capital market and began to implement a series of reform measures towards the latter part of the 1960s.

POLICY MEASURES FOR THE DEVELOPMENT OF THE
CAPITAL MARKET

The enactment of the Law for Fostering Capital Markets, November 1968, was the first in the series of such policy measures. This law aimed at creating a favorable environment for the growth of the capital market by encouraging major corporations to go public. In this way, the authorities hoped to facilitate the diffusion of corporate ownership through increased capital participation by the public. At the same time, to make corporate equity shares more attractive to investors, private stockholders of government-controlled enterprises were entitled to claim dividends up to a specified level. This level was set at 10 percent of par value until August 1974, when it was raised to equal the level of interest on one-year time deposits.

Regular employees (except executives) of publicly held corporations were given the opportunity to subscribe to new stock issues up to the limit of 10 percent of the newly issued share or 10 percent of the combined new and existing issues after 1972. In addition, the Minister of Finance was given the discretion to sell government-owned stocks at below market prices to the general public, government officials, or employees of the government, if he deemed it desirable. Furthermore, to enhance the value of equity shares, stocks traded on the Exchange were permitted to be used as guarantee deposits for contract bids with central and local governments or government enterprises.

Tax incentives were another important instrument used to encourage closed corporations to go public. For corporate income in the highest bracket, the (marginal) tax rate was fixed at 35 percent for publicly held companies (see Table 16 for the requirements of these companies) against 45 percent for closed corporations. From 1969 to 1971, the rates were changed to 25 percent and 45 percent, respectively, for publicly held and closed corporations, and, since 1972, to 27 percent and 40 percent respectively (see Table 17). In addition, closed corporations were subject to a 5 percent tax on their internal saving.

Furthermore, a reduction of the base of tax assessment was allowed until 1976 for publicly held corporations, according to the proportion of newly raised capital to total capital prior to 1975. In this connection, a publicly held firm was also automatically treated as a "green-returns" corporation and accorded privileges such as (1) the payment of corporate income tax in installments, (2) treatment of reserves for overseas marketing as a cost, (3) an additional 20 percent special depreciation allowance on fixed assets over the regular depreciation allowance, (4) a one-year extension (from three to four years) of the income deduction for carried-over loss.

Favorable tax treatment was also given to investors in securities. Tax exemption was granted for dividends received by "small" stockholders owning less than 3 percent of the total shares outstanding, as well as interest income on corporate bonds sold to the public through financial institutions and held by investors owning less than 10 percent of the total bonds outstanding. Even the dividend income of "large" stockholders was taxed at 5 percent, a rate much lower than the 20 percent applied to dividends from closed corporations.

Government efforts to stimulate the demand for securities were not limited to tax incentives. They also included underpricing of new stock issues and discouraging holding other assets, in particular real assets and claims on the unregulated financial institution. Prices of new issues were deliberately kept below their market values so that, when these shares were placed in the secondary market, their prices rose markedly.[29] This expected short-term capital gain was a strong incentive to investors

TABLE 16 Requirements for Publicly Held Corporation Status

Effective from	1968	31 July 1969	1972	1975
Minimum number of small stockholders	30	100	200	300
Minimum percentage of shares held by all small stockholders	20	30	30	40
Maximum percentage of shares held by a principal stockholder	60	60	51	51
Maximum percentage of shares an investor can hold and still qualify as a small stockholder	3	3	3	1

Source: Ministry of Justice, *Taehanmin'guk hyŏnhaeng pŏmyŏngjip.*

in securities. While it succeeded in attracting a large number of savers into the capital market, the underpricing created several other problems. On the supply side, the high cost of raising equity capital caused by the undervaluation discouraged the existing owners of firms from going public or encouraged them to dilute the value of securities before offering new shares, or to go public in a disguised manner in which the owners themselves purchased most of the new issues. On the demand side, the underpricing led to over subscription aimed at short-run capital gains on new shares, with the consequences of wild speculation in the capital market and illegal trading outside the Exchange before or after the listing.

In determining the issue-price (see below on underwriting), the authorities placed more emphasis on asset values than expected earning of the firms to be listed and applied the same capitalization rate based on the official interest rates to all firms irrespective of the differences in the risk, growth potential, and financial conditions of different firms. As a result, some of the new stock issues were traded below the issue prices, whereas others experienced a doubling or tripling of their issue prices immediately after being placed in the secondary market.

TABLE 17 Differential Corporate Income Tax Rates[a] for Publicly Held and Closed Corporations

Yearly Taxable Income	1968	1969–1971	1972–1974	1975–1976	1977–	
Less than 1 million wŏn	20[b]	15[b]	16[b]	20[b]	20	20[c]
	25	25	20	20		25[cc]
1–3 million wŏn	30[b]	20[b]	20[b]	20[b]	30	
3–5 million wŏn	35	35	30	30		
More than 5 million wŏn	35[b]	25[b]	27[b]	27[b]	40	27[c]
	45	45	40	40		33[cc]

Source: Ministry of Justice, *Taehanmin'guk hyŏnhaeng pŏmyŏngjip.*

Notes: [a]The tax rates are marginal rates applicable to the specified portion of total taxable income.
[b]For publicly held corporations.
[c]For publicly held corporations whose principal stockholder owns less (or more, [cc]) than 35 percent of the total shares. The rates apply only to firms whose business year starts after January 1, 1977. For publicly held corporations as of January 1, 1977, the rates are effective from the business year closing after January 1, 1979.

Between January 1976 and September 1977, as many as 25 stocks among the 126 issues newly offered in the market were traded below the issue price, while another 25 issues were sold at a level more than double the issue price at the end of September 1977.

In order to discourage real-estate investment, capital gains on designated types of land were taxed at the heavy rate of 50 percent starting in 1968. These regulations were further tightened in 1974, when property and acquisition tax rates for idle land and luxury dwellings were again raised. As a result, land prices rose only moderately during 1969–1973 (with the exception of 1971), a fact that no doubt contributed to the expansion of the demand for securities.

Another target of attack was the unorganized money market (see Chapter 5). By the Presidential Emergency Decree of August 1972, unorganized money-market loans to business enterprises exceeding three million wŏn in value were rescheduled to be repayable over eight years with a three-year grace period at an interest rate of 1.35 percent per month. This decree not only greatly reduced the capitalized value of outstanding loans, but also raised the public's perception of the risk of lending money to the unregulated institutions. The unregulated institutions were moribund for some time, but gradually began to revive again one year later. Furthermore, the informal money market loans made by large stockholders or executives to their firms, so-called "disguised" informal money market loans, were converted into capital subscriptions by the decree.

Long-term time deposit interest rates, which were raised to 30 percent per annum after the adoption of the high-interest-rate policy in 1965, were lowered gradually to 22.8 percent in June 1969, to 20.4 percent in June 1971, and further to 16.8 percent and 12.0 percent, respectively, in January and August 1972. This downward adjustment of bank deposit interest rates was not necessarily intended to support the capital market, but nevertheless constituted an important part of making securities investment relatively more attractive.

Tax and other incentive measures were buttressed by the government efforts to improve institutional facilities of the market. As a first step, the Korea Investment Corporation was created in 1968, based on the Law for Fostering Capital Markets, through the subscription of the government and private banks. The Korea Investment Corporation was a leading distributor of new shares and corporate bonds until it was dissolved at the end of 1976. It provided best-effort arrangements and outright or stand-by underwriting, guaranteed corporate bonds, gave credit to subscribers in public offerings, and made general loans against the collateral of designated securities. The Korea Investment Corporation also traded securities for the management of the investment trusts established in 1970 and for the stabilization of stock prices. The establishment of securities investment trusts was a means of attracting small savings from the public, and it contributed significantly to the development of the securities market. This business was transferred to newly opened investment trust companies and banking corporations in 1976.

At the same time, existing securities companies were encouraged to increase their equity capital, and large-scale securities companies were established with the equity participation of insurance companies and the Korea Trust Bank. All these measures were designed to enhance public confidence in securities companies and the securities market in general.

Beginning in February 1969, the method of transactions was changed from the previous forward transactions and clearance settlement to "regular" or spot transactions, with the exception that the Korea Securities Finance Corporation, through securities companies, was permitted to engage in forward lending of stocks and money to sellers and buyers. This was to discourage speculative transactions aimed at short-run capital gains. In reality, however, the exceptional rule became the dominant form of transaction and did not cure the problems that had beset previous forward transactions and clearance settlements. Consequently, after June 1971, the "regular" transactions system was revised so that the Korea Securities Finance Corporation strictly confined itself to financing margin transactions, while settlement financing was transformed to securities collateral loans.

PROMOTION OF THE ISSUE MARKET
AND NEW INSTITUTIONS FOR AN ORDERLY
AND EFFICIENT MARKET

Designating Firms to Go Public

Because of the government's efforts, the demand for securities grew significantly. The supply of securities, however, did not expand commensurately. In the four years following the enactment of the Law for Fostering Capital Markets in 1968, only 32 new firms listed their equity shares at the Exchange, bringing the total to 66 listed corporations at the end of 1972. Total listed equity capital increased only 80 percent from 1968 to 1972. This imbalance between demand and supply was reflected in stock prices, which rose sharply during 1971 and 1972. In 1972 alone, the composite stock price index more than doubled, although the dividend yield remained at the 20 percent level based on par value.

Faced with this situation, the authorities decided to adopt a series of strong measures to increase the supply of stocks. The Public Corporation Inducement Law of December 1972 empowered the Minister of Finance to designate eligible corporations and force them to go public. Eligible firms were to be chosen from among companies that had borrowed heavily from foreign sources or domestic banks or had rescheduled unregulated money market borrowings of more than 100 million wŏn under the August 3 Decree in 1972. Eligible firms were also designated in consideration of the size of their equity capital, their ability to pay dividends, and their prospects on the stock market.

Designated firms that actually went public enjoyed some tax benefits, while those that did not were subject to heavier personal and corporate income taxes and restrictions on access to bank credit. Designated firms, as well as corporations that had gone public previously, were allowed to revalue their non-operating land subject to an appreciation tax rate of 27 percent, or much lower than the 40 percent rate applied to other firms. This law also provided other incentives in the underwriting of stocks and the tax burden on large stockholders of publicly held corporations. The capital gains earned by underwriters from selling residual shares within six months after the initial public offering of underwritten stocks were tax-exempt until 1976. Large shareholders of a publicly held corporation holding less than 30 percent of the total shares who were subject to the global income tax were allowed to deduct 50 percent of the tax on dividend income earned before 1977.[30]

Due to these efforts, in 1973 alone, 38 corporations listed their equity shares, while 35 new issues and 12 outstanding issues were offered in the stock market, mobilizing 21.5 billion wŏn. Furthermore, the sales value of shares more than doubled from 71 billion wŏn in 1972 to 161 billion wŏn in 1973.

Joint Underwriting System: A Strong Foundation for the Issue Market

Until 1968, there was no organized issue market. Government bonds and public debentures were issued mainly to finance government deficits and specific public projects. Because of their unattractive terms, those bonds and debentures were not offered for public sale to investors but were simply "allocated" to financial institutions or forcibly sold in administrative dealings with the public. Being unable to indulge in similar forced sales of debt, private corporations were reluctant, on the other hand, to try to compete with the high interest rates on bank time deposits. Instead, they relied mainly on bank loans and foreign loans for their debt financing. As for equity shares, new equity capital was rarely raised through public offering but typically among the relatives of the company owners.

Securities companies were not involved in the underwriting business but rather functioned as intermediaries in the secondary market, because of both their lack of capital and the high risk associated with underwriting in unfavorable market situations. In 1969, the Korea Investment Corporation initiated the formation of the Council of Securities Underwriters, consisting of securities companies, banks, and insurance companies, in order to encourage the underwriting business. Underwriting activities were virtually discontinued after 1970, however, when only seven cases of underwriting were recorded. The insufficient capitalization of most securities companies and the lack of incentives for banks and insurance companies were the major reasons behind this poor performance.

In 1974, the government again prepared a plan to develop a viable underwriting system, this time placing emphasis on financing for securities underwriters. On the basis of this plan, a joint underwriting system was established, in which the Korea Investment Corporation, larger-scale securities companies, banks, investment and finance companies, and insurance companies all participated. For each case of underwriting, a managing underwriter was empowered to organize the underwriting syndicate, to analyze and price issues, and to transact other relevant business. The role of managing underwriter was generally played by the Korea Investment Corporation or one of the seven large securities companies with experience, demonstrated ability in securities analysis, and adequate capital.

Securities financing facilities made available through the Korea Securities Finance Corporation to underwriting institutions have been vital to the growth of this activity. Such financial support encouraged underwriting and issuing securities and made it possible for underwriters to participate flexibly both as demanders and suppliers to stabilize the market. Underwriters would normally distribute securities evenly over time in line with market conditions at a flexible premium over the underwritten price.

The financial support available to underwriters, however, has not always been sufficient. Due mainly to the lack of financing, some underwriters have sold the securities immediately after the underwriting at the underwritten prices. This practice has made the market less stable than it might have otherwise been.

PROMOTING FAIRNESS AND EFFICIENCY
IN THE MARKET

The rapid growth of the capital market was not accompanied by corresponding institutional improvements to deal effectively with emerging problems. A Securities and Exchange Commission and its executive body, the Securities Supervisory Board, were established only in 1977 to remedy structural weaknesses remaining in the capital market and, thereby, to maintain fairness in transactions and protect the investors. The establishment of the Securities Supervisory Board greatly facilitated the development of a centralized and specialized capital market.

In addition, the government's supervision and guidance of the operations of securities companies has increased. To secure fairness in transactions and thus protect investors, auditing of listed corporations by certified public accountants has been required, and an improved system of margin transactions and subscription to new equity issues has been established.

To encourage corporate disclosure of financial information essential for a competitive market and the optimal price determination of new issues, registration is required for corporations wishing to list their securities on the Exchange, for unlisted corporations wishing to sell securities or to merge with a listed firm, and for other designated firms. This registration system is a further development of the government's policy of inducing corporations to go public. Through it, unlisted registered firms could be encouraged to enhance managerial efficiency and to build up a healthy capital structure before they go public.

Although the law provides that a corporation may require any officer, employee, or principal stockholder to tender his profit to the firm when it is earned by trading securities of the firm making use of confidential corporate information within a period of less than six months, this provision has not been effective, and experience suggests that it is difficult to identify and regulate such transactions. Principal stockholders, defined as those holding more than 10 percent of the total shares of a corporation, are required to report to the authorities any change in their holdings of the securities, but this does not apply to the officers and employees of the listed corporations.

An orderly over-the-counter market can provide liquidity to unlisted high-grade shares, odd-lot shares of the listed stocks, and delisted or transaction-suspended shares. But, in Korea, as of 1978, this market had not yet developed. By nature, transactions outside the Exchange are made on a small scale and in a decentralized manner at negotiable prices. Thus, close supervision and supportive measures of the authorities are often needed to secure fair transactions in this market. If this market were better organized, however, it would have the potential to play a critical role in providing valuable information about the issue price, especially when market-value pricing is employed for newly offered issues in the Exchange.

GOVERNMENT INTERVENTION IN THE CAPITAL MARKET

The Korean capital market, though it grew rapidly after the mid-1960s, still lacked depth, breadth, and resiliency. In order to protect investors in this immature market, government intervention has been extensive. Frequent intervention, however, led to a new source of uncertainty, causing inexperienced investors to leave the market disillusioned, and inducing many investors to speculate merely on the timing and degree of expected intervention.

The limit of price change allowable within a trading day was introduced supposedly to protect investors from abrupt price changes. In reality, however, when there was strong upward or downward pressure on price, virtually no trading was concluded for several consecutive days until the price was fully adjusted to the underlying factors. This rigidity in price changes led to a similar change among stocks in the same industry, aggravating the rigidity further. Thus, the arbitrary limitation of the maximum possible price change simply delayed and amplified price adjustments without protecting non-speculative investors.

Major tools used by the authorities to stabilize the stock market have included changing credit availability for margin transactions and urging institutional investors to buy or sell specific stocks in a stabilizing manner. Investors may borrow money from securities companies to buy stocks or may borrow stocks to sell them. These margin transactions increase demand and supply and thus stimulate the circulation of equity shares. Furthermore, unusual and erratic swings in a stock price could, to a great extent, be damped by the supplementary and adjustment role played by transactions on credit. Margin transactions have, however, other side effects. Only investors closely connected with securities companies have access to the limited credit. These investors could manipulate prices in order to obtain short-run speculative gains.

Institutional investors have contributed to the development of the capital market by distributing the high returns from securities investment to individuals with limited capital and little experience. By the concentrated purchase of particular shares, however, the big institutional investors tend to reduce the circulation and exert significant impact on the stock prices.

At the end of 1977, about 54 percent of the total listed shares were held by the government and public entities, banks, securities, and insurance companies, and other legal entities. The ratio held by individuals decreased from 59 percent at the end of 1974 to 46 percent three years later. Thus, the institutional investors are a major factor in the market, but the investment activity of institutional investors has been hampered by frequent government intervention; institutional investors have not been able to play a stabilizing role by countering speculative transactions.

GROWTH OF THE KOREAN CAPITAL MARKET

Expansion of the Organized Securities Markets

Growth of the Korean stock market during the last decade has been very rapid. The number of companies listing their stocks at the Exchange increased from 24 at the end of 1967 to 356 eleven years later. New stock listings have been particularly numerous since 1972, when the Public Corporation Inducement Law was enacted (see Table 18).

Similarly, the number of shareholders, which was only 33,000 in 1967, rose to 963,000 at the end of 1978. The total market value of listed stocks also has shown enormous growth, with rapid increases in both the quantity and the price of listed stocks. With the exceptions of 1967, when the composite stock price index more than doubled, and of 1964 and 1968, when there was a fairly high (above 20 percent) stock price increase, the stock market was, in general, very sluggish during 1963–1970 (see Table 18). It was only after 1971 that the total market value of listed stocks exceeded the book value. Table 19 displays stock prices and yields from 1972 to 1978.

The government and public bond market declined from 1963 to 1967, but, thereafter, it grew steadily, with an increasing number of issues. Because of relatively low coupon rates on these bonds, most of them were bought up by government-controlled financial institutions rather than by individual investors. Thus, the growth of the market has been relatively slow. A total of 253 issues of government and public bonds with a face value of 340 billion wŏn were listed on the Exchange at the end of 1977. Nevertheless, the rate of turnover has been falling to as low as 0.08 during 1969–1976 (see Table 20).

For many years, few corporations issued bonds on the open market. Instead, they depended heavily on indirect financing through banks. The Law for Fostering Capital Markets of December 1968 was mainly concerned with the stock market. With the recovery of business conditions after 1972, firms

TABLE 18 Growth of the Korean Stock Market, 1963–1978

	Number of Listed Companies	Number of Brokers	Number of Shareholders (1,000 persons)	Book Value of Capital Stock Listed (billion wŏn)	Total Market Value (billion wŏn)	Turnover of Market
1963	15	40	14.8	17.0	10.0	2.23
1964	17	36	13.9	22.2	17.1	3.64
1965	17	35	14.8	23.2	14.6	0.65
1966	24	26	31.8	32.5	19.5	0.57
1967	24	25	33.1	46.1	38.5	0.74
1968	34	27	40.0	96.6	64.3	0.48
1969	42	29	54.3	119.9	86.6	0.55
1970	48	28	76.3	134.3	97.9	0.46
1971	50	28	81.9	141.4	108.7	0.37
1972	66	27	103.3	174.3	246.0	0.39
1973	104	30	200.0	251.6	426.2	0.45
1974	128	30	199.6	381.3	532.8	0.38
1975	189	28	290.7	643.4	916.1	0.48
1976	274	28	a	1,153.3	1,436.1	0.54
1977	323	27	395.3	1,492.4	2,350.8	0.78
1978	356	27	963.0	1,913.5	2,892.5	0.66

Source: Korea Stock Exchange, Stock (February 1979).

Note: [a]The number of shareholders reported by the Korean Stock Exchange for 1976 is 568,100, but this is probably an incorrect estimate and is therefore omitted in the table.

TABLE 19 Stock Prices and Yields, 1972–1978

	Composite Stock Price Index–Average (4 Jan. 1972=100)	Yearly Stock Price Index Average Range (first trading day of each year=100)		Dividend Yield (%)	Government and Public Bonds Yield (%)	Corporate Bonds Yield (%)	Stock Price-Earnings Ratio
		Average	Range				
1972	162.1	—	—	13.8	18.7	22.9	—
1973	308.5	—	—	7.5	16.6	20.0	—
1974	303.4	105.4	95.3–118.5	13.7	21.0	21.0	4.8
1975	337.1	126.0	100.0–142.9	13.7	21.1	20.3	5.3
1976	414.1	109.9	100.0–115.8	12.7	21.6	20.4	6.6
1977	437.1	113.5	100.0–137.0	14.2	20.7	20.1	5.9
1978	573.8	118.0	100.0–129.8	12.9	21.6	21.1	5.9

Source: Securities Supervisory Board, *Chŭnggwŏn chosa wŏlbo*, various issues.

TABLE 20 Growth of the Bond Market, 1963–1978

	Government and Public Bonds			Corporate Bonds			
	Number of Issues	Listed Amount (billion wǒn)	Sales Value	Number of Companies	Number of Issues	Listed Amount (billion wǒn)	Sales Value
1963	16	6.0	1.1	—	—	—	—
1965	14	3.6	0.2	—	—	—	—
1967	8	1.4	0.0	—	—	—	—
1969	26	17.5	0.3	—	—	—	—
1970	35	26.7	3.6	—	—	—	—
1971	55	44.1	7.2	—	—	—	—
1972	80	64.1	8.3	12	16	4.7	0.1
1973	128	120.4	7.2	14	18	5.3	0.2
1974	197	169.5	3.0	42	54	22.4	0.2
1975	234	167.9	12.7	71	110	52.2	0.6
1976	254	280.1	30.0	105	180	118.4	6.7
1977	253	339.7	114.3	165	293	232.3	16.2
1978	240	431.2	195.1	278	553	538.9	43.5

Source: Korea Stock Exchange, *Stock* (February 1979).

found they could no longer finance all their investment needs with bank and foreign borrowings alone, nor, after the August 3, 1972 Decree, could they borrow on the unorganized money market. At the same time, due to the downward adjustment of bank deposit rates in 1971 and 1972 and the introduction by the Korea Investment Corporation of a corporate bond guarantee system, large firms with good credit ratings could finally afford to issue bonds at competitive interest rates. Thus by the end of 1975, 71 corporations were listing 110 bond issues on the Exchange amounting to 52 billion wŏn. By 1977, the number of listed corporate bonds had increased to 293 issues offered by 165 corporations worth 232 billion wŏn, or 16 and 10 percent of the book and market value of listed equity capital, respectively. The turnover of listed corporate bonds rose from almost zero to 6-7 percent after 1976.

Reflecting high opportunity costs and rate of inflation, government and public bond yields for secondary market transactions were very high until 1971, ranging from 44 percent in 1967 to 28 percent in 1974. The yield fell below 20 percent only during 1972-1973, but stabilized at a 21-22 percent level thereafter. The yield on corporate bonds was 3-4 percent higher than that on government and public bonds for the first two years after their introduction, at about the same level during the following year (1974), and about 1 percent below them thereafter. Since 1973, the corporate bond yield has remained stable at around 20-21 percent, while the interest rate on time deposit has fluctuated between 12 percent and 16.2 percent (see Table 19).

Most of the corporate bonds currently issued and circulated are those guaranteed by banks with relatively short maturity, and few long-term bonds with more than three-year maturity and transferable bonds have been issued. One of the reasons for the slow growth of the bond market has been the absence of a well-developed secondary market which makes bond holdings illiquid and thus unattractive compared with other assets.

The income tax system has not been very conducive to investment in bonds. Under the current personal income tax system, interest income earned by those who hold more than 3 percent of the total bonds of a corporation is as heavily taxed as income from money market loans which is subject to the global income tax after a 25 percent tax at the source. It sharply contrasts with a 5 percent withholding tax for those holding less than 3 percent.

Securities in Corporate Financing and Asset Portfolios

Corporate funds raised in the capital market have increased rapidly since 1972 when the corporate bonds and outstanding stocks of unlisted companies started to be offered. Before 1972, capital increases of listed corporations and rare cases of new stocks issued before listing comprised all market activities.

During the last decade, public offerings of new and outstanding stocks prior to listing accounted for 20 percent of the total capital market financing, while 45 percent was accounted for by the paid-in capital increases of listed corporations. The other 35 percent of total corporate funds raised in the capital market was raised through bond issues which have been growing in popularity. In the two years 1977 and 1978, 500 billion wŏn were raised by bond issues, almost half of all capital market financing (see Table 21).

It is conceivable that the organized capital market could have provided a larger share of corporate financing through greater reliance on equities and bonds, in earlier years. Financing through equities and corporate bonds accounted for as much as one-fourth of total corporate external financing in 1964 (see Table 22). Following the high-interest-rate policy and large capital inflows from abroad in the mid-1960s, this ratio fell to 8 percent by 1968. Thereafter, government efforts to foster the capital market raised the dependency on equities and bonds to a level of 28 percent in 1972. But rapid growth of non-bank financial institutions and the acceleration of foreign capital inflows after 1973 again pushed the ratio down to 12

TABLE 21 Corporate Funds Raised in the Securities Market, 1968–1978 (amount in million wŏn)

	Public Offerings of New Stocks Before Listing		Public Offerings of Outstanding Stocks Before Listing		Offerings of Stocks by Listed Companies		Corporate Bonds		Total
	Case	Amount	Case	Amount	Case	Amount	Case	Amount	Amount
1968	2	160	—	—	10	20,317	—	—	20,477
1969	12	2,211	—	—	8	6,145	—	—	8,356
1970	9	2,068	—	—	13	5,083	—	—	7,151
1971	4	850	—	—	7	2,090	—	—	2,940
1972	6	955	1	125	31	13,733	35	9,928	24,741
1973	35	17,756	12	3,719	52	29,623	12	3,450	54,548
1974	12	9,227	7	5,110	61	32,080	59	27,870	74,287
1975	48	27,287	14	12,588	68	82,929	67	33,450	156,255
1976	56	40,559	31	33,445	81	101,941	112	86,280	262,225
1977	34	31,073	15	13,040	97	141,859	196	176,480	362,453
1978	23	23,777	10	17,744	148	285,201	306	326,340	653,062

Source: Korea Stock Exchange, *Stock* (February 1979).

TABLE 22 Corporate Investment, Saving, and External Financing, 1963–1977
(billion wŏn)

	Investment	Saving	Total External Financing	Bonds	Equities	Borrowings from Banks Insurance and Investment & Finance Companies and Government	Other Borrowings (Unofficial Money Market Borrowings)		Trade Credits	Foreign Liabilities
1963	49.6	24.2	36.2	1.1	9.0	9.3	7.5	(2.1)	1.0	8.3
1964	46.8	27.1	26.9	0.0	7.2	5.7	7.0	(3.3)	4.3	2.7
1965	82.2	39.7	48.4	0.0	9.4	21.4	7.8	(2.3)	4.8	4.7
1966	131.1	48.9	107.9	0.3	12.9	17.1	20.2	(9.6)	8.6	48.8
1967	185.2	63.8	198.6	1.3	16.0	64.3	30.9	(23.2)	21.5	64.6
1968	257.5	89.7	321.7	-0.1	25.0	116.2	32.6	(13.1)	39.3	108.7
1969	308.9	107.9	412.9	2.1	68.5	130.9	67.5	(21.8)	19.8	124.1
1970	373.8	126.1	471.0	4.9	62.1	153.3	67.5	(25.3)	36.9	146.3
1971	476.1	161.9	528.2	6.3	91.2	189.7	67.8	(24.4)	36.1	137.1
1972	490.2	246.4	560.6	29.6	125.9	158.1	90.3	(-24.2)	53.9	102.8
1973	774.4	431.2	928.6	17.8	169.1	411.7	83.3	(0.4)	62.6	184.1
1974	1,394.5	599.1	1,497.8	1.5	174.8	694.9	92.2	(-23.2)	288.1	246.3
1975	1,650.1	792.8	2,095.0	27.9	303.0	594.0	165.1	(8.5)	211.7	793.3
1976	1,861.4	984.1	2,252.2	64.8	459.0	660.9	264.2	(-5.8)	379.7	621.9
1977	2,509.0	1,254.9	2,936.3	155.4	593.6	885.0	480.3	(45.4)	361.9	573.7
1978	3,969.2	1,514.2	4,958.0	303.0	1,043.1	2,107.3	706.2	(101.8)	429.9	358.5

Source: BOK, *Flow of Funds Accounts in Korea* (1978).

Note: These numbers don't match with p. 103 and don't look to be internally consistent, especially for saving and external financing.

percent in 1974 before it rose to 16 and 24 percent respectively in 1975 and 1976.

Holdings of bonds and equities in the asset portfolios of individuals and corporations show roughly the same trend as the share of total external financing in the form of corporate bonds and equities (see Tables 22 and 23). At the end of 1962, individuals held 44 percent of their total financial assets in bonds (principally government bonds) and equities. Mainly due to high bank deposit rates since 1965, the ratio decreased to 20 percent at the end of 1968 then rose again to the stable level of 28-31 percent during 1972-1976. Corporations have also reduced their holdings of bonds and equities from 44 percent of their total financial assets to a 23-25 percent level since 1971.

These ratios, however, are based on book value or issue price of securities. In view of the substantial increase in stock prices since the beginning of the 1970s, the relative importance of bonds and equities in the asset portfolios of individuals and corporations must have increased significantly in recent years. Crudely, the ratios based on market value are estimated to be at 37 and 28 percent for individuals and corporations, respectively, at the end of 1976, against 31 and 23 percent in terms of book value.

Looking across the thirty-year history of institutional development in the regulated financial sector in Korea since 1945, one can discern a rough pattern of differential evolution which can be broken down into approximately five-year time periods. The first period, from 1945 to 1950, was a time of confusion and decline following the departure of the Japanese. No institutional innovations were made and the ineffectiveness of financial controls contributed to rapid inflation.

The new central bank was the dominant institution from 1950 to 1955, but its main role was to finance the war effort, a task which drew it ever more tightly into the orbit of governmental control. During the next five years, the commercial banks were shifted to private ownership and brought under the stricter

TABLE 23 Holdings of Financial Assets by Individuals and Corporations, 1962–1978 (billion wŏn)

Individuals

End of	Total	Money	Time & Savings Deposits	Insurance, Trust, and Investment & Finance Companies Deposits	Bonds and Beneficiaries' Certificates	Equities	Unregulated Money Market Loans
1962	73.3	25.7	10.5	3.5	6.3	25.9	1.4
1965	164.2	49.7	28.3	11.4	3.4	62.4	9.0
1968	577.0	147.5	200.8	59.7	2.9	111.2	54.9
1971	1,392.7	270.0	533.6	139.2	48.6	274.9	126.4
1972	1,811.9	347.9	674.3	165.0	63.9	458.6	102.2
1973	2,412.4	486.2	899.4	237.7	82.4	604.1	102.6
1974	2,991.8	605.6	1,100.0	322.0	99.8	785.1	79.3
1975	3,786.0	749.7	1,447.0	399.0	122.7	979.8	87.8
1976	5,043.9	973.8	1,847.4	576.8	231.2	1,332.6	82.1
1977	6,848.8	1,378.9	2,495.6	790.0	416.7	1,640.0	127.6
1978	9,285.5	1,618.8	3,535.4	925.5	692.6	2,283.8	229.4

TABLE 23 (continued)

Corporations

End of	Total	Money	Time & Savings Deposits	Insurance, Trust, and Investment & Finance Companies Deposits	Bonds and Beneficiaries' Certificates	Equities	Unregulated Money Market Loans
1962	15.8	8.0	2.6	0.5	1.1	3.6	—
1965	29.0	8.8	5.8	1.5	1.3	11.6	—
1968	125.9	19.4	60.2	10.4	1.8	34.1	—
1971	353.3	77.6	175.4	20.7	20.2	59.4	—
1972	565.5	143.1	252.2	41.2	26.1	102.9	—
1973	884.6	220.6	390.0	49.4	33.9	190.7	—
1974	1,107.3	288.3	466.7	70.0	38.1	244.2	—
1975	1,464.5	352.0	661.9	94.9	44.1	311.6	—
1976	2,047.3	491.7	934.3	142.0	107.1	372.2	—
1977	2,960.7	702.3	1,345.4	232.2	210.5	470.3	—
1978	4,214.9	882.0	1,940.5	424.7	319.1	648.6	—

Source: BOK, *Flow of Funds Accounts in Korea* (1978).

supervision of the central bank. They also declined in relative importance as the new special banks—the Korea Reconstruction Bank and the Agriculture Bank—became the main dispensers of credit which was based heavily on the inflows of foreign aid. (Aid goods were sold in the domestic economy, thereby generating counterpart funds that were either loaned directly to the special banks by the government, or used to offset central bank credit to those banks.)

The years from 1960 to 1965 were another period of relative confusion, as the new government renationalized the commercial banks, reorganized the Agriculture Bank, created several new special banks, took complete control of the central bank, engaged in excessive credit expansion and then carried out an ill-conceived currency reform that further undermined confidence in the financial system.

During the following five years, this pattern was again dramatically reversed, as the commercial and special banks became major mobilizers of domestic financial resources and the Korea Reconstruction (Development) Bank together with the commercial banks became participants (or silent partners) in the massive foreign-loan-guarantee business. There were also some institutional innovations during this period when the way was opened for organizing local, private commercial banks; several new special banks were created.

In the 1970–1978 period, the growth of the banking system slowed markedly as greater emphasis was placed on non-banking financial institutions. The financial crisis of 1972 led to a frontal attack on the unregulated financial institutions, which drastically reduced the real value of their assets. At the same time, new institutions were created to promote the growth of both short-term commercial bills and longer-term securities.

Since 1965, there has been both significant growth and institutional differentiation within the financial system. The government has continued to give strong guidance to all parts of the system and to see that the institutions serve the broader interests of the national development program. Recently, the local banks and the short-term finance companies have provided a limited outlet for private initiative, and have probably encroached on some of the previous domain of the unregulated markets. The longer-term securities markets are, however, very much a product of governmental incentives and direction. While they have led to some broadening of the ownership of the major corporations, they have not generated significant amounts of new capital or reduced the heavy reliance on bank and foreign-loan financing, nor have they much effect in reducing the direct links between the government and the principal owner-managers of the large corporations.

FOUR

The Unregulated
Financial Institutions and Markets

The concept of the unorganized money market was first introduced to the literature in a 1957 article by U Tun Wai to describe financial markets in which institutional financial intermediaries, such as commercial banks, are in general not involved in the exchange of either existing or new financial claims.[1]

Although U Tun Wai describes in some detail the nature and working of the UMM, he has very little to say about the assets and liabilities traded in these markets. While the characteristics of borrowers as well as lenders and the operational procedures are important to the understanding of these markets, equally important would be the nature of the financial claims exchanged between lenders and borrowers, and the nature of their relationship or lack of relationship to the regulatory authorities and to the regulated parts of the financial system.

DEFINITION AND STRUCTURE OF THE
UNREGULATED FINANCIAL MARKETS (UFMs)

We also believe that the terminology—*organized* versus *unorganized*—is misleading in that it implies the existence of organization and order in the former and an absence of those qualities in the latter. This seems to suggest that competitive markets, freedom of entry, and flexible prices are evidence of lack of organization. We regard these as important organizing forces that lead to greater efficiency, if not always to greater equity, than the regulated prices and restrictive practices of what U Tun Wai calls the organized financial sectors. In our view, the basic distinction is one of regulation rather than organization. The regulated part of the financial system is that part where governmental bodies control entry through some type of licensing system and either set prices directly or permit the limited entrants to set prices by mutual agreement, and where the government imposes numerous regulations on behavior to try to preserve some of the qualities of a competitive system. An unregulated system has the opposite characteristics, and, while it need not result in a purely competitive system, it is likely to be much closer to that than is a regulated system.

The unregulated financial markets (UFMs) in Korea are markets for short-term primary securities which are close substitutes for the short-term indirect securities issued by regulated financial institutions and which generally mature in one year or less. As in the regulated money and capital markets, ultimate borrowers and lenders are households and business enterprises. The unregulated markets and institutions have the following characteristics:

1) Credit transactions are carried on outside the system of regulated financial institutions and therefore are not subject to control of either the monetary or the tax authorities. [2]

2) Some of the primary securities in this market, such as IOUs, are not tradable.

3) Tradable securities are mostly distributed among surplus

economic units through brokers and dealers who are not legally approved for such activities. Regulated financial intermediaries seldom purchase these securities. On the other hand, the unregulated financial institutions often hold part of their assets in the form of claims on the regulated institutions (as, for example, currency and demand deposits).

The unregulated credit sector of the Korean economy may be divided into five sub-markets in terms of the characteristics of intermediaries, borrowers, and lenders in each market:

1) rudimentary private credit market
2) the *kye* market
3) informal bill market
4) curb market
5) the private financial companies, a gray credit market for consumers and small enterprises

It should be pointed out, however, that one can not, in practice, easily draw a clear demarcation among these markets. Nor does the market classification necessarily imply that these sub-markets are not coordinated or interdependent. It would be more realistic to say that they are linked to each other, and thus loanable funds flow among them, as they flow between the regulated and unregulated institutions. Our classification is designed to bring out the structural characteristics of the UFMs and thereby facilitate our discussion.

RUDIMENTARY PRIVATE CREDIT MARKET

One of the major characteristics of this market is that there are no visible professional intermediaries. Credit transactions, in general, take the form of face-to-face arrangements between ultimate borrowers and lenders. Most loans are granted on a personal basis, unsecured beyond a verbal pledge. Sometimes ultimate borrowers acquire funds by issuing primary securities such as IOUs, promissory notes, and postdated checks. These securities are not, however, tradable. The majority of borrowers are households in need of consumption loans and small business enterprises, such as small traders and small-scale producers, and farmers who can not obtain sufficient funds from the organized credit sector. The suppliers of credit in this market are heterogeneous and consist of non-commercial moneylenders (relatives, acquaintances, and neighbors) and local commercial moneylenders.[3]

Non-commercial lenders extend credit because of kinship and friendship. Moneylenders, who usually combine moneylending with other business activities, do not have either facilities for mobilizing credit or formalized procedures of lending. They operate mostly with their own funds and do not have detailed knowledge of a broad market, so their lending activities are confined to a small geographical region in which they live and are thus quantitatively limited. Because of these characteristics of lenders and borrowers, this market appears to be more fragmented and imperfect than others and, consequently, the interest rates are relatively high and varied. Although this market is likely to be large, in terms of numbers of participants, it is the least important sub-market for business financing.

THE ROTATING CREDIT CLUB: *KYE* MARKET

The *kye* is a form of rotating credit association commonly found in East Asia, Southeast Asia, and Africa, called by various names, such as *ko, hui, dashi, arisans,* and *esusu.*[4] The rotating credit association is essentially "a device by means of which traditional forms of social relationships are mobilized so as to fulfill non-traditional economic functions, and which has grown within peasant social structure to harmonize agrarian economic patterns with commercial ones and to act as a bridge between peasant and trader attitudes towards money and its uses."[5]

Though the origin of the *kye* is not clear, a similar institution is often mentioned in historical records several hundred years old in Korea. They were initially social clubs, but, in the process of economic development and gradual transition from a barter to money-using economy, the *kye* have lost their traditional elements of mutual help, community solidarity, and harmony and have evolved into informal, but more economically rational, financial institutions.

The *kye* are an installment system for deposits and loans—a scheme designed to pool small savings to make a large sum of money. The basic principle on which the *kye* is founded is rather simple: a lump-sum fund (*kye* fund) composed of variable contributions, based on an interest payment calculation, from each member of the *kye,* is distributed (or, more properly, loaned out), at fixed intervals and as a whole, to each member in order of a predetermined sequence (sequence *kye*), by auction (auction *kye*), or by lottery.[6]

As a saver-depositor, the longer the duration of a *kye* member's deposit (that is, the later his position in the sequence *kye*), the higher the rate of return on his installment deposit. As a borrower, the longer the duration of his loan (that is, the earlier his position in the sequence *kye*), the higher the rate of interest to be paid. The interest rate calculations in most *kye* are not, however, all too rational.[7] The holder of the first position in a sequence *kye,* who is usually the *kye* organizer, is a pure borrower; the last, a pure saver.

Although the *kye* market appears to be very extensive, there is no way of measuring its size. We can only present some qualitative evidence. A 1959 survey suggests that 90 percent of 2,691 households sampled in Seoul participated at one time or another in *kye.*[8] Another survey undertaken in 1963 shows that about 45 percent of households in Seoul were at the time of the survey participating in various *kye.*[9] A nationwide survey from 1971 shows a participation rate of 65 percent with households contributing up to 32 percent of their monthly average incomes to *kye* installment payments.[10] Contrary to the common belief that the *kye* funds are used mainly for consumption financing, this survey found that 40 percent of the members lent their *kye* funds to others. The income from such loans represented 7 percent of total household income. Some of these funds were channeled to the business sector directly or through other sub-markets of the UFM. The *kye* organizers often act as credit brokers in the curb market. The estimated return on saving through *kye* was about 4 percent per month in 1971.[11]

Despite the sustained growth of the organized financial sector over the years, the *kye* continues to enjoy enduring popularity as an informal savings association among households, as evidenced by the nationwide survey of the savings behavior the BOK has taken every three years since 1967. These surveys have consistently shown that a majority of Korean households take part in various *kye* to raise lump-sum funds and to take advantage of relatively high rates of interest on *kye* deposits.[12]

INFORMAL COMMERCIAL-PAPER MARKET

The regulated commercial-paper market, described in the previous chapter, represents a small fraction of the total outstanding DMB bank credit (4 percent at the end of 1978).[13] One reason for this low proportion may be that, in Korea, the commercial bills eligible for discount at the DMBs and, for that matter, even at the investment and finance companies, are in practice limited to those "real" bills based on the production, distribution, or sale of goods and services.[14] The DMBs do not purchase either industrial or finance paper, such as unsecured promissory notes issued to finance unspecified short-term credit needs.

Commercial paper in most developed-country money markets is not based on a specific transaction or process but on the general credit rating of the issuer reflected by his past and prospective income and expenses, assets, and liabilities (both short and long). Such a credit rating system, it is often suggested, is essential for the development of a commercial-paper market.

In Korea, the BOK designates the prime enterprises whose bills are eligible for rediscount, and the IFCs have their own credit evaluation system whereby the quality of commercial bills is rated. The IFCs produce periodically a list of prime enterprises, usually an enlarged version of the BOK's list, and they purchase or accept the bills issued by these prime firms. Because of the nature of its operations, the Korea Credit Guarantee Corporation has its own credit evaluation system, but its ratings of businesses are not available to the general public. Other than these, there are no private or public institutions specializing in credit evaluation. The absence of adequate rating services may have impeded the growth of the commercial-paper market in Korea.

Finally, it is often alleged that the system of presumptive taxation usually applied to small non-public business firms in Korea has been detrimental to the development of the commercial-paper market. Since commercial bills in Korea must be based on commodity transactions, the volume of bills issued could be used as a presumptive measure of business taxes.[15]

Prior to the establishment of the investment and finance companies in 1972, the informal commercial-paper market had developed initially among the firms in the same industry or trade and gradually expanded into other industries and trades. Although it is extremely difficult to measure the size of this market, the volume of trade credit indicates that it was very large before August 1972.

In an effort to absorb this informal-bill market into, and establish a short-term credit market within, the regulated sector, investment and finance companies—bill-discounting houses—were established in 1972. As discussed in Chapter 3, these have grown rather rapidly since their inception, their growth believed to have been at the expense of the informal-bill and the curb markets.

In the beginning, the interest rates on bills and discounts at the IFCs were allowed to fluctuate, depending upon market conditions, within an upper limit set by the Ministry of Finance, thereby supposedly allowing these companies to compete effectively with UFM lenders. In practice, however, while the interest rates in the UFM have been well over 30 percent per annum, maximum interest rates of the IFCs have been maintained far below the market rates.[16] This rigidity in the interest rates appears to have hampered IFCs' competitiveness vis-à-vis UFM lenders.

Such inflexibility has also induced these companies to enter the UFM as covert brokers. The typical practice of these companies as brokers takes the following pattern. They sell their own commercial paper to private buyers—usually UFM lenders—on the condition that they purchase in return the paper issued by the individual or firm designated by these buyers. The private lenders then receive a premium, which is usually 1 or 1.5 percent per month over the discount rate of the IFCs, from the ultimate borrower. In this way, private lenders eliminate the risk of default on their loans, and the IFC, in addition to receiving commission either from the lender or borrower, can increase its volume of business and market share.[17]

Of the eleven IFCs at present, nine are owned or directly controlled by large business conglomerates, and these companies have allegedly become the financial arms managing short-term liquidity of these conglomerates. The IFCs, like other banking institutions, mostly cater to the short-term credit needs of large businesses. Since they are purchasing or discounting mainly the paper issued by the large firms whose bills are also eligible for rediscount at the Bank of Korea, they have not been effective in supplying short-term working capital to small-sized enterprises. Nevertheless, it must be conceded that the establishment of the short-term finance companies has been one of the few successful institutional reforms of the government designed to integrate the UFIs with the RFIs. If they have not succeeded in reducing the relative size of the informal-bill market and curb market, they have at least succeeded in building a bridge between the two credit sectors.

THE CURB MARKET: LARGE-SCALE INFORMAL CREDIT BROKERS' MARKET

Before the proclamation of the Presidential Emergency Decree of August 3, 1972, it was reported that there were at least a hundred large-scale informal credit brokers or houses clustered around the business center of Seoul.[18] In order to avoid taxes and encounters with legal authorities, they were often disguised as legitimate business concerns, such as publishing firms, employment agents, or telephone-line ownership dealers, but they were in reality engaged exclusively in mobilizing funds from informal lenders and channeling them to large business firms.

In addition to these professional money brokers, a large number of real-estate dealers, warehouse operators, jewelery shop owners, and foreign-exchange dealers in the black market were heavily involved in informal lending as intermediaries. They were drawn into the UFM largely because they had the expertise and experience of dealing in real properties that are often used as collateral in the UFM.

As a group, these brokers and dealers exerted considerable influence on their borrowers,[19] and set the terms of and the interest rates on informal loans. They exchanged information about borrowers and ultimate lenders, sometimes made loans to each other, and had market-sharing arrangements. The interest rates in this market were considered as the prime rates of the UFM, which were closely followed by the other sub-markets.

These brokers had an efficient system of credit evaluation of borrowers, lending policies and procedures, a network of agents, and even a collection agency. There were two types of agents. One type were the regular employees of the brokerage houses. These agents were assigned to the borrowers, usually large corporations—as liaison men to evaluate the borrowers' financial conditions and immediate future prospects, and to follow up the loans made to them. Another type were the officers of the overdraft section and managers of commercial bank branches. They introduced potential borrowers among their bank customers to the brokers and provided information as to their credit-worthiness. For instance, if any of their bank customers was unable to balance his accounts, such a bank officer would arrange a short-term loan for him at the going market rate of interest in the UFM with the funds supplied by the informal credit brokers.

Another popular method of informal credit transaction that involved bank officers took the following form. An informal lender would make a savings deposit at a bank branch. With this additional deposit, the branch would extend a loan to a particular firm or individual that the depositor (the UFM lender) agreed to in advance. The informal lender then earned the savings deposit rate plus 1.5 to 2.0 percent premium per month from the borrower without any risk of default.[20] As far as the borrower was concerned, this arrangement was more attractive than borrowing directly from the informal lender, because he could often renew the loan at the bank lending rate. In this sense, these bank officers were secondary credit brokers. Since informal lenders and borrowers carried on their credit transactions through the media of commercial banks, the banks in such cases provided an important linkage between the brokers and borrowers.[21]

In this market, borrowers were mostly large corporate firms. Ultimate lenders, on the other hand, were heterogeneous and consisted of a variety of people—owners or major stockholders of closed corporations, high-ranking government officials, large *kye* organizers, educational and religious foundations, real-estate brokers, large wholesale traders and various entertainment establishments with large cash flows.[22]

Since informal credit brokers' operations were technically subject to the usury law, which limited the maximum interest rate on private loans to 30 percent per annum after August 1965, their credit transactions were carried out with considerable secrecy. Borrowers seldom disclosed their sources of credit or broker. If a borrower disclosed his source of credit, he was automatically barred from this market, risking possibly the only short-term credit source he had.

The size of loans in this market was relatively large—anywhere from 500,000 wŏn to 100 million wŏn, with a term in general no longer than a month and usually secured by notarized property deeds. Borrowers also signed an agreement that they would not contest their cases in court in the event they were unable to repay their debts.

After August 3, 1972, this market disappeared or went underground for a while, only to surface again a year later (see the discussion on the effects of the August 3, 1972 Decree on this market in Chapter 6). A recent newspaper article[23] indicates that the curb market has ever since been thriving as an important source of short-term loans to large businesses and has retained its major characteristics and mechanics of credit transactions described above. The market has, in particular, been active in periods of monetary restraint, as during the oil crisis and again since 1977. Various estimates place the size of the market at the beginning of 1979 at somewhere between 800 billion and 1,000 billon wŏn, close to 15 percent of total DMB loans at the end of 1978.[24]

Another newspaper article shows that practically all the large and reputable corporations classified as the prime enterprises by the BOK borrow heavily from this market. These borrowers are rated into four classes depending upon their financial conditions and future prospects. The lending rates (discount rate) range from 3 percent for the prime A class to 4.2 percent for the D class per month.[25] The market has, in fact, been so well integrated with the regulated markets that changes in the interest rates or the volume of loans in the unregulated market appear to be good indicators of the tightness or ease of monetary policy.

SEMI-REGULATED FINANCIAL INSTITUTIONS: THE GRAY FINANCIAL MARKET FOR CONSUMERS AND SMALL ENTERPRISES

Before the August 3, 1972 Presidential Emergency Decree, there were basically three types of registered private credit institutions that had operated in a mid range between the regulated and unregulated financial markets.[26] In order of importance, they were (1) *mujin,* a form of mutual savings and loan institution, (2) private finance companies or popular funds (henceforth (PFs), some of which were also operating *mujin* business, and (3) *kaekchu,* a private financial intermediary specializing in short-term financing of fishing households. Except for *kaekchu,* most of these institutions were incorporated in various forms under the "Chosŏn (Korea) *Mujin* Business Ordinance," which had been enacted in 1931 during the Japanese colonial rule, until 1961, and under the commercial code thereafter.[27] In this limited sense, they could be treated as regulated credit organizations. Since they were not licenced under the Banking Law, however, they remained outside the control of the monetary authorities.

After August 3, 1972, a majority of these credit institutions, through merger and consolidation, were reorganized into the mutual savings and finance companies (MSFCs) established under the MSFC Act of August 1972 and subsequently placed under the direct control of the Ministry of Finance.

At the time of reorganization, it was reported that there were 936 *mujin* and PFs. As shown in Table 24, these private intermediaries were small: the average equity capital of the *mujin*—the largest of the three—was 8.4 million wŏn, whereas the PFs were less than half the size of *mujin.* The volume of loans extended by these institutions amounted to 27.7 billion wŏn, approximately 9 percent of total informal credit reported to the government in compliance to the 8/3/72 Decree, or about 43 percent of the volume of similar loans extended by the Citizens' National Bank, which specializes in small-loan business. The total volume of *mujin* and mutual installment deposits of these institutions stood at 27.5 billion wŏn (see Table 25), more than 80 percent of the CNB's mutual installment deposits at that time.

This figure represented an almost 80 percent increase over the volume at the end of 1971 estimated by the Bank of Korea (see Table 26).

TABLE 24 Number of Private Financial Institutions as of
September 1, 1972

	Number of Institutions[a]	Total Equity Capital (million wŏn)	Average Equity Capital (million wŏn)
Mujin	451 (48%)	3,800	8.43
PFs	222 (24%)	700	3.15
Combinations of *Mujin* and PFs	263 (28%)	1,600	6.08
Total	936 (100%)	6,100	

Source: "On the Acts Establishing the IFCs, MSFCs, and Credit Cooperatives: Their Purposes and Significance," BOK, *Chosa wŏlbo* (November 1972), p. 18.

Note: [a]Includes branch offices.

TABLE 25 Loans and Installment Deposits of *Mujin* and PFs
as of September 1, 1972
(billion wŏn)

	Amount		Amount
Mujin remunerations (*Mujin* loans)	22.8	*Mujin* installment deposits	24.3
Loans on mutual installment deposits of PFs	2.2	Mutual installment deposits at PFs	3.2
Short-term loans	2.5		
Discount on bills	0.2		
Total	27.7	Total	27.5

Source: "On the Acts Establishing the IFCs, MSFCs, and Credit Cooperatives: Their Purposes and Significance," BOK, *Chosa wŏlbo* (November 1972), p. 18.

KAEKCHU

Kaekchu are a form of private finance that operate mainly in fishing villages and towns. They make equipment as well as operational loans to small fishing households, mostly with their own funds. As a sideline business, they also act as brokers or consignees in the fish market or operate warehouses for fish products.

TABLE 26 *Mujin* Installments and Mutual Installment Deposits
at PFs and Citizens' National Bank (CNB),
1963–1974[a]
(billion wŏn)

Year	Mujin *and PFs*	CNB *Mutual Installment Deposits*[c]
1963	0.8	
1964	1.1	
1965	1.4	3.5
1966	3.1	5.3
1967	5.2	7.0
1968	9.1	11.1
1969	11.7	17.1
1970	14.2	25.1
1971	15.4	31.5
1972[b]	47.7	36.6
1973[b]	113.0	47.6
1974[b]	160.8	57.6

Source: BOK, *Flow of Funds.*

Notes: [a]BOK figures were likely to have been underestimated because they were based on sample surveys.
[b]Include short-term financing companies and mutual credit companies.
[c]BOK, *Economic Statistics Yearbook.*

Since the establishment of the fisheries cooperatives in 1962, a large number of *kaekchu* have been absorbed into the cooperative system and, as a consequence, their role as informal lenders has been considerably diminished in recent years. A recent financial survey of fishing households shows that only 27 out of 300 sample households had outstanding loans obtained from the *kaekchu*, whereas 72 percent of the sample were liable for debt to various informal lenders.[28]

PRIVATE FINANCE COMPANIES (PFs)
Private finance companies were, in all respects, moneylenders, but they differed from the ones in the rudimentary sub-market in that they were urban-based corporate firms established under

the Commercial Code and were engaged in mutual installment deposits and loans. In this limited sense, they had facilities for mobilizing liquid funds and formalized procedures for applying for loans.

These companies specialized in small-loan business: they extended small loans for consumption and working capital to small retailers, wholesale traders, and owners of various small service establishments in urban areas, mostly with their equity capital and mutual installment deposits.

At the end of August 1972, when the PFs were reorganized into the MSFCs, it was estimated that there were approximately 485 PFs including branch offices, 263 of which were engaged in both PF and *mujin* business. Unfortunately, however, there is no reliable information on the number of PFs, let alone the size of their assets and liabilities, for other years. The available data from various sources are fragmentary and often inconsistent.

According to a Ministry of Finance survey, there were 123 PFs with 56 branch offices at the end of 1971. Of these, 18 PFs with 7 branch offices were also engaged in *mujin* business and 107 companies were incorporated in various forms under the commercial code.[29] It is interesting to note that more than 90 percent of these PFs were established after the monetary reform in 1965; 63 PFs sprang up in 1971 alone.

MUJIN COMPANIES

The *mujin* organizes a large number of individual accounts into a group contract. A group contract may have anywhere from 12 to 37 members and a lump sum of *mujin* remuneration (or *mujin* loan) from as little as 30,000 to 5 million wŏn. The company then holds a monthly auction to determine which member of the contract receives the *mujin* remuneration or loan.[30]

The *mujin* is a credit institution rather unique to the East, and has a long history in Japan. It is said to date from as far back as the thirteenth century.[31] Originally, it was one of the non-profit social organizations—the rotating credit club variety—for mutual assistance. However, in the process of industrialization of the economy these institutions lost much of their social function and became more economically oriented financial institutions. One such evolutionary form was the *mujin.*

A commercial *mujin* was first established in Japan in 1901,[32] and, through Japan, it was introduced to Korea in 1912. Thereafter *mujin* grew rapidly. It was, however, during the post-Korean War period (1954–1959) that *mujin* mushroomed, due in part to the increasing number of *kye* failures, but mostly due to repressive financial policies.[33] The majority of *mujin* were no better than local moneylenders and heavily involved in the UFM transactions. But, since most of them were incorporated, they had the facade of legal credit institutions, which, in turn, helped enchance the public image of and confidence in these institutions. In addition, the scheme of installment payment of loans in small sums was attractive to small enterprises. Even the government was actively involved in the development of these *mujin* in an effort to reduce the number of *kye* and to prevent *kye* failure.[34]

Most of the *mujin*—particularly larger ones—were reorganized in 1962 as a privately owned commercial bank, the Citizens' National Bank (CNB), specializing in small-loan business for consumers and small enterprises. The CNB took over the mutual loans and savings (installment deposits) and other businesses handled by the *mujin.*

After a year, however, in line with the deprivatization policy of commercial banks, the government obtained a controlling share of the CNB. After that, the CNB grew steadily but could not keep up with the pace of growth of the economy. As the CNB lagged behind in the small-loan business, private *mujin* companies began to reappear in 1964 and grew rapidly until they were reorganized in 1972 into the MSFCs.

ESTIMATES OF ASSETS AND LIABILITIES
AND THE RATES OF INTEREST IN THE UFM,
1963–1978

SIZE OF THE UFM

This discussion of the characteristics and nature of the UFM suggests that there is no clear demarcation between the RFM and UFM and that some of the UFM sub-markets can not easily be defined. Given this conceptual difficulty and unavailability of reliable data, it would be almost impossible to estimate the size of the UFM. Nevertheless, there have, over the past decade, been several attempts to measure the size of the informal financial sector, focusing on its outstanding liabilities, with, in most cases, dubious results.

Since 1963, the Bank of Korea has estimated outstanding loans in the UFM,[35] but the BOK figures cover only the informal borrowings of the corporate sector. In 1964, it was estimated that outstanding assets and liabilities in the UFM were on the order of 40 to 45 billion wŏn, all within the private sector. This figure was almost double the commercial bank loans outstanding at that time. Although it was claimed that this estimate was likely to be low, there is no way of examining the claim because the study does not elaborate on how the estimate was obtained.[36]

Another study undertaken in 1970 shows that the outstanding volume of informal loans was close to 180 billion wŏn at the end of 1969, which was about 4.5 times larger than the level of 1964. This figure was, however, only half the volume of commercial bank loans at that time, suggesting that the size of the UFM had been reduced during the high-interest-rate period.[37] A 1972 study places the volume at 190 billion wŏn at the end of 1969, which rose to 300 billion wŏn a year later (see Table 27).[38]

All these estimates understandably encompass numerous conceptual and statistical difficulties. They are, in general, based upon such unreliable information as corporate-tax-return data

TABLE 27   Estimates of the Size of the UFM, 1963–1972

	I	II	III	IV	V
1963		22.2	19.1		49.1
1964	40.0–45.0	39.4	30.2		53.1
1965		–	43.8		72.1
1966		68.7	64.9		102.7
1967		–	112.4		178.0
1968		–	140.4		331.2
1969		178.7	188.7		563.0
1970			254.3		722.4
1971			300.6		919.5
1972				345.6	1,198.0

Sources: I Gurley, Patrick, and Shaw, p. 8.
II Sogang University, p. 47.
III Shim et al., p. 96.
IV The volume of informal loans declared by enterprises on August 3, 1972.
V BOK, Loans and discounts of Deposit Money Banks, *Monetary Statistics of Korea*, 1963–1973.

and various unofficial sample survey results. Their estimation methods are ad hoc, ambiguous, and, in some cases, erroneous. As such, these estimates reflect neither the actual size of, nor changes that have taken place over time in, the unregulated financial sector.

The only reliable information on the size of the UFM is the outcome of the 8/3/72 Decree in which all enterprises with a business license were required to report their informal debts, raised directly or indirectly from sources other than regulated financial institutions, to the government. As already pointed out, the total of informal loans declared by business enterprises under this Decree amounted to 345.6 billion wŏn, equivalent to 80 percent of the then supply of money and to 34 percent of the then outstanding domestic credit of the banking sector. About 25 percent of these borrowings were "disguised informal loans," in that they were made by the owners, major stockholders, or executives of the borrowing firms.

It was also widely believed at that time that many debtors and creditors simply did not bother to report their claims and debts, especially when the amounts involved were small, despite the apparent inducement to the borrowers for declaration. If these loans had been included, one report suggests that the total volume of credit would have been well over 500 billion wŏn.[39] It should also be pointed out that informal borrowings by households and small enterprises without business licences, both in urban and rural areas, were not required to be reported. All in all, it would be fair to speculate that the size of the UFM in 1972 was about half the deposit money banks in terms of the volume of credit outstanding.

A recent study estimates the volume of informal credit and its composition between the household and business sector for the years 1964–1973.[40] These estimates, reproduced in Table 28, are largely based on urban and rural household budget surveys conducted by the government and other business surveys by banking institutions. While this study utilizes more reliable and consistent estimation methods than previous studies, it does not succeed in measuring the actual size of the market. For example, the total outstanding volume of UFM loans at the end of 1972 was estimated to be 204.2 billion wŏn, 150 billion wŏn less than the 8/3/72 figure.

As noted earlier in this chapter, various newspaper articles suggest that the size of the market (the curb market according to our definition) early in 1979 was close to one trillion, but this figure is not based on any reliable studies and is no more than conjecture.

THE RATES OF INTEREST IN THE UFM

A number of organizations, including the Bank of Korea, publish periodically the estimates of the interest rates in the UFM. Of these the BOK estimates, based on quarterly business financial surveys, cover the longest time period and appear to be relatively more consistent than others.

As shown in Table 29, the interest rates in the UFM, which

TABLE 28 Estimates of the Volume of Credit in the UFM, 1964–1978 (billion wŏn)

	Business Sector			Household			Total
	(I) *Corporate*	*(II)* *Unincorporated*	*Sub-Total*	*(III)* *Urban*	*(IV)* *Farm*	*Sub-Total*	
1964	3.9	—		1.2	6.6	7.8	—
1965	8.1	—		1.8	10.5	12.3	—
1966	10.4	—		3.4	8.8	12.2	—
1967	19.1	—		7.1	12.7	19.8	—
1968	37.8	17.0	54.8	7.9	15.5	23.4	78.2
1969	59.0	22.2	81.2	17.5	13.4	30.9	112.1
1970	88.8	57.7	146.5	18.9	16.2	35.1	181.6
1971	113.5	80.0	193.5	14.0	10.9	24.9	218.4
1972	102.2	68.2	170.4	19.0	14.8	33.8	204.2
1973	102.6	112.1	214.7	14.8	16.9	31.7	246.4
1974	79.3	—	—	—	—	—	—
1975	87.8	—	—	—	—	—	—
1976	82.1	—	—	—	—	—	—
1977	127.6	—	—	—	—	—	—
1978	—	—	1,000.0[a]	—	—	—	—

Sources: I. Bank of Korea, *Flow of Funds Accounts in Korea* (1978). II, III, IV. Y. C. Park, p. 72.

Note: [a]*Dong-A Ilbo.*

TABLE 29 The Rates of Interest in the UFM, 1963–1978 (monthly, %)

	1/4	2/4	3/4	4/4	annual average
1963	4.30	4.30	4.40	4.50	4.38
1964	4.80	5.80	5.00	5.00	5.15
1965	5.01	4.84	4.87	4.90	4.91
1966	4.93	4.87	4.87	4.90	4.89
1967	4.71	4.76	4.72	4.64	4.71
1968	4.70	4.59	4.51	4.86	4.67
1969	4.36	4.21	4.25	4.28	4.28
1970	4.41	4.16	4.14	3.89	4.18
1971	3.86	3.87	3.90	3.84	3.87
1972	3.54	3.44	3.18	2.83	3.25
1973	2.49	2.48	2.85	3.28	2.77
1974	3.32	3.39	3.41	3.40	3.38
1975	3.42	3.65	3.33	3.37	3.99
1976	3.18	3.37	3.49	3.45	3.37
1977	3.51	3.38	2.96	2.84	3.17
1978	3.20	3.20	3.60	3.90	3.48

Source: BOK, *Kiŏp kŭmyung mit sagŭmyung silt'ae chosa* (quarterly report, various issues since 1963).

are average interest rates, have been very high as compared with those in the RFM. At the same time, they have been rather stable, displaying no visible seasonal and other fluctuations over the business cycle. This stability, however, should not be construed as implying that informal credit markets are also stable. On the contrary, the characteristics and workings of the UFM suggest that informal loan markets are likely to be sensitive to the stance of monetary policy in the RFM and that the interest rates in these markets would fluctuate over a wide margin in the short run. The seemingly stable interest rates may be due to the limited information one can obtain from a sample survey and the biased averaging scheme.

The BOK survey asks sample firms to quote the interest rate

TABLE 30 The Rates of Interest on Bank Loans and Rates of Return to Fixed Assets in the Manufacturing Sector, 1959–1978 (%)

	(I) Nominal Interest Rates on General Loan (one year maturity)	(II) Rate of Return to Fixed Assets in the Manufacturing Sector	Rates of Interest on UFM Loans
1959	17.5	—	—
1960	17.5	—	—
1961	17.5	—	—
1962	16.7	43	—
1963	15.7	33	52.56
1964	15.9	32	61.80
1965	18.5	34	58.92
1966	26.0	40	58.68
1967	26.0	37	56.52
1968	25.8	28	56.04
1969	24.5	28	51.36
1970	24.0	25	50.16
1971	23.0	23	46.44
1972	17.7	27	39.00

TABLE 30 (continued)

	(I) Nominal Interest Rates on General Loan (one year maturity)	(II) Rate of Return to Fixed Assets in the Manufacturing Sector	Rates of Interest on UFM Loans
1973	15.5	34	33.24
1974	15.5	30	40.56
1975	15.5	29	47.88
1976	16.1[a]	33	40.47
1977	15.0[a]	—	38.07
1978	17.1[a]	—	41.70

Sources: I. BOK, *Economic Statistics Yearbook*, various issues.
II. Wontack Hong, *Trade, Distortions, and Employment Growth in Korea* (Korea Development Institute, Seoul, 1979), pp. 188, 201.

Note: [a]Prime enterprises.

TABLE 31 Estimates of Rates of Return to Capital in
Manufacturing[a], 1954–1975
(%)

	Gross[b]	Net[b]
1954–1961	52	48
1962–1966	52	48
1967–1971	52	47
1972–1975	59	52

Source: Wontack Hong, *Trade, Distortions,* p. 184.

Notes: [a]Non-labor shares excluding indirect taxes
[b]Annual averages

bearing on their informal loans, irrespective of the terms, sizes, and collateral requirements of these loans. The quoted interest rates are then weighted by frequency—the number of loans by different interest rates—to derive an average interest rate. Since small loans are likely to account for a larger share of the total and they carry, in general, higher interest rates, the weighting would result in an average interest rate higher than otherwise. For these reasons, one should be careful about relying upon these interest rates for any analysis of the credit conditions in both the RFM and UFM. Nevertheless, it appears that the interest rates in the UFM reflect the nominal rate of return to fixed assets and to capital in the manufacturing sector (see Tables 30 and 31).

FIVE

Interactions of the Regulated and Unregulated Financial Markets

One of the most important financial characteristics of Korea over the past century has been financial dualism. Its origin may be traced in part to the dualistic economic structure—the coexistence of a modern industrial and commercial sector and the traditional agricultural, handicraft, and service sectors—created and sustained by the Japanese during their colonial rule of the country from 1909 to 1945, and continued until recent times.

As shown in Chapters 2 and 3, in the colonial period there was rapid growth of both financial assets and superstructure. The modern financial system, however, was designed and fostered to accommodate the financial needs of the Japanese community—the modern sector—and grew along with its expansion. The modern financial system, as a result, penetrated into the traditional sector only to a limited degree. Nor did the system attend to the financialization of savings or intermediation within this traditional sector, whose financial needs were left to be served by indigenous financial intermediaries. Most of the financial assets of the organized sector were owned by the Japanese; and practically all the financial resources were channeled to them.

This characteristic of the system, together with the antagonism of the Korean people towards their colonial ruler, bred distrust of the modern financial system, which was further deepened in the final years of World War II when the Japanese attempted to force private savings by means of inflation and forced sales of debentures to finance their war efforts.

After independence, the dualistic financial structure persisted, but the relationships between the financial and the other sectors of the economy have changed. Not only has the unregulated financial sector expanded over the years, despite government efforts at suppression, but the unregulated institutions have broadened their services to meet the financial needs of large as well as small borrowers and lenders, of both the modern and the traditional sectors.

This continued existence and expansion of the UFIs, in the face of rapid growth and modernization of the economic structure, may be explained largely by the repressive, ostensibly anti-inflationary financial policy that impeded growth of the regulated institutions and led to the consequent inability of those institutions, so closely controlled by government, to adapt to changing economic situations, savers' asset preferences, and industrial and commercial patterns. Opportuntity has thus existed for an important role to be played by the UFIs.

STRUCTURAL CHARACTERISTICS

One cause of the growth of the UFIs in Korea, particularly relevant to the early post-war period, is to be found in the incompatibility among the nature of the production structure, the distribution of wealth, and the financial system. Where there are few restraints imposed on financial intermediaries, the financial structure of an economy would, to a large extent, tend to reflect the underlying production activities and wealth distribution of the economy. For instance, in an economy characterized by the predominance of the primary sector, a small light manufacturing base, and small-scale commerce, the majority of borrowers would consist of small industrial firms, farm households, and small retailers and wholesale traders, who would require financial resources for short-term periods distributed in relatively small blocks. In a competitive unregulated situation, this would be conducive to the development of atomistic money and financial markets, consisting of many small-sized and specialized financial intermediaries.

Until the early 1960s, when the government launched its First Five-Year Development Plan, Korea had been an agrarian economy with a small manufacturing base. The underlying economic structure, therefore, would have been more compatible with a financial system characterized by atomistic money and capital markets. But the so-called modern portion of the system in Korea was controlled by the government and could not adapt to that pattern. Instead, the legacy of a system appropriate to the development of industrial enclaves during the Japanese rule persisted, and was dominated by a few large commercial banks and non-bank intermediaries, both owned and closely regulated by the government. Such a system was functionally unable to cater to the financial needs of the majority of borrowers—small and medium firms, agriculture, and consumers. This inflexibility of the RFIs to adapt to the existing economic patterns, therefore, created a vacuum in the nation's finance and provided strong incentives for informal intermediation by small-sized financial entrepreneurs.

Similarly, on the supply side, there were savers who, despite the relatively high risk of default and government suppression, preferred to accumulate the short-term, high-yielding informal primary securities. The cost of intermediation in the UFIs, contrary to some observations in the literature, has not been high as compared with that of the RFIs. It was economically viable and profitable to enter the UFM as an intermediary.

The predominance of the agriculture sector, which accounted for more than 40 percent of total output up to the mid-1960s, might have been another structural reason for the expansion of the UFIs. Such an agriculture-dominated economic structure would, other things being equal, be less conducive to the formation of modern banking habits and financialization of private savings and, in general, unresponsive to financial policies, but more suitable to the expansion of small-scale informal credit institutions like *mujin,* private financial companies, *kye,* and moneylenders.

The lack of public confidence in the modern money and credit system, germinated by the high rates of inflation in the late stages of the Japanese period, may also explain in part the growth of the UFIs. Subsequent economic breakdowns, social disorder, political confusion and uncertainty caused by the two intervening wars, a student revolution in 1960, a military coup in 1961, and some drastic economic policy measures, such as currency reforms, which blocked the deposits at the banks in 1962, contributed little in the way of cultivating public confidence in the RFIs.

Finally, there was a lack of incentives for active intermediation on the part of banking institutions owned and controlled by the government and periodically supplied with limited amounts of low-cost funds from the Bank of Korea or the government. This hindered the growth of the RFIs and hence provided room for the UFIs' activities.

THE INTEREST-RATE POLICY

As discussed in Chapter 3, the official interest rates adjusted for inflation have been kept far below the free-market level, except for the high-interest-rate period from 1965 to 1971. Even during that period, however, the real rates of interest, in particular real lending rates, were much lower than those that prevailed in the UFM.

The low-interest-rate policy of the banking sector generated an insatiable demand for its credit, while at the same time discouraging the public from accumulating claims on the banks. Under the circumstances, the monetary authorities had to exercise a stringent credit rationing. As might be expected, the priority of credit distribution was given first to the main government-owned or -controlled enterprises, then to those industries strategic to economic development, such as exporters and large producers, with very little to the others. Those who have not been accommodated by the banks have had to raise funds outside the RFM, mostly in the UFM. The low-interest-rate policy has been the single most important cause of the continued expansion of the UFM in Korea and the persistence of financial dualism.

One reason for the low-interest-rate policy before the monetary reform in 1965 might, as Shaw points out, have been the historical antipathy to usury.[1] Throughout the Yi dynasty and the Japanese colonial rule, the public had suffered from very high interest rates. Real interest rates in excess of 50 percent per year were not unusual in the private credit market during the period: there are documents showing that even the government had charged 40 percent real interest rates per annum on their loans in kind, mostly grain and cloth.[2] Another reason may have been related to the conduct of monetary policy. The inability or unwillingness to impose effective control over the growth of liquidity, which had occurred frequently in Korea and led to high rates of inflation (see Chapter 8) meant that, if interest rates had been determined freely in the market, they would have risen to very high nominal levels.

Most important of all, there was a widespread presumption, not only in Korea but in much of the development literature, based on the Harrod-Domar growth model, that low interest rates were necessary to stimulate investment, which was the key to growth. In order to promote a high rate of investment, and thus a high rate of growth, it was thought that the cost of capital should be kept low, with little regard to the fact that such a policy might discourage saving and thereby encourage inflation. Saving was presumed to depend only on income and therefore to be unaffected by interest rates. It was further argued that reconstruction of the Korean economy after two wars demanded a large block of capital with a long gestation period and that, to induce such an investment in an uncertain environment, the cost of capital should be low.

Bloomfield, writing in 1956, noted that the Monetary Board had repeatedly requested the government to revise the Interest Rates Restriction Act to permit an increase in rates above the existing legal maximum of 20 percent per annum. His own views on interest-rate policy were more skeptical, as indicated in the following passage:

> I find it difficult to take any firm position in this matter, largely because of my skepticism of the efficacy, in general, of higher loan rates as a means of curbing excessive bank credit expansion under the present conditions, and because of my concern, on the other hand, that at least some deserving categories of bank borrowers might be hard hit. In any case, with more effective use of the ceiling device . . . application of higher interest rates on bank loans would technically be unnecessary.[3]

Bloomfield obviously attached little importance to the efficiency role of interest rates in guiding credit allocation, although he had previously noted that "the real rate of interest on bank loans in general has actually tended to be negative," and that this "amounted to a subsidy to borrowers in general and has tended to increase the reluctance of many borrowers to repay their bank borrowings at maturity."[4] The average bank lending rate at the time, according to Bloomfield, was 16.5 percent per annum, while the inflation rate was in the 20–25 percent range and the prevailing open market interest rates ranged between 10 and 15 percent *per month.*

Bloomfield gave no consideration to the potential impact of interest rates on bank deposits, suggesting an even greater skepticism of the efficacy of such measures, which was consistent with the prevailing view in the international economic community at that time.

Prior to the 1960s, the intellectual community—both abroad and in Korea—had not yet provided the arguments for maintaining positive real interest rates in capital-scarce economies.[5] Thus, in Korea at that time, there was little intellectual awareness of the benefits that might accrue from a positive real-interest-rate policy. Also, the policy-makers, even if they had realized the merits of the policy, were not willing to pursue such an unpopular course in the face of strong opposition from the then favored borrowers.

Korea was one of the countries that demonstrated the potential effects of interest rates on the demand for bank deposits in the latter half of the 1960s, as discussed in Chapter 7. Initially, this resulted in a major shift of financial asset holdings from the unregulated to the regulated institutions. Subsequently, there was an offsetting or reverse flow as businesses channeled some of their excess short-term liquidity, arising from increased loans of the banking system, into short-term claims on the unregulated institutions. Overall there was a substantial increase in the claims on both the regulated and unregulated institutions, with a relatively smaller gain in the latter.

Again, since 1972, the real interest rates in the regulated sector have, on average, been close to zero or sometimes negative, due to the downward adjustment of the nominal interest rates and higher rates of inflation. As a result, the growth of the regulated sector has slowed down, and much of domestic savings has shifted either back into the UFIs or into other forms of assets. Yet, there has been a strong resistance to maintaining positive real interest rates in the regulated sector on the ground that the resulting high nominal interest rates would undermine competitiveness of Korean exports in the world markets and would induce a cost-push inflation.

CREDIT ALLOCATION OF THE RFM

Some of the causes for the expansion of the UFM have been related to the characteristic of DMBs' asset portfolios, dominated by what were in fact long-term loans and the DMBs' traditional preference for large industrial borrowers. Deposit money banks have been, and remain, the dominant financial intermediaries in Korea's financial system. They have also been, over the years, transformed mainly into long-term lending institutions, while there have been no adequate institutional arrangements for short-term credit needs within the RFS. Despite the rapid growth of the IFCs since their inception in 1972, the size of the short-term money market still remains relatively small. The UFS has filled this gap in the RFS by supplying largely short-term credit.

There are a number of reasons for the predominant role of the DMBs in the business financing of long-term funds.[6] As discussed in Chapter 3, the capital market, the major source of long-term funds in advanced countries, was nearly moribund until the 1970s in Korea. Non-bank financial institutions, though they have grown rapidly in recent years, still remain a secondary source of credit. The DMBs have also been the cheapest source of financing. Even during the high-interest-rate period (1965–1971), the average lending rate of the DMBs was about 13 percent in real terms because of various concessionary rates on loans for export financing, machinery-industry promotion, equipment for export industries, and for others, whereas the real rate of return to capital in manufacturing was on average over 30 percent per annum.[7]

Another institutional reason for the heavy involvement of the DMBs in long-term finance has been the government development strategy in which the regulated financial system has been the predominant means for allocating resources to preferred sectors. Financial institutions in the RFS have been little more than government agencies engaged in mobilizing savings at home and abroad and allocating them to development financing and to capital formation in the preferred sectors which have consisted of large-scale exporters and manufacturers. To promote this pattern of capital formation, it would be equally logical to allow—at least implicitly—the industrial borrowers to roll over or renew continuously their short-term loans, thereby making these loans in effect medium- or long-term loans.[8]

In 1971, the monetary authorities finally recognized existing practice and authorized the commercial banks to grant term loans, and limited general loans to a period of one year with a maximum extension of six months of 80 percent of the original loan. The experience over the past few years indicates that the term loan has not been popular among businesses, and demand for it has been rather sluggish, representing about 2 percent of total outstanding bank loans at the end of 1978.[9] Despite the limitation on the extension of general loans, the tendency of the roll-over and renewal in practice still remains: denied an extension, borrowers simply apply for a new loan in place of the old one.

At the end of 1978, the share of short-term loans—as classified by the BOK—in total bank loans was about 78 percent, including export-financing loans. Excluding these, the share went down to 65 percent. Given the pervasive roll-over and renewal, many of these loans should, in fact, be classified as medium- or long-term loans.

This renewal or roll-over practice is not a recent phenomenon; as early as in 1952, Bloomfield was concerned about this practice and suggested that there was a relatively large share of long-term loans in commercial banks' portfolios.[10] An official publication of the BOK conceded that "general loans on bills are often utilized to meet long-term equipment fund requirements by means of roll-overs and renewals."[11] A sample survey conducted by the BOK in 1968 showed that the actual term of general loans on bills was on average about three and a half years and that of all bank loans other than overdrafts was a little over a year.[12]

Finally, there is the common belief among policy-makers in most LDCs that the only productive way of using financial resources is to invest them in durable capital goods and machinery embodying modern technology. They attach little importance to the vital role of working capital as an essential input of production, and the financing of trading activities is often regarded as unproductive. This tendency has led policy-makers to neglect both the development of short-term financial markets within the RFM and the channeling of some of the commercial loans to financing short-term working capital requirements.[13]

DETERMINATION OF THE RATES OF INTEREST AND VOLUMES OF CREDIT IN THE UFM

FRAMEWORK OF ANALYSIS: THE FINANCIAL SECTOR

This section develops a simple financial sector model to analyze the process through which the rates of interest and volumes of credit are determined both in the UFM and RFM and the interaction between the two financial markets. Hence, we assume the following:

1) In this economy, there are four asset markets—high-powered money, commercial bank loans, UFI credit, and real assets. There are no markets for either bonds or equities. Asset-holders in this economy allocate their stocks of wealth among currency, bank deposits (demand and time deposits), informal primary securities, and real assets. Commercial banks—the only type of financial intermediary in the RFM—are not allowed to hold either real assets or UFM securities.

2) There exists, though one cannot observe it directly, a representative rate of interest of the economy, the nominal rate of return on real assets or, if you will, the nominal marginal product of capital. The supply of real assets is assumed to be given in the short run. The rate of interest in the UFM moves always closely with this representative rate of interest, r. In theoretical terms, this is equivalent to the assumption that promissory notes, informal bills, postdated checks, and other securities traded on the UFM are good substitutes for real assets. The rate

of interest on bank loans can be market-determined, in which case the UFM may disappear or the size of the market would be of little significance. However, if the rates of interest on bank deposits and bank loans are fixed at a level below the market equilibrium rate and credit rationing is in effect, the intervention would lead to the formation of the UFM.

The dualistic financial structure has been in existence for some time, due to financial repression and, over time, these two credit markets have developed into two separate and independent credit markets with their own characteristics (though the UFM still retains some features of a black credit market). Hence, bank deposits and informal securities are not perfect substitutes for each other in wealth-owners' portfolios; neither would bank credit and informal loans be perfect substitutes in borrowers' portfolios.

3) Bank loans supplied by the RFM and informal loans available from the UFM can be either substitutes or complements in the portfolios of ultimate borrowers. The complementarity relationship, as will be shown later, stems basically from the institutional characteristics of the financial system rather than the characteristics of the two liabilities.

4) In the real world, there are many types of bank and informal UFM loans with different interest rates, terms, and varying degrees of risk. We represent all these loans by a composite loan of representative risk and term both in the RFM and UFM.

These are undoubtedly unrealistic assumptions; however, they reduce our problem to manageable proportions without altering the essential aspects of the workings of both the UFM and RFM and the basic conclusions of our analysis. Under these assumptions, we may specify the asset demand and supply functions and the conditions for equilibrium in each market.

The high-powered money market

$$C = C^d\ (r,\ i^d,\ \pi^e,\ Y,\ W) \tag{5.1}$$

$$R = R^d\ (i;k)\ D \tag{5.2}$$

$$A = C + R \tag{5.3}$$

Equations 5.1 and 5.2 are behavioral relations, explaining the public's demand for currency and banks' demand for reserves, where C is the stock of currency, r is the representative rate of interest or the interest rate in the UFM, i^d the bank deposit rate; π^e the expected rate of inflation; Y and W are income and wealth; R represents bank reserves; k the required reserve ratio on bank deposits; D is bank deposits (the sum of demand and time deposits), and A is the exogenously determined supply of high-powered money.

Bank credit market

$$DD = D^d \ (r, \ i^d, \ \pi^e, \ Y, \ W) \tag{5.4}$$
$$TD = TD^d \ (r, \ i^d, \ \pi^e, \ Y, \ W) \tag{5.5}$$
$$D = DD + TD \tag{5.6}$$
$$L^s = [\,1 - R^d \ (i, \ k)\,]D + B \tag{5.7}$$
$$L^d = L^d \ (r, \ i, \ \pi^e, \ \frac{dY}{Y}, Y) \tag{5.8}$$
$$L^s = L^d \tag{5.9}$$
$$i = i^d + e \tag{5.10}$$

Equations 5.4 and 5.5 are the demand functions for demand (DD) and time deposits (TD). The total volume of bank deposits is defined in Equation 5.6. The supply function for bank loans (L) may be derived from the commercial bank balance sheet identity as is given in Equation 5.7. The demand for commercial bank loans is specified in Equation 5.8. Equation 5.10 is the relationship between the bank deposit and loan rates where e is a constant.

The unregulated financial market

$$U^s_d = U^s_d \ (r, \ i, \ \frac{dY}{Y}, \ Y) \tag{5.11}$$
$$U^d_s = U^d_s \ (r, \ i^d, \ \pi^e, \ Y, \ W) \tag{5.12}$$
$$U^d = U^s \tag{5.13}$$

Equation 5.11 is the demand function for UFM credit, whereas U^s is the supply function for the UFM loans or alternatively the demand function for informal securities by wealth-owners.

In this model, A, Y, W, π^e, k, and B (bank borrowings from the central bank) are exogenously determined outside the system.

The workings of the model as specified by Equations 5.1 to 5.13 may be represented diagramatically in Figures 3 and 4.

The demand for bank credit by the public is, other things being equal, assumed to be negatively related to i, which is shown by the DD curve in Figure 3. An increase in r would, *ceteris paribus*, shift the curve to the right, since the cost of bank financing is now relatively cheaper. The supply of bank credit, the SS schedule, which is directly related to the public demand for indirect securities issued by commercial banks, is assumed to be an increasing function of i, given r and other variables exogenous to the system. An increase in r, *ceteris paribus*, would cause a leftward shift of SS, as the increase would induce wealth-owners to shift out of the bank deposit market and into the UFM. On the other hand, an increase in B—commercial bank borrowings from the central bank—or a reduction in k would shift the SS schedule to the right.

If the bank credit market, as represented by Figure 3, were competitive and subject to no government intervention, it would be cleared at i_0, and, as noted earlier, there would be little or no demand for informal credit. On the other hand, if the government authorities set the bank loan rate (and the deposit rate) at i_1, far below the market equilibrium rate, this intervention would generate an excess demand for bank credit measured by $Q_1 Q_2$ in Figure 3. In order to maintain i_1, therefore, the authorities will have to supply $Q_1 Q_2$ by means of additional lending to commercial banks or reducing k. The supply schedule would then be perfectly elastic at i_1. Otherwise, they will be required to exercise credit rationing among borrowers through various means to suppress the excess demand $Q_1 Q_2$. Borrowers who are excluded from this credit market for their credit accommodations and ultimate lenders who are not happy about the low deposit rates would then come together in direct finance and thereby form an informal credit market.

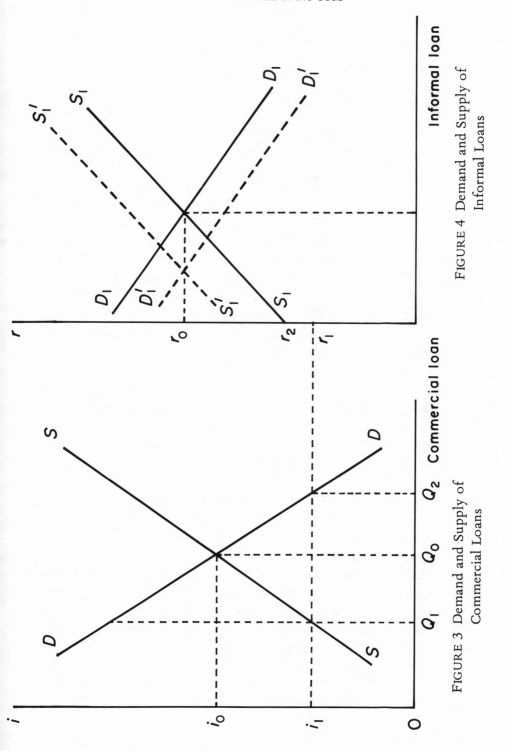

FIGURE 4 Demand and Supply of
Informal Loans

FIGURE 3 Demand and Supply of
Commercial Loans

Suppose this financial repression has been imposed upon the economy for some time. The excess demand for bank credit would then spill over into the UFM as the demand for informal credit as shown by the D_1D_1 schedule in Figure 4. This curve is basically related to the DD schedule in Figure 3 and, if commercial bank and informal money market liabilities are perfect substitutes, it may be obtained by subtracting QQ_1 at all levels of i from the DD curve.

Lenders in the UFM are subject to a relatively high degree of risk of default and the risks associated with the violation of the usury regulation and income-tax evasion, and possibly high costs of information due to market imperfections. They would, therefore, demand a risk premium over the rate of return they could earn in the RFM as a compensation for their informal loans. Suppose this risk premium, which is invariant to the size or term of loan, is measured by r_1r_2 in Figure 4; that is, r_1 is comparable to i_1 in the RFM, so that there will be no supply of informal loans forthcoming below r_2 and that, above r_2, the supply schedule S_1S_1 would be an increasing function of r. And if bank deposits and informal securities are perfect substitutes in lenders' portfolios, it can be obtained by subtracting QQ_1 from the SS schedule in Figure 3 at all levels of the interest rates, i. Given the demand for and supply of informal credit, the UFM would reach an equilibrium at r_0.

SUBSTITUTABILITY BETWEEN BANK LOANS AND INFORMAL CREDIT: TRADITIONAL VIEW

In order to elaborate on the workings of the model, let us consider the effects of an exogenous change in B, i, and k on both credit markets. We shall first examine the simplest case, in which bank deposits and informal securities are perfect substitutes in lenders' portfolios and borrowers are indifferent as to the sources of credit so long as the cost of borrowing is the same. An increase in B would then cause a rightward shift in the SS and thus a leftward shift in the D_1D_1 by an equal distance without changing the position of the DD; at a new equilibrium in the UFM, both the volume of credit and r would be lower than before.

An exogenous increase in i would shift both the $D_1 D_1$ and $S_1 S_1$ schedules by an equal distance but in the opposite directions, thus raising r, but without causing any changes in the DD and SS schedules in Figure 3.

If these assets and liabilities are imperfect substitutes, the comparative static analysis becomes a little more complicated because both the DD and SS schedules in Figure 3 would now shift in response to changes in r. The basic conclusions of the preceding analysis would, however, remain intact.

An increase in i would, in the first instance, cause an asset substitution in favor of bank deposits in ultimate lenders' portfolios and subsequently induce them to move out of the UFM and into the RFM, therefore shifting the $S_1 S_1$ to the left. As this asset substitution takes place, commercial banks will be able to extend more loans with their increased resources at a higher i. They are now able to accommodate some of the credit demand that has been hitherto satisfied through the UFM: the SS would shift to the right. As a result of these shifts, the rate of interest, r, would initially tend to rise. The rise in r would then set in motion a rightward shift in the DD and a leftward shift in the SS, which will in turn moderate the initial shifts in both the $D_1 D_1$ and $S_1 S_1$ and thus the rise in r.

At a new equilibrium in the UFM, the volume of credit would be smaller than before, but the effect of the increase in i on r would be, in general, ambiguous. It would, *inter alia,* depend upon the relative magnitudes of the shifts in the $D_1 D_1$ and $S_1 S_1$. One might argue that the magnitude of the leftward shift in the $D_1 D_1$ is likely to be greater than that of the $S_1 S_1$, and therefore r would fall in the end on the ground that the credit supply multiplier of the RFM is greater than unity, whereas that of the UFM is, by definition, unity. The foregoing analysis, it appears, basically reflects the views of McKinnon, Shaw, and Brown on the interaction between the RFM and UFM.[14]

FINANCING BEHAVIOR OF FIRMS IN A DUAL
FINANCIAL STRUCTURE: COMPLEMENTARITY
BETWEEN COMMERCIAL LOANS
AND INFORMAL CREDIT

Real Expenditures and Financing

In the preceding section, we have assumed that commercial loans and UFM loans are substitutes in borrowers' portfolios, in the sense that the borrowers would be indifferent as to the sources of loans insofar as the costs of loans are equal. The Korean experience over the past two decades, however, suggests that they can be and in fact have been complements. This complementarity relation would be, *ceteris paribus,* more pronounced (in LDCs) where the rates of interest in the organized financial sector are kept below the market equilibrium rates and the expected rate of inflation is relatively high. The objective of this section is to examine the rationale for and evidence of this complementarity relationship and to discuss its implications for short-run as well as long-run financial policies.

As noted earlier, however, there is no reliable information either on the volume of credit or the rates of interest in the UFM. The nonexistence of these statistics prevents us from any meaningful empirical examination of the hypothesis: we can only provide qualitative and some indirect quantitative evidence.

The complementarity relation between commercial and informal loans essentially hinges upon the ways in which business firms finance each component of their real expenditures—fixed and inventory capital, trade credit, and other liquid assets—in the two loan markets. Therefore, the financial sector model on pp. 157–158 will be modified so as to reflect the causal relationships between firms' real expenditures and financing decisions.

Although the two decisions are likely to be made simultaneously in a general equilibrium framework, a common assumption in partial analyses like this one is that the firm's real expenditure decisions are made prior to the financing decision, provided commercial banks do not ration their customers.[15] In the presence of credit rationing in the commercial loan market, however, this assumption may not necessarily hold: the availability of credit as well as its cost in the commercial loan market may well determine the level of the firm's sales and production inputs. Even in this case, however, it should be pointed out that, to the extent that firms are allowed access to funds in other markets—informal and trade credit—the commercial loan market rationing would be offset if not completely avoided. This consideration suggests that it may be acceptable to assume that firms first decide how much they will invest and then modify their investment decisions in light of any borrowing contraints they may face in the commercial loan market.

Once the firm's total need for financing is determined, the firm must decide on the division of financing between commercial loans and the UFM, which will, *inter alia,* depend upon the structure of the firm's assets with respect to maturity, liquidity, acceptability as collateral, and on the relative cost and availability of the two types of loans.

Insofar as the term and cost of commercial loans are more favorable than those of informal loans, one would expect that the firm would attempt to finance all its required need for funds in the commercial loan market and none at all in the UFM. The firm would not be able, however, to obtain the loan size it requests. Finding the loan it desires not available, the firm has two options with regard to its real expenditure and financing decisions. The firm could reduce its real expenditures to a level consistent with the commercial loan it does have on hand. The firm would accordingly adjust its net assets, but it is not clear which assets it would reduce and by how much.

Another alternative, which appears to be more realistic, is that the firm enters the UFM in need of supplemental financing. The entry then raises two questions. One is the extent to which the firm would borrow from the UFM and another is the classes of its assets informal loans would most likely finance.

*Division of Financing between the Commercial Loan and
Informal Credit Market: The Case of Aggregate Investment*
To answer these questions, we shall assume the following.
First, there exists an aggregate investment function based on
either the present value maximization or the Keynesian marginal
efficiency of investment criteria. Aggregate investment includes
both fixed and working capital investments. Second, firms have
no disposable income of their own and finance everything.[16]
This assumption implies that the total demand for funds is a
function of total investment, which, in turn, is a function of
the interest rates, income, and other variables. Third, firms are
not subject to non-price rationing in the UFM.[17]

Under these assumptions, the total demand for funds or the
demand for investment goods for the economy as a whole may
be shown by the *I-I* schedule in Figure 5. We may also be able
to derive an aggregate supply of funds (the sum of both commercial and informal loans) from Equations 5.7 and 5.12.[18]

The flow supply is shown by the *L-L* curve in Figure 5. It
shows that the cost of credit is constant at i_0 up to the point
Q_1, the distance QQ_1 measuring the financing obtained through
the commercial loan market. Beyond this point is the range of
the UFM financing, the cost of which is the UFM rates of interest. The intersection of the two schedules then determines the
level of investment.

Suppose that *i* is raised to i_1, but that the magnitude of the
increase is such that there still exists an excess demand for
credit in the commercial loan market, as was the case during the
high-interest-rate period 1965–1970 in Korea. The increase
would initially induce ultimate lenders to accumulate bank deposits at the expense of, *inter alia,* informal securities. The
increase in the demand for bank deposits would allow commercial banks to expand their supply of credit. As a result of
these changes in both loan markets, the *L-L* schedule would
shift upward to $L_1 L_1$, but the *I-I* curve would remain unchanged as shown in Figure 5. The increase in *i* reduces the

FIGURE 5 Investment and the Supply of Loans

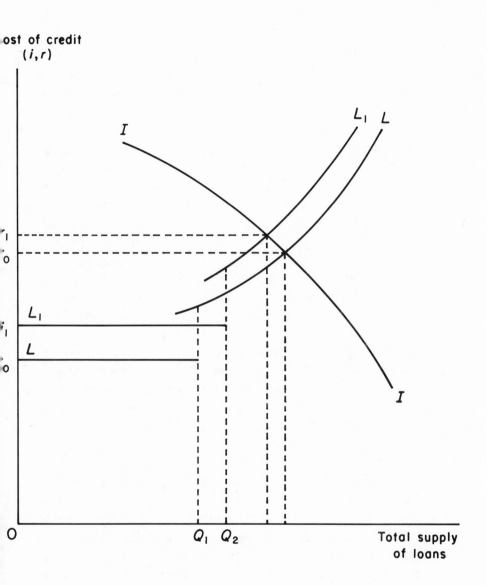

level of investment, and, in response to the relaxation of the commercial loan market rationing, firms simply replace some of their informal credit with commercial loans.

DIVISION OF FINANCING BETWEEN THE COMMERCIAL AND INFORMAL LOAN MARKET: THE CASE OF DISAGGREGATED INVESTMENT FUNCTIONS

While the preceding analysis may indeed have some relevance to the actual workings of the two loan markets, it is deficient in two important respects. The analysis does not take into consideration the differing characteristics of the two markets, one being a long-term and the other a short-term loan market.

It also makes no distinctions between fixed and working capital investment, although the underlying theoretical structures of the two types of investment are entirely different and empirically they have widely different patterns of behavior over the business cycle.[19] The existence of an aggregate investment function, in fact, implies that the firm's decision on the financing between the two markets depends only upon the relative cost and availability of the two liabilities and is invariant to the nature of the assets the firm attempts to finance. Only when disaggregation of investment between fixed and working capital is made would the structure of the firm's assets become an important factor which would influence the firm's decision on the division of the financing between the two markets. For this reason, we shall disaggregate total investment into two components, fixed capital and inventory investment. As before, we shall retain the present value maximization or the Keynesian marginal efficiency of investment criteria for fixed investment. As for inventory behavior, it will be assumed that the desired stocks of inventory are a function of the expected sales of the firm and insensitive to either the cost or availability of funds.[20]

As we have argued in this chapter, business firms in Korea tend to regard commercial loans as long-term liabilities and must also provide collateral of fixed real assets against these loans. Given these characteristics and the low cost of commercial loans, one would normally expect a large proportion of fixed business investment to be financed by commercial loans and very little by informal loans, though the issue is essentially an empirical one. It would also be expected that a relatively large percentage of working capital requirements would be financed through the UFM, because the working capital of business firms embodied in inventory has a shorter gestation period between the borrowing of funds and the revenue generation due to these funds.[21] The terms of informal loans are short, and their cost, though far more expensive than that of commercial loans, is likely to be irrelevant to inventory financing.

Consequently, if commercial loans are rationed, then the brunt of the impact of the rationing will be on the firm's fixed capital investment; that is, in response to credit rationing in the commercial loan market, firms would most likely adjust by curtailing investment in fixed capital rather than reducing all their assets. In the presence of high and continued credit rationing, therefore, the level of fixed investment will be, *ceteris paribus,* strongly influenced by the availability of commercial loans.

This does not necessarily mean that firms will not finance their fixed capital through the UFM. In the short run, informal loans may serve a buffer function that is the result of the partial adjustment of long-term liabilities towards the long-run level. Some firms, in particular large ones with a good credit standing, may be able to renew their short-term loans, making them available for fixed capital investment. This tendency would be stronger, the larger the discrepancy between the rate of return to capital and the rate of interest in the UFM. In the long run, however, the proportion of fixed capital financed by UFM loans will be quantitatively insignificant for a number of reasons other than the cost and term of these loans, and the existing evidence bears out our view.[22]

The credit transactions in the UFM are subject to the usury law; any interest charges higher than 25 percent per annum are illegal and prohibited. Business firms would be reluctant to plan on long-term investment with financial resources obtained from illegal sources, though the government has never seriously attempted to enforce this usury regulation. It would, nevertheless, be too risky. Another reason is that ultimate lenders, though they also allow roll-overs of their loans, are, in general, reluctant to tie up their resources with a particular borrower for an extended period of time. This may endanger their anonymity as lenders in the UFM and lead to subsequent encounters with the tax as well as criminal authorities. Even if the credit standing of the current borrower is good, it may be desirable, as a precautionary measure, not to stay with him for a long period of time. Two attempts at currency reforms—not to mention the 8/3/72 Decree—and other explicit and implicit suppression of curb-market transactions have generated enough uncertainty as to the dangers of an unexpected government crackdown on them. As a way of protecting against this danger, informal lenders would prefer to maintain their loan portfolios highly liquid. The third possible reason is that these lenders—the UFM brokers in particular—have been ruthless in that, at the first sign of poor performance of their borrowers, which may be a short-run problem as far as the borrowers are concerned and in no way reflects the long-term prospect, they pull out their loans. The fourth reason, perhaps the most important one, appears to be that the supply of credit is subject to a high degree of seasonal and other fluctuations.

Once business investment is disaggregated and it is accepted that firms' fixed investment is, *ceteris paribus,* constrained by the availability of commercial loans, it can be easily shown that commercial and informal loans can be complements in borrowers' portfolios.

For this purpose, consider the case of the exogenous increase in the commercial loan rate in the preceding section. The expansion of commercial loans associated with this increase will in the first instance lead to an increase in the demand for investment goods, which, in turn, would cause income to rise.[23]

In the short run, the increased demand for investment can not be matched by an equal increase in production because of a production lag. As a result, an unintended decumulation of the inventories will take place, allowing firms to reduce their informal market liabilities.[24] At the same time, however, there occurs a positive discrepancy between the desired and actual inventory stocks due to the initial inventory decumulation and the increase in the expected sales associated with the expansion of investment and income. Firms will soon have to start building up their inventories to a new desired level which will be higher than before. Firms will have to finance their inventories, trade credit, and other liquid assets in part by commercial loans but mostly by informal loans, given the assumption that inventory investment and the demand for other liquid assets are insensitive to the cost of credit. Thus, firms reduce their informal market liabilities in the short run, but, over the long run, they will borrow more from the UFM as their desired level of inventory stock gradually rises. At the new equilibrium, therefore, it is not clear whether firms' short-term liabilities from the UFM would rise, fall, or remain unchanged, but the interest rates in the UFM would certainly rise.

As noted above, the expansion of loans in the commercial loan market will also, through the linkage effect, stimulate the demand for investment by those small firms who have no access to commercial bank loans and finance most of their real expenditures through internal funds or the UFM. This effect will also increase the demand for UFM loans. In view of these considerations, one must conclude that, in a dual financial system with two distinctive loan markets, a high-interest-rate policy may not necessarily reduce the volume of loans in the UFM.

THE PRESIDENTIAL EMERGENCY DECREE
OF AUGUST 3, 1972

Despite the important contributions of the UFM to the functioning of the Korean economy and the complementary relationship between the regulated and unregulated parts of the financial system, the Korean government has repeatedly tried to suppress and eliminate the unregulated financial institutions, or at least to bring them under some form of regulation. These efforts might be attributed to the desire to recoup lost revenues from the unreported financial transactions and the profits of the "illegal" institutions. Alternatively, they might reflect concern that the effectiveness of monetary policy measures, especially to restrain demand, was vitiated by the capacity of the UFM to reallocate credit and raise the velocity of money during periods of tight credit. While both these concerns are probably well founded, and might be considered as costs to be weighted against the benefits of services performed by the unregulated institutions, it is our impression that the main objection of succeeding governments to the existence of the unregulated institutions was the fact that they were "unregulated." Given the very tight rein exercised by government over all other parts of the financial system, it was disturbing to have these entities about which so little was even known playing such an active role in the day-to-day financial activities of the country. Because little was known, there was a tendency to attribute all kinds of sinister acts to these institutions and thus to build up an argument for their suppression or regulation. The most dramatic example of an attempt to eliminate the UFM occurred in 1972, and it provides some insight into the role of the unregulated institutions, and finally the limit to governmental regulatory powers in the face of strong private market forces.

ECONOMIC BACKGROUND OF THE DECREE

On August 3, 1972, the Korean government announced a Presidential Decree for Economic Stability and Growth (henceforth referred to as the 8/3/72 Decree), which entailed a set of policies designed to achieve twin objectives—stability and growth of the economy. The Decree was a drastic measure, inconceivable in a free-enterprise economy, and as such had considerable repercussions throughout the economy. The 8/3/72 Decree was also significant in that it marked the end of the partial financial liberalization policy the government had initiated with the reforms in 1965 and a complete return to the financial repression of previous years. The Decree was noteworthy in that it was an attempt to eradicate by administrative fiat a market that had served useful functions. For these reasons, the background and the effects of the Decree deserve close examination; however, as with many other policy measures, changes in the economic events preceding and following the Decree—the collapse of the international parity exchange-rate system in 1971, instability in the world financial markets, and the petroleum crisis—blur much of the effect the Decree would have had on the economy. And much of the statistical information about the UFM obtained in the implementation process of the Decree remains confidential. These constraints make it difficult to present an adequate quantitative analysis.

The performance of the Korean economy for the four or five years following the reforms in 1965 had been spectacular. Over that period, the real GNP grew more than 10 percent a year on average; the per capita income (in U.S. dollars) almost doubled; and inflation was brought below 8 percent per annum. In 1970, it looked as though the economy was cooling off, as there was an appreciable drop in investment demand, caused in part by the tight monetary policy pursued over the preceding three years, which had reduced the rate of expansion of domestic credit from 85 percent in 1968 to 27 percent in 1970. The growth of export demand was also declining from its previous very high levels. The rate of growth of exports fell from a high of 42 percent in 1968 to 34 and 28 percent in 1969 and 1970. The reduction in the growth of aggregate demand continued throughout 1971 and into most of 1972. Therefore, expansionary measures were deemed appropriate to stimulate the economy in the short run. This was one of the objectives of the Decree. There were, of course, other long-term structural problems that appear to have provoked the Decree. Foremost among the concerns in the minds of policy-makers were the chronically unstable and weak financial structures of business firms, especially large ones.

The exceptional performance of the economy during 1965–1969 had bred an expectation in the business community that the expansion would continue indefinitely. This optimism, in turn, led business firms to maintain a high rate of investment with funds obtained from domestic financial institutions and foreign sources, supplemented, when necessary, by short-term funds from the UFM. The average cost of capital in real terms was relatively low so long as prices kept rising and depreciation of the exchange rate was gradual. However, the major (18 percent) devaluation in 1971, designed mainly to stimulate exports, also caused a sudden jump in the wǒn cost of foreign debt servicing. This created severe short-run financial problems for those firms that had borrowed abroad most heavily, particularly the case for larger firms. Many of them, faced with deteriorating debt-equity ratios and short-run cash shortages, turned to their customary source of emergency financing—the unregulated money markets. Also, as an increasing number of these firms found themselves unable to meet the principal and interest payments to their foreign creditors, the guaranteeing banks were forced to make good on their commitments.

Conceivably, the Korean government could have let these debt-ridden firms go bankrupt and weathered the painful consequences. In fact, some policy-makers were in favor of this course of action, on the ground that the time had come to "rationalize" industries and the financial structure of firms through market forces. This alternative, however, posed a number of serious problems. It was feared that poor performance of the economy and an increasing number of business failures would undermine the nation's credit standing in the international capital markets and would thus hamper the inflow of much-needed foreign loans. This option also ran counter to the high growth objective of the government. As a result, a more costly but less painful alternative was chosen; it was simply to bail out these troubled firms.

A second structural problem at that time was the concern that a rising real cost of capital, together with a rising exchange rate, was emerging as an element of cost-push inflation. It was argued that the high cost of capital itself and its cost-push inflation effect would weaken exporters' competitiveness in the international markets and threaten a setback in the implementation of the export-led growth strategy. An overall downward adjustment in the interest rate was thus called for in some sectors of the economy.

A third structural issue that led to the Decree was related to the need for changes in the industrial development strategy. In the preparation stages of the Third Five-Year Development Plan (1972–1976), there emerged a general consensus that a high growth objective would require major shifts in the development strategy from emphasis on the expansion of labor-intensive light manufacturing industries to heavy and chemical industries. In view of the enormous capital investment requirements with a long gestation period and uncertain future prospects of these industries, private firms could not be induced to invest in these sectors unless they were given substantial government subsidies. The existing interest-rate structure and financial policies based upon indirect control of the financial sector were not consistent with this new development strategy.

The authorities were aware of the possible adverse effects an overall reduction in the interest rate might have on domestic resource mobilization. There was a widespread feeling at that time, however, that the savers' confidence had been established over a period of the high-interest-rate policy so that saving would be more dependent upon real income and that the interest rate could be safely reduced. Also, it was anticipated that the rate of inflation could be brought down to a low level (for example, 3.5 percent per year was the target for 1972), which would have resulted in a positive real rate of interest even at relatively low nominal rates.

A fourth institutional problem was the growth of the unorganized financial sector. In spite of the relatively high real interest rates in the OFM after 1965 and other measures for the development of this sector, the volume of informal loans was climbing and this aggravated further the interest burden of large as well as small business firms. Some of the owners of private firms and even public corporations were employing their own funds in their firms in the form of loans to the firm rather than as equity capital, in part to take advantage of the corporate tax system that allowed interest paid on borrowed funds as a cost in determining profits (that were subject to tax at a rate of about 40 percent) whereas interest income—for example on bank deposits—was subject to tax of only around 10 percent.[25]

In order to curb the expansion of the UFM and alleviate the interest burden of business enterprises, it was felt, therefore, that some drastic measures had to be taken. Thus, the 8/3/72 Decree had two purposes. On the one hand, it was intended to stimulate economic activity by reviving investment demand, a short-run objective. On the other, it was designed to eliminate some of the structural problems of the economy.[26]

THE EFFECT OF THE DECREE

The main features of the 8/3/72 Decree were:

1) All the loan agreements between business firms with a business license and lenders in the UFM as of August 2, 1972 were nullified and replaced by new ones. The borrowers would have to repay their informal loans over a five-year period after a

three-year grace period, carrying a 1.35 percent monthly interest rate, or the lenders had the option to switch their loans into shares of the borrowing firms.

2) Some of the short-term high-interest-rate bank loans by business firms were replaced by long-term loans at 8 percent annual interest rate payable over a five-year period after a three-year grace period. The amount of the replacement was 200 billion wŏn.

3) Establishment of a credit guarantee fund for small and medium industries, and agriculture and fishing businesses, amounting to 2 billion wŏn with government funds, would allow the banking system to make loans up to ten times the amount of the fund without collateral requirements.

4) Establishment of an industrial rationalization fund, to which the government supplied 50 billion wŏn, and which was to be used for long-term, low-interest loans to the business firms that could meet the criteria of the rationalization standards.

5) An overall reduction in the interest rates of banking institutions lowered the time deposit rate from 17.4 percent to 12.6 percent and general loans up to one year from 19 percent to 15.5 percent.

As discussed in Chapter 4, the volume of informal loans reported by all enterprises with a business license—both corporate and unincorporated—amounted to 345.6 billion wŏn, approximately 80 percent of money supply at that time (see Table 33). There were also other startling revelations of the informal credit sector:

1) Of the total informal loans, one third, 113.7 billion wŏn, were the so-called disguised informal loans, that is, those loans extended by corporate owners or stockholders to themselves.

2) At the end of July 1972, there were about 9,000 corporate firms. Only 3,819 of those firms, about 42 percent, had been paying taxes on type C income, that is, a withholding tax on interest payments; 10,753 enterprises out of a half million unincorporated firms, about 2 percent of the total, had reported taxable type C incomes. These figures suggest how secretive the UFM credit transactions were at that time.

TABLE 32 Size Distribution of Informal Loans Reported by
Creditors as of August 3, 1972

	Number of Loans	Percentage	Amount (billion wŏn)	Percentage
Below 3 million wŏn	189,245	89.8	114.25	32.3
3 to 5 million wŏn	9,958	4.7	36.22	10.1
5 to 10 million wŏn	7,028	3.3	44.92	12.6
10 to 50 million wŏn	4,145	1.9	75.29	21.1
50 to 100 million wŏn	331	0.2	21.87	6.1
Over 100 million wŏn	198	0.1	64.55	18.1
Total	210,905	100.0	357.10	100.0

Source: BOK, Report of the Results of the August 3, 1972 Presidential Emergency
Decree (August 1973), p. 190.

3) Although it was never made public, it was reported that
one-third of these loans were extended without any collateral
requirements at the monthly rate of interest of 2–2.5 percent
on the average.[27]

4) About 80 percent of total loans were reported in the two
largest cities—Seoul and Pusan—suggesting a heavy concentration of the UFM transactions in urban areas.

5) The size distribution of informal loans (see Tables 32 and
33) indicates clearly that the UFM was not limited to making
small short-term loans; and thirty firms borrowed more than
100 million wŏn each. The outstanding volume of loans of over
100 million wŏn accounted for 53 percent of the total (see
Table 33).

6) The distribution of the loans by industry was quite similar
to that of the banking institutions, as shown in Table 34. It is
not clear how one should interpret this result, but, in view of
our discussion on the structure and characteristics of the UFM,
it could be presented as evidence supporting our complementarity hypothesis.

After the Emergency Decree, the UFM disappeared from the
scene for a while, but the Decree failed to eradicate the institutional factors or economic forces that had led to its existence.

TABLE 33 Size Distribution of Informal Loans Reported by Borrowers as of August 3, 1972

	Number of Loans	Percentage	Amount (billion wŏn)	Percentage
Below 3 million wŏn	30,756	75.6	24.75	7.2
3 to 5 million wŏn	2,924	7.2	11.09	3.2
5 to 10 million wŏn	2,766	6.8	19.42	5.6
10 to 50 million wŏn	3,123	7.7	68.35	19.8
50 to 100 million wŏn	561	1.4	39.04	11.3
Over 100 million wŏn	547	1.3	182.98	52.9
Total	40,677	100.0	345.63	100.0

Source: Same as Table 32.

The Decree simply resulted in a large capital levy on the lenders to the UFM and an equivalent transfer of capital to the borrowers, thereby causing a temporary disruption of the short-term credit market in its performance of a role still neglected by the RFM.

It was inevitable that the UFM would reappear and expand, and, in fact, the revival of the UFM started about a year after the Decree with the beginning of the oil crisis at the end of 1973. During that interval, almost a year, the UFM activities were drastically curtailed, and, as usual, the underprivileged small enterprises, traders, and agriculture suffered the most.

The disorganization of the UFM could have had more serious repercussions for the economy in the following years, had there not been offsetting factors that precipitated a rapid expansion of the economy. Beginning from the fourth quarter of 1972, due in part to a 25 percent depreciation of the wŏn vis-à-vis the yen, exports skyrocketed, and in 1973 expanded by 90 percent. The economy grew by 16.5 percent in 1973, the highest rate of growth in the nation's history. The sudden increase in exports lifted the economy out of the mild slowdown in 1971 and 1972, and more than offset the effects of the disruption of the credit system. Then the oil crisis and the worldwide recession and inflation hit the economy. A worsening

TABLE 34 Loans by Industry

	Informal Credit Sector as of August 3, 1972		Commercial Banks at the End of June, 1972[a]		Deposit Money Banks and the Korea Development Bank at the End of July 1972[a]	
	Amount	%	Amount	%	Amount	%
Mining & quarrying	8.8	2.5	20.82	3.2	34.14 (11.32)[c]	4.2
Manufacturing	195.5	56.6	414.87	64.2	487.55 (72.68)	59.3
Construction	26.2	7.6	59.77	9.3	71.44 (11.67)	8.7
Commerce	42.7	12.4	58.60	9.1	60.51 (1.91)	7.4
Transportation, storage & communication	17.5	5.1	23.40	3.6	39.86 (16.46)	4.8
Electricity, gas & water	—	0	7.30	1.1	63.2 (55.9)	7.6
Services	27.9	8.1	42.29	6.5	42.47 (0.18)	5.2
Others	27.0	7.8	18.70	3.0	23.39[d] (4.69)	2.8
Total	345.6	100.0[b]	645.75	100.0[b]	822.56[b]	100.0[b]

Source: Same as Table 32.

Notes: [a]For the purpose of comparison, loans to agriculture, forestry, hunting, and fishing by commercial banks and special banks are excluded from the total. Since only the business firms with business licenses were required to report their informal loans, it is reasonable to assume that most of the informal loans extended to these industries were not reported and that the reported amount would be insignificant. [b]Do not add up to 100 because of rounding. [c]Figures in parentheses are those of KDB. [d]Include the Citizens' National Bank remunerations.

balance-of-payments situation and speculation on imported raw materials in the early part of 1974 brought about a substantial credit squeeze in the RFM. With this signal, borrowers and lenders started getting together, as conspicuously as before the Decree.

In retrospect, it appears that the Decree succeeded in achieving none of the objectives for which it was designed. It had very little impact on the recovery and subsequent expansion of the economy. The upsurge in export demand was the major cause of the expansion in 1973. Nor did the Decree contribute to a permanent improvement in the financial structures of the corporate sector. After the Decree, the rate of business profits shot up markedly, and the improvement in the debt position of business firms was equally impressive. These were, however, short-lived improvements. Within a year, most of the indicators measuring the soundness of business financial structures, profitability, and other management efficiency began to deteriorate and returned to the levels that had prevailed before the Decree, as businesses pressed ahead with large-scale debt financing of new investment, and the government arranged for massive external borrowing to cover the increased energy and other production costs of the private sector.[28]

The August 1972 reforms were another attempt to eliminate the unregulated financial market and, in the process, relieve the financial stress on large borrowers from that market. The latter objective was achieved and, as a bonus, major businesses were reassured that the government would be likely to assist them in any future periods of stringency. This did much to relieve the fears among the new entrepreneurs of any risks of over-expansion and excessive indebtedness. As long as they stayed on good terms with the government, they would be rescued.

The UFM, while not destroyed, was given the opposite message, that is, that they could expect repeated assaults whenever it served the government's interests and that theirs was a risky business. Still, the demand for their services remained, mainly because of the inefficiencies of the DMBs. Despite the emergence of some new officially sanctioned short-term financing institutions, the UFM resumed business after a brief hiatus.

SUMMARY OF INTERACTIONS

The cost and potential long-term nature of bank loans have been favorable for long-term investment in Korea. Together with a potentially rich field of investment opportunities with high rates of return in an inflationary environment, they have induced businesses with access to the banks to rely heavily on bank loans for the financing of their fixed investment in machinery, equipment, and plant. With the limited ability of the banking sector to mobilize financial resources, therefore, there has been a chronic shortage of bank finance for working capital. As a result, business firms have had to finance the bulk of their working capital through retained earnings or through the UFIs.

Traditional discrimination of banks against small borrowers has been an equally important institutional factor for the expansion of UFI credit. Furthermore, the government allocated a large share of bank credit to the so-called essential industries, and very little to the unprotected sectors of small-scale industries, small farmers, and small-sized processing enterprises.

In most developing countries, the bigger commercial banks avoid small-scale borrowers, irrespective of their productivity, because large firms can provide secure collateral against loans and the administrative cost of a loan for them is on the average lower than it is for small borrowers. Small borrowers are often unable to offer collateral acceptable to these institutions because their net worth is small. It has been argued that, because of these inherent built-in biases in their lending practice, commercial banks are likely to limit the use of their resources to the well-established borrowers with secure collateral and, "once having exhausted these possibilities, prefer to keep their funds idle rather than to channel them to the second or third best customers."[29] In Korea, however, there has been such consistent excess demand for bank loans by large borrowers because of the low-real-interest-rate policy, that the commercial banks have never had idle funds.

On the contrary, the RFS in Korea has tended to channel any additional amount of loanable funds they mobilize to those large firms in the industrial sector that use it mainly for new investment. Thus, this increase in the supply of credit to the industrial sector has led eventually to a greater demand for short-term working capital, much of which has been financed in the UFIs. The expansion in the large-scale industrial sector has led to a subsequent increase in the demand for goods and services produced by small-scale industries and processing firms. This, in turn, has caused a corresponding increase in the demand for informal credit by these small borrowers without access to the banks.

Because of these characteristics of the asset structure and loan policy of the banking system, there have been two main types of borrowers coming to the UFIs: those larger firms that have access to the bank resources which they use mainly for financing fixed investment and, from time to time, require credit to satisfy their short-term working capital needs; and those smaller firms that have no access to the banks, and therefore need to rely on the UFIs for most of their working capital and some financing of fixed capital. On the supply side, as pointed out, savers who would otherwise have gone into the RFIs have been encouraged to enter the UFIs as lenders induced by the high rates of return in that market. Also, enterprises that found themselves with excess liquidity in the short run were able to maximize profits by channeling that liquidity into the unregulated market on a short-term basis.

Thus, there has been a close and symbiotic relationship between the regulated and unregulated financial markets over the years in Korea. Businesses have been borrowers and lenders in both markets and have moved funds from one to the other as needs and opportunities permitted. Households have been suppliers of funds to both markets, but borrowers mainly from the unorganized markets. The disparity of interest rates in the two markets has varied over time and has been a major factor affecting the allocation of savings to one or the other market. Longer-term deposits have been attracted to the regulated financial sector because of both a stepped interest-rate structure and greater security. Similarly, longer-term loans have come mainly from the RFIs, leaving the unregulated markets to specialize in short-term deposits and loans.

SIX

Policies to Influence Resource Allocation

As Chapter 1 has suggested, a financial system can influence the allocation of real resources by mobilizing financial resources and transferring those resources from one economic unit to another, thus permitting the receiving unit to buy a different package of real resources, which it uses in a way different from what the unit supplying the financial resources would have done. In addition to simply intermediating between surplus and deficit units, a financial system can be used (manipulated) to channel financial resources to certain favored categories of deficit units that are expected to use the resources for certain purposes, or the terms on which the financial resources are provided can be manipulated so as to influence the decisions of the potential users of the resources.

Some economists argue that an unfettered, competitive financial system is the best means to achieve optimal allocation of resources. Such a system is believed to result in a set of prices that correctly reflects the marginal productivity of the resource uses of borrowers and the marginal utility of deferred income of lenders. It is also seen as a system that is able to grow in response to a society's needs and wishes and to contribute thereby to the growth of the economy. Finally, if its international linkages are similarly unconstrained, the financial system may draw in external financial resources and allocate them along with the domestic resources to the most productive uses.

Few governments in developing countries seem to believe in the allocational efficiency of the financial system. As documented by Shaw[1] and McKinnon,[2] the financial sector is perhaps the most heavily regulated industry in developing countries. The governments in these countries intervene extensively, setting interest rates on both deposits and loans and allocating credit, in the apparent belief that, without such intervention, credit allocation would not reflect the social and economic priorities often set by the governments themselves. The Korean government is no exception. It has behaved as if, in the absence of its interference, some sectors would receive more credit than socially and economically desirable, while others would receive too little, and that, with uncontrolled interest rates, some industries that are "important for development" would not survive, while other less critical sectors, such as commerce and home construction, would be the only ones able to pay the "high" interest rates.

Government controls over credit allocation in Korea were initially exercised through a system of guidelines which set forth a ranking of loan priorities for different sectors and within each sector. Credit guidelines were formally introduced in 1958 under Regulations Pertaining to the Uses of Funds in the Financial Sector and have been modified from time to time since.[3]

As stated in the Regulations, the credit guidelines were comprehensive in the coverage of industries and businesses, but provided only a general ranking of loan priorities and a broad categorization of the types of businesses to be accorded preferential treatment in credit allocation. Thus, the guidelines were too general to be translated into operational terms, thereby giving the BOK, which was in charge of administering the guidelines, considerable room for discretion in the actual allocation of credit. There was always excess demand for credit as a result of a low-interest-rate policy, and the financial institutions were generally not able to meet the total credit demand of the preferred sectors at the prevailing interest rates. Under the circumstances, the financial institutions had to ration the available credit even to preferred borrowers, and were thus entrusted with considerable economic power.

Beginning in the early 1960s, the government took a more active role in guiding resource allocation through the formulation of both multi-year development plans and annual overall-resource-allocation programs. With the assumption of this leading role, the government increasingly interfered with the allocation of credit and gradually took over the rationing of credit from the BOK and financial institutions. Accordingly, the system of general credit guidelines contained in the Regulations has given way to a system of government directives, ranging from general guidelines to the earmarking of funds or prescription of bank loans for specific sectors, industries, and even individual firms and projects. In formulating the annual financial stabilization plan, the government allocates anywhere from 50 to 70 percent of domestic credit, depending upon the classification of "directed" or "policy" loans, to predesignated sectors, industries, and uses. The remainder is then, in theory, allocated at the discretion of the DMBs, but, in reality, these banks exercise little control over even the residual banking funds.

Also, over time the government adopted an increasingly complex structure of interest rates intended to give varying amounts of favored treatment to different categories of borrowers. In some cases, the preferential interest rates and large credit allocations went together, as with export producers. In other cases, such as much of agriculture, the interest rates were kept low, but loan amounts were limited.

Such manipulation of financial prices and quantities raises some obvious questions. One is the rationale of the interventions: What allocation objectives was the government trying to accomplish? A second question is whether the credit instruments of interest rates and loan allocations were effective means of achieving the objectives. A third set of questions relates to which groups bore the burden and which received the benefits of the credit incentives. These are all difficult questions to answer.

OBJECTIVES AND INSTRUMENTS
OF CREDIT-ALLOCATION POLICY

Government policy in the post-Korean War decade was directed towards the following main goals: facilitating the inflow of foreign aid, promoting new import-substituting industries, and maintaining sufficient support for the agriculture sector. Not only was the foreign aid important as a real resource transfer, but also the local currency generated from the imports of aid-financed consumer and intermediate goods was a major source of funds for both the government budget and bank lending programs. Thus, a smooth aid flow was important, and government wanted to assure that importers of aid goods had sufficient financing at low interest rates to provide incentives to bring in the imports.

At the same time, the import-substitution objectives called for a combination of long-term credit at low interest rates plus protection of the domestic market through tariffs and quotas for the chosen industries. The new import-substitute industries also needed sufficient power and fuel for their operations, so that investment in electric generation and coal mines was encouraged through low-cost, long-term loans.

Finally, the government sought to support the agriculture sector to raise its productivity. But, in this post-war era, there appears to have been some ambivalence. Although the government did want to improve the livelihood of the farmers and consolidate the results of the earlier land reform, it also wanted to hold down urban food prices and maintain a justification for continuing imports of food-grain under the aid program. Thus, the guidelines for agricultural credit policy were to finance current inputs of the many small farmers, but not to undertake any major investment or expansion schemes. Low interest rates on the limited supply of agricultural loans were consistent with the objectives of benefiting both the farmers through lower costs and also the urban population through lower food prices.

When the government's development strategy shifted from import substitution to export-led growth in the 1960s, there was a major reorientation of credit policies. The heart of the new system was automatic approval of low-interest loans by the commercial banks to any producer with an export letter of credit (L/C) or other valid evidence of an export order.

In the early years, the amount of loan granted mounted to 80 percent of the domestic production costs of the exports, and it ran for 90 to 120 days at an annual interest rate of 6.5 percent. The same basic procedures applied for sales to the U.N. Forces in Korea or other sales that directly earned foreign exchange. Special measures were taken to see that suppliers of exporters also shared in the favorable bank-loan schemes. This was done through the use of a domestic letter of credit covering orders of exporters from their domestic suppliers.

In addition to the short-term loans for financing current production, export producers were also given preferential consideration for the guaranteed foreign loans used to finance imported machinery for expansion of productive capacity. These loans were not granted automatically like the export-production loans, but had to be approved by both the guaranteeing banks, the Economic Planning Board, and, in many cases, the National Assembly. Inevitably, the cost incurred in obtaining approval of such loans was greater than it was for those granted automatically. But they probably were still less expensive and difficult to obtain than the earlier loans for investment in the protected import-substitution industries.

Finally, in the 1970s, the focus of government policy broadened to include more of the intermediate-goods industries, such as steel and petrochemicals, that supplied the export industries, and also the machinery and construction industries, including shipbuilding. These were all seen as potential exporting industries or intermediate suppliers of export industries.

The government set up special loan programs for the machinery industries as well as preferential financing for domestic purchases of Korean-made machinery. In addition, the government assisted with the arranging for large-scale, multi-source financing of the major capital-intensive investment undertakings in steel and petrochemicals. Such financing packages included funds from international financing institutions, foreign government-owned and private banks, domestic banks, and, sometimes, even Korean government equity contributions. These large schemes generally carried fairly low nominal interest rates as well as extended grace and repayment periods, but they were also quite difficult and costly to arrange.

EFFECTS OF GOVERNMENT INTERVENTION ON RESOURCE ALLOCATION

In intervening in the financial markets, the government was not interested in the sectoral allocation of credit per se, but in effecting the allocation of physical resources; that is, the ultimate objective of the government controls over credit allocation was to bring about an allocation of physical resources that might not be optimally efficient but was desired on other grounds. To what extent has the Korean government succeeded in attaining this objective? It is an extremely difficult question to answer even at a theoretical level and one that requires sophisticated microeconomic data for an adequate empirical examination. Unfortunately, such data are not available.

The key to the answer lies in the fungibility of credit. If credit fungibility is of a high degree, the government cannot expect to be successful in effecting what it considers to be an optimal allocation of physical resources. The problem is that it is almost impossible to measure the degree of credit fungibility. With limited data and information, we could make, at best, some tentative and often impressionistic observations.

During the 1950s, the primary and social overhead sectors and some of the import-competing manufacturing industries received preferential treatment. As can be seen in Table 35, the manufacturing sector was the predominant recipient of bank loans. It absorbed on average almost 45 percent of total bank lending, though this sector accounted for only 12 percent of GNP. Next came the agriculture sector, with about 25 percent, to be followed by the social-overhead sector with a disproportionately large share of 15 percent in comparison to its share in GNP of less than 8 percent. Services and other sectors constituted more than 37 percent of nominal output; yet they received less than 10 percent of bank credit, much of which went to wholesale and retail traders. Electricity, gas, water, and sanitation industries, all dominated by government enterprises, accounted for about 9 percent of bank loans, though the share of these industries as a whole in GNP was less than 1 percent (see Table 36). Such a large share of bank loans for this sector in comparison to its GNP share reflects both the lumpiness and long gestation periods of investment in social-overhead capital and the government's emphasis on building infrastructure.

Different industries are bound to have different financing requirements. Financial needs would, other things being equal, vary from industry to industry, depending upon the differences in factor intensity, capital-output ratio, investment gestation period, and cash-flow requirements. For example, agriculture would, in general, need less financing per unit of output than manufacturing industries, and both would need less than social overhead. For these reasons, one could argue that the ex post information on loan distribution reflects largely the differences

TABLE 35 Loans by DMB and KDB by Industry, 1955–1978 (in billion wŏn)

	1955		1960		1965		1970		1975		1978	
	Amount	%	Amount	%	Amount	%	Amount	%	Amount	%	Amount	%
Agriculture, forestry, hunting & fishing	1.69	25.8	12.27	30.5	19.48	18.7	100.23	12.4	304.90	9.2	669.35	8.6
Mining and quarrying	0.32	4.9	1.74	4.3	2.87	2.7	19.69	2.4	53.35	1.6	95.46	1.2
Manufacture	2.89	44.3	16.90	42.0	47.49	45.7	385.72	47.5	1873.08	56.2	4247.56	54.8
Light industries	1.75	26.9	7.51	18.7	22.34	21.5	175.64	21.6	928.99	27.9	1720.75	22.2
Heavy industries	1.14	17.4	9.39	23.3	25.15	24.2	210.08	25.9	944.09	28.3	2526.81	32.6
Social overhead	0.95	14.5	4.93	12.2	17.43	16.7	132.93	16.4	675.39	20.3	1586.90	20.5
Construction	0.12	1.7	2.38	5.9	3.98	3.8	63.10	7.8	272.96	8.2	651.85	8.4
Electricity, water & sanitation	0.64	9.8	1.69	4.2	11.19	10.7	43.28	5.3	216.25	6.5	442.98	5.7
Transport, storage & communication	0.19	3.2	0.86	2.1	2.26	2.1	26.55	3.3	186.18	5.6	492.07	6.4
Services and others[a]	0.70	10.5	4.32	10.7	16.57	15.9	172.50	21.3	422.72	12.7	1146.69	14.8
All industry	6.55	100.0	40.16	100.0	103.84	100.0	811.07	100.0	3329.44	100.0	7745.96	100.0

Sources: BOK, *Economics Statistics Yearbook* (1958–1978); BOK, *Monthly Economic Statistics* (1979), 1, 3; BOK, *National Income in Korea* (1978).

Note: [a]Includes wholesale and retail trade, restaurants and hotels, financing, insurance, real estate, ownership of dwellings, public administration and defense, social and personal services, education, and rest of world.

TABLE 36 Industrial Origin of GNP, 1955–1978
(billion wŏn)

	1955		1960		1965		1970		1975		1978	
	Amount	*%*	*Amount*	*%*	*Amount*	*%*	*Amount*	*%*	*Amount*	*%*	*Amount*	*%*
Agriculture, forestry, hunting & fishing	50.27	43.9	89.31	36.5	303.28	37.6	710.71	26.6	2311.87	24.0	4717.54	21.2
Mining and quarrying	1.22	1.1	5.23	2.1	16.21	2.0	38.96	1.4	148.16	1.5	323.33	1.5
Manufacture	13.08	11.4	33.51	13.7	143.79	17.9	558.65	20.9	2590.35	26.9	5946.82	26.7
Light industries	10.27	8.9	24.97	10.2	96.60	12.0	341.41	12.8	1360.13	14.1	—	—
Heavy industries	2.81	2.5	8.54	3.5	47.19	5.9	217.24	8.1	1230.22	12.8	—	—
Social overhead	6.91	6.0	21.38	8.7	69.78	8.7	373.00	13.9	1230.67	12.7	3605.88	16.2
Construction	3.51	3.0	8.20	3.3	27.39	3.4	146.77	5.5	497.78	5.2	1959.11	8.8
Electricity, water & sanitation	0.58	0.5	1.85	0.8	9.98	1.3	43.98	1.6	126.22	1.2	321.36	1.4
Transport, storage & communication	2.82	2.5	11.33	4.6	32.41	4.0	182.25	6.8	606.67	6.3	1325.41	6.0
Services and others[a]	43.01	37.6	95.50	39.0	272.66	33.8	994.08	37.2	3363.19	34.9	7662.16	34.4
All industry	114.49	100.0	244.93	100.0	850.72	100.0	2675.40	100.0	9644.24	100.0	22255.73	100.0

Sources: BOK, *Economics Statistics Yearbook* (1958–1978); BOK, *Monthly Economic Statistics* (1979), 1, 3; BOK, *National Income in Korea* (1978).

Note: [a]Includes wholesale and retail trade, restaurants and hotels, financing, insurance, real estate, ownership of dwellings, public administration and defense, social and personal services, education, and rest of world.

179

in industrial characteristics with regard to financial requisites rather than the consequences of government's allocational policy. There was, in fact, a marked increase in both the ratio of bank loans to nominal output and the credit shares of the manufacturing and social overhead sectors during the 1950s. This piece of evidence does not imply any causality, but, combined with the credit rationing exercised by the government at that time, suggests that a large part of bank loans may in fact have been allocated according to the loan priority ranking consistent with the policy direction of the primary-import-substitution period. But it is still difficult to determine the extent to which selective credit allocation was responsible for the changes in industrial structure envisioned by the government.

During 1965–1969, the period of rapid financial growth, the manufacturing sector, which accounted for the bulk of exports and registered the highest rate of growth, was accorded a growing share of bank loans. More important, during the 1959–1966 period, 72 percent of private foreign borrowings were allocated to this sector.[4] For the next five years, this percentage went down, but was still close to 60 percent. Although self-sufficiency of grains continued to be one of the stated policy objectives, agriculture's loan share declined gradually to about 12 percent at the end of 1969, reflecting the relative slowdown in the growth of this sector. The social-overhead sector remained one of the priority sectors and received a large share of bank loans relative to its output as in the 1950s, though less in terms of loans per unit of output (see Table 37). The government also allocated a large share of its foreign borrowings to this sector during the period.[5]

In the 1960s, the loan share of services and other industries which were relatively less preferred sectors almost doubled compared with the figure in the 1950s, mostly at the expense of agriculture. This was not necessarily the result of relaxation of credit rationing by the government, but of a greater availability of financial resources realized by the interest-rate reform.

In the 1970s, heavy industries in the manufacturing sector

TABLE 37 Ratios of Loans by DMB and KDB to Output by Industry, 1955–1978 (%)

	1955	1960	1965	1970	1975	1978
Agriculture, forestry, hunting & fishing	3.3	13.7	6.4	14.1	13.2	14.2
Mining and quarrying	26.2	33.2	17.7	50.5	36.5	29.5
Manufacture	22.0	50.4	33.0	69.0	72.3	71.4
Light industries	17.0	30.0	23.1	51.4	68.3	—
Heavy industries	40.5	109.9	53.2	96.7	76.7	—
Social overhead	13.7	23.0	24.9	35.6	54.9	44.0
Construction	3.4	29.0	14.3	43.0	54.8	33.3
Electricity, water & sanitation	110.3	91.3	112.1	98.4	171.3	137.8
Transport, storage & communication	6.7	7.5	6.9	14.6	30.7	37.1
Services and others[a]	1.6	4.5	6.0	17.4	12.6	15.0
All industry	5.7	16.3	12.8	30.3	34.5	34.8

Sources: BOK, *Economics Statistics Yearbook* (1958–1978); BOK, *Monthly Economic Statistics* (1979), 1, 3; BOK, *National Income in Korea* (1978).

Note: [a]Includes wholesale and retail trade, restaurants and hotels, financing, insurance, real estate, ownership of dwellings, public administration and defense, social and personal services, education, and rest of world.

received a growing share of bank credit. This reflected a change in Korea's development strategy in which heavy and chemical industries were promoted for both import substitution and export promotion. As shown in Table 37, heavy industries accounted for 33 percent of bank loans at the end of 1978. The decline in agriculture's loan share continued into the 1970s. This trend could be explained by the relative decline in the size of the agricultural sector, together with the institution of a price-support program in 1969 in place of a credit-support program for agriculture.

It is possible to compare the relative loan shares of the industrial sectors with their sectoral capital-output ratios to assess whether the loans are proportional to capital requirements. This is done in Table 38. While recognizing that the capital-output ratio reflects only fixed capital, and that bank loans are used to finance both fixed and working capital, we have the impression, as discussed in Chapter 5, that bank loans are used mainly for investment in fixed capital. Thus, the comparison of loan ratios with fixed capital-output ratios has some relevance. In Table 38, we show the sectoral capital-output ratios over an eighteen-year period, 1956–1974 in Column 1, and then the sectoral ratio as compared to the all-industry capital-output ratio in Column 2. This shows that the sectoral ratio for agriculture, forestry, and fishing was 67 percent, or two-thirds, of the overall ratio, whereas the sectoral ratio for electricity, water, and sanitation was three times the overall ratio. Finally, in Column 3, we show the comparable ratios for loan allocations using averages for the three years 1970, 1975, and 1978, as shown in Table 37. The average ratio of bank loans to value added for those years for all industries was 33.2 percent. Column 3 shows that the ratio of loans to value added in the agriculture, forestry, and fisheries sector was only 42 percent of the ratio for all industries, whereas the manufacturing-sector ratio was more than double (214 percent) the overall ratio.

By comparing Columns 2 and 3 of Table 38, it is possible to see which sectors received a larger than proportionate share

TABLE 38 Comparison of Loan Ratios to Capital-Output Ratios

	Marginal Fixed Capital-Output Ratio, 1956–1974	*Ratio of Sectoral to Overall Capital-Output Ratio*	*Ratio of Sectoral to Overall Ratio of Loans to Value Added 1970, 1975, 1978*	*Column 3 divided by Column 2*
Agriculture, forestry, and fishing	1.54	0.67	0.42	0.63
Mining and quarrying	1.48	0.64	1.17	1.83
Manufacturing	1.37	0.59	2.14	3.63
Construction	0.61	0.26	1.32	5.08
Electricity, water, and sanitation	7.08	3.06	4.09	1.34
Transport, storage, and communication	7.70	3.33	0.83	0.25
All industries	2.31ᵗ	1.00	1.00	

Sources: Column 1 is from Wontack Hong, *Factor Supply and Factor Intensity of Trade in Korea* (Seoul, 1976). Column 3 is derived from Table 37.

of total loans if the criterion for allocation had been the fixed capital to output ratio. Such a comparison, shown in Column 4, indicates that the construction and manufacturing sectors received relatively very large allocations, that mining and electricity, water and sanitation were moderately favored, and finally that agriculture, transport, storage, and communication, as well as all other services (not shown in the table), received much less than their proportionate share. While repeating the caveat that capital-output ratios are only one factor influencing the need for resources and, thus, for external financing, we think that they are a significant factor for most industrial sectors and, therefore, that the figures in Column 4 of Table 38 do suggest that manufacturing and construction have received favorable treatment from the loan allocators in recent years.

CONSEQUENCES OF FUNGIBILITY AND UFM INTERMEDIATION

It is often alleged that, when the financial markets are imperfect and the financial sector is still an infant industry, government intervention may be both warranted and effective. The effectiveness stems from the fact that financial market imperfections reduce credit fungibility; that is, in a financial regime where the financial markets are fragmented among regions and different classes and groups of borrowers so that funds do not flow freely among the separated and segmented markets, government intervention has a better chance of success in channeling bank credits to bring about the desired use of physical resources.

The fungibility issue could be examined at the two stages of credit allocation. At the first stage, which is related to the lending behavior of the financial institutions, it is possible that the financial intermediaries may simply evade or ignore the government's credit guidelines and directives; that is, the financial intermediaries may be guilty of credit diversion. This problem does not appear to be serious in Korea because of the government's close supervision of the day-to-day operations of the DMBs and other regulated financial intermediaries. The financial institutions, however, have consistently evaded the guideline for the allocation of credits to small-scale enterprises. At one stage in the latter part of the 1970s, the DMBs were required to make available a minimum of 30 percent of their total loans to small- and medium-scale industries. No one believed the actual performance of these institutions was anywhere close to the guideline quota. Because of the ambiguities in the definition of small and medium enterprises, the banks were easily able to meet the quota without necessarily lending the required amount to small-scale businesses. Given their traditional aversion to small borrowers, the banks may have taken advantage of the definitional loopholes and thereby facilitated credit diversion.[6]

At the second stage of credit allocation, which is related to the behavior of borrowers, it is quite conceivable that a large part of bank credit has been diverted to uses other than those predesignated by the government. One possible reason for this diversion is that the DMBs and KDB do not have an effective system of credit-use supervision. Even if they had one, the management of these financial institutions would not be very much concerned about, and hence would not actively supervise, the actual use of bank credits because the management was not really responsible for the decisions on directed and policy loans. The lack of autonomy in bank management may have aggravated credit diversion.

The financial market fragmentation that existed in Korea can be attributed largely to government controls over the interest rates and management of the regulated financial institutions. In other words, the fragmentation may be viewed as a result of a deliberate effort on the part of the government to facilitate its directed credit allocation. We have shown in the preceding chapter that the growth of the unregulated money market was in part due to the financial market fragmentation engineered by the government and that one of the major functions of the UFM has been to facilitate the flow of funds among the markets that are geographically separated and artificially segmented. The existence of a large and active UFM, therefore, suggests a considerable degree of credit fungibility in Korea, which would, in turn, reduce the effectiveness of government intervention and the extent of effective fragmentation. These unregulated markets have acted as both a short-term money market for large business borrowers and a retail-credit market for consumers and small businesses. In so acting, the UFM provided a linkage among the segmented regulated markets and hence a channel for a diversion of credit from the intended uses.

As shown in Chapter 4, large businesses often borrow their working capital from, and lend their idle funds through, the UFM. In fact, they may combine their regular business activities with those of a financial intermediary. They have done so largely because there was no active short-term money market until recently, and the government-dominated financial institutions could not provide adequate short-term credit facilities.

Different sectors and industries have different fund requirements for their production activities. Some sectors need mostly long-term outside financing, whereas others seek short-term loans from the financial institutions. Seasonality in the demand for loans varies from industry to industry. Except for overdrafts, the processing of a bank loan takes a long period of time from application to an actual loan disbursement. No matter how sophisticated and detailed a credit guideline system the government could devise, it could not expect to account for all those factors that figure importantly in determining the sectoral demand for loans in formulating its control system. Indeed, if the credit allocation guidelines and directives had been enforced to the letter, the financial system would have been brittle and could not have functioned. The unregulated money markets have complemented and compensated for the rigidities of the regulated financial system and thereby facilitated smooth flows of funds between the different markets.

Another defect of the government credit allocation was that it made no effective provision for the credit demand of consumers and small- and medium-scale firms which were traditionally discriminated against by the regulated financial institutions. Most of the financial institutions, including non-bank financial intermediaries in Korea, are essentially engaged in wholesale banking. Except for the CNB, the DMBs and KDB are wholesale banks. In the deposit market, they mobilize only a fraction of their loanable funds from household savers. Most of their deposit customers are large businesses with access to institutional credits. In the commercial loan market, a majority of DMBs' loan customers are large industrial and commercial borrowers. The DMBs seldom extend consumer loans such as the loans for the purchases of consumers' durables and other consumption purposes. These banks also shy away from dealing with small-scale businesses, because they often cannot post secure collateral and have a weak credit base. The unregulated financial market has been the major source of credit for these small borrowers. In this sense, the UFM has served as a retail credit market in Korea.

As an integral part of Korea's financial system, the UFM has contributed to unifying otherwise segmented financial markets and thereby to allocating part of the nation's resources to the sectors with higher private rates of return. At the same time, the average cost of capital may have been above the level that would have prevailed if there had been no government intervention. The reason for this is that lending through the UFM is riskier than through the RFM, because the UFM has been the frequent target of government suppression and has no institutionalized system for protecting its creditors.

As noted earlier, it is difficult, if not impossible, to gauge empirically the extent of credit reallocation through the UFM. At best, we could provide indirect evidence. It is common knowledge that one of the major sources of funds in the UFM is large corporations with access to institutional credits.

Among the favored bank borrowers, exporters have been the major beneficiaries of government credit allocation. Short-term credit and other export-related preferential loans have been a powerful incentive for exporting, and the subsidy element in export credits has been large enough that exporters in many instances have been willing to accept prices for their products that were below production cost, knowing that the interest subsidies could more than offset the losses incurred in exporting. For example, exporters could expect to receive automatically an amount of loans nearly equal to their firm export orders, at a concessionary rate of 6–7 percent per annum. They could re-lend export loans through the UFM and earn an annual rate of interest over 30 percent. Such a large interest rate differential could, therefore, allow the exporters to sell abroad below cost. The possibility of diverting export credits through the UFM in effect reduced the cost of production and increased the profits of the exporters. It also provided the means for translating a potential credit subsidy into a real subsidy.

Along with the UFM, the real-estate market provided another important channel for credit reallocation in Korea. Businesses invested heavily in land and other real assets. A recent government report, according to newspaper reports, shows that business groups and corporations hold a large share of their total assets in the form of real assets, such as land and buildings. Their holdings of these assets, it has been argued, far exceed the level normally required for their production activities. The presumption here is that businesses invest in real assets as a hedge against inflation and finance their holdings with bank loans. One large business group that was once a ranking exporter was so heavily involved in real-estate speculation with export loans that it went bankrupt in 1978 when its export earnings fell sharply and the real-estate boom cooled off. Not surprisingly, there were numerous similar cases among relatively smaller business groups and individual exporters.

Finally, it should be noted that most guaranteed foreign loans were less susceptible to reallocation than domestic loans because, in most instances, the foreign loans were used to finance imports of machinery and equipment that went directly into plant expansion or modernization. There were undoubtedly some cases where the imported machinery was sold to raise funds that were then used for other purposes. Also, in some cases, the foreign financing covered imports of raw materials or intermediate goods, which then freed up some domestic financing for other uses. The ingenuity of Korean businessmen in maximizing returns from differential interest rates has been amply demonstrated. Nevertheless, it was more difficult for them to transform lumpy imported machinery into a liquid asset than it was to so transform a line of credit from a domestic bank.

INTEREST-RATE SUBSIDIES: WHO PAID? WHO BENEFITED?

In a financial regime where the interest rates are controlled and kept below a market clearing level, all loans supplied by the financial institutions, whether short- or long-term, are, by definition, subsidized. Those able to obtain institutional credits are subsidized either by the government which has the seignorage right or by those who hold financial assets. The Korean government has not only directed the DMBs, KDB, and other financial institutions to lend to particular sectors and borrowers, but also to charge those borrowers lending rates below the market rates, thereby varying interest-rate subsidies from sector to sector and from borrower to borrower. See Table 39 for the pattern of controlled lending rates from 1950 to 1978.

There are several issues concerning interest-rate subsidies. The first is a matter of measurement—how to estimate a market clearing rate when there is no effective free market. The unregulated markets have special risks and distortions that probably push their interest rates above an equilibrium level. The second issue, assuming the size of the subsidy could be measured or approximated, is who actually pays for the subsidy? A third issue is whether the differential interest-rate subsidies have an impact on sectoral resource allocation. The last issue centers on the

TABLE 39 Illustrative Loan Interest Rates of the Central Bank, Deposit Money Banks, and Special Banks, 1950–1978

(% per annum as of end of each year)

	1950	1955	1960	1965	1970	1975	1978
BOK rediscount	5.84	6.57	10.22	28.00	19.00	13.00	14.50
BOK export credit rediscount		6.57	10.22	3.50	3.50	3.50	4.00
DMB discounts on bills	14.24	17.52	13.87	24.00	24.00	15.50–19.00	18.50
DMB export loans	9.86	13.87	13.87	6.50	6.00	7.00	9.00
NACF agriculture production loans			8.00	10.00	10.00–15.00	12.00	13.00
KDB investment loans				7.50–12.00	7.50–12.00	7.50–12.00	7.50–15.00
Annual inflation rate of wholesale price index		18.10	10.70	10.00	9.10	26.50	11.70

Source: BOK, *Economic Statistics Yearbook*, various issues.

question of whether credit controls coupled with differentiated sectoral interest subsidies have had a more powerful impact on sectoral resource allocation than a credit control system with a uniform subsidy.

In a recent study, Wontack Hong estimated interest-rate subsidies associated with DMB and KDB loans for the manufacturing sector and also for all industries, using his own estimates of the rates of return to capital in different sectors. According to this study, the interest-rate subsidies ranged from 7 to 28 percent of the gross capital stock of the manufacturing sector between 1970 and 1976. Similar figures for all industry were lower and in the range of 2 to 9 percent.[7]

In Hong's study, an interest-rate subsidy on bank loans is computed by subtracting the real (weighted average) interest rates on these loans from the real rate of return on capital. The real rate of return on capital, defined as the ratio of incremental value added of capital, net of indirect taxes, to investment, represents the rate of return to all factors but labor. That is, it includes the returns to technical progress, economies of scale, market imperfection, and entrepreneurship and hence is higher than a true estimate of the return to capital. As a result, both the rates of return to capital and interest-rate subsidies on bank loans are overestimated.

A more serious problem with Hong's estimates is that he omits any consideration of the extra payments a borrower must make in the process of obtaining a loan. Such payments are likely to be inversely related to the degree of automaticity and the priority of the loan, but there is still much random variation.

While Hong's estimates are undoubtedly high, they suggest that the preferred borrowers have received a substantial amount of interest subsidy, which brings us to the next question: Who has actually paid for these subsidies? As a first approximation, it could be argued that those who hold money and other financial assets bear the brunt of the subsidies, as the real rate of return on these assets has consistently been negative except for the high-interest-rate period in the latter part of the 1960s.

The interest-rate subsidies have been financed mainly by inflation taxes on the holdings of financial assets. Unlike other taxes, it is relatively easy to avoid inflation taxes simply by not holding financial assets. When the real yields on savings and time deposits are negative, as they have been at various times in Korea, it is difficult to believe that rational savers would hold financial assets as an instrument of savings and willingly pay inflation taxes.

A large portion of financial assets held by household savers consists of currency and short-term savings and time deposits. As far as households are concerned, currency and short-term deposits serve primarily as the means of payments rather than a savings instrument. As the means of payments, they yield a positive productivity which could be measured in terms of the saving of transactions costs associated with the use of money. Insofar as currency and short-term deposits yield a stream of income (an implicit return), the holders of these assets do not necessarily pay inflation taxes, for the implicit return on these assets could cancel out the tax payment.

The bulk of demand and long-term deposits is held by businesses. The former are used as the means of payments for them and the latter are often held as compensating balances, which represents a further reduction in the hypothetical interest-rate subsidy. Since the business sector as a whole is the major beneficiary of underpriced institutional loans, it is the recipient of interest-rate subsidies as well as the payer of inflation taxes on compensating and working balances. Therefore, the actual magnitude of income transfers in the form of credit subsidies from lenders to borrowers through the financial institutions has probably not been very large in Korea. Much of the credit subsidies should be regarded as a transfer to the borrowers of the productivity gains from the use of money and deposits as means of payments. This does not mean that such a transfer does not have any welfare implications. In a stable economy with realistically priced financial assets, some of the productivity gains stemming from an improvement in transactions technology would accrue to households. In this sense, the holders of financial assets assume the payment of the credit subsidies.

EFFECTS OF DIFFERENTIAL INTEREST RATES ON RESOURCE ALLOCATION

There have been only a few attempts at investigating empirically the effects of the differential-interest-rate system on sectoral resource allocation. One of the most rigorous studies is the one by Hong, which estimates changes in the factor intensities of exports and imports and relates these changes to interest-rate subsidies on bank loans. According to this study, exports were becoming more capital-intensive than import substitutes in the 1970s.[8] Aggregate capital intensity of exports (capital valued at 1970 dollars divided by the number of workers employed for export production) rose from 0.6 to 1.5 between 1960 and 1970.

Since then, it has continued to rise rapidly and, within a five-year period, has more than doubled and has become higher than the capital intensity of imports. Although it is difficult to associate directly changes in the factor intensity with those in the wage-rental ratio, Hong shows that the credit subsidies could be held responsible in part for the increasing use of capital-intensive technology in the export sector.[9]

Undoubtedly, exporters have been by far the most preferred borrowers at the financial institutions. They have automatic and unlimited access to short-term export credits which carry a concessionary interest rate far below other lending rates. Exporters have also received other preferential long-term loans for the financing of export-related activities.[10] The elasticity of substitution between capital and labor may be far from zero and responsive to changes in the wage-rental ratio. These considerations, however, do not necessarily imply that exporters would choose a capital-intensive technology. The issue hinges on whether they would use the official interest rate or the opportunity cost of loans in the UFM in their estimation of the wage-rental ratio. If credit fungibility had been severely limited, then the exporters would have faced a distorted wage-rental ratio and might have selected a relatively capital-intensive technology. On the other hand, if they had alternative uses of the subsidized credits with a higher rate of return, the proper rental variable should have been that higher opportunity cost of capital. For example, when the UFM interest rates are used as a proxy for the rental cost, the wage-rental ratio does not rise as rapidly as Hong's study shows. We have argued that exporters do relend at least some of their export credits through the UFM to take advantage of the interest-rate differential. To the extent that this alternative use of funds was available, it is difficult to relate directly the rising capital intensity to the credit subsidies and to argue that the exporters would employ more capital relative to labor. Rather, it has probably been the ready availability of bank-guaranteed and government-promoted foreign financing of imported machinery and equipment that has led to the rapid and, many suggest, excessive expansion of the capital-intensive industries.

This chapter contains more speculation than hard facts because we have been trying to say something about the impact of the financial system on the allocation of resources and the distribution of income. These topics are rendered obscure by the fungibility of credit and the many hidden costs of obtaining credit. Some writers, in analyzing these questions, have chosen to take the statistics at face value—to assume that borrowers use money for the stated purposes and that there is no substitution of one source of financing for another; and to further assume that recorded interest rates reflect the actual total cost of borrowing money. We have opted, instead, to acknowledge the practice of reallocating finance from specified to unspecified uses and of making side payments in one form or another in addition to the nominal interest rates. Thus, we are saying, in a sense, that there are hidden markets operating behind the scenes of the controlled markets. Economic theory tells us something about how those hidden markets function (as discussed in the previous chapter), and we have attempted to apply that theory plus some anecdotal history to the analysis of how the regulated and unregulated parts of the Korean financial system have interacted to guide resource allocation. The results are tentative—more in the form of hypotheses or strong impressions rather than firm conclusions.

Bank loans have gone predominantly to the manufacturing, construction, and public utility industries; and the relative shares were greater than could be explained by the differences in capital-output ratios between these and other sectors. On the other hand, these tended to be the most rapidly growing sectors and therefore required abundant funding. It is our belief that bank loans and foreign loans have been used mainly to finance fixed investment, although they may have been used as working capital or held as financial assets for some time before being transformed into fixed assets. Here again, fungibility obscures reality. But over the decade and a half from 1964–1978, bank loans and foreign loans were clearly the main source of financing of the capital formation of the high-growth sectors.

These allocation decisions were not made by the financial institutions on the basis of careful analysis of the relative profitability of alternative investments. Rather, the choices emerged mainly from the interaction of private-sector businessmen and government ministries that were engaged in arranging foreign financing, approving domestic financing, and setting investment and production targets for particular industries. Throughout this period, potential export markets provided the basic reference point for investment allocation by both business and government. All supporting services and infrastructure tended to derive first from the needs of the export sectors and secondarily from other elements of domestic demand.

To the extent that the regulated financial system made serious misallocations of credit either temporally or sectorally, the unregulated part of the system carried out the appropriate market-oriented reallocation. Thus, the UFM contributed significantly to both the fungibility of finance and integration of what would otherwise have been a very fragmented financial system. We believe this improved the efficiency of resource allocation substantially.

Subsidized or differential interest rates probably had little impact on resource allocation (we discuss the effects on savings in the next chapter), except in connection with exports. Here the combination of low interest rates and automatic approval of loans by the banks plus the possibility of relending excess funds at high interest rates in the UFM made for effective incentives. But these were just a few of the incentives for exporters, so it is difficult to sort out the relative impact of each in promoting high growth of exports.

Most other forms of interest-rate subsidy were illusive or ephemeral. The common but unofficial practice of requiring compensating deposit balances or various types of contributions and payments in order to obtain most other types of bank loans eliminated most, if not all, the subsidy often attributed to such loans. One might speculate that this informal market mechanism probably led to a relatively efficient solution, whereby the funds flowed to the borrower who could earn the highest returns. On the other hand, the larger enterprises were generally in a stronger bargaining position than the smaller ones and thus were able to get a disproportionate share of total bank and foreign loans. This could have resulted in investment by large firms that was less efficient than what smaller firms might have done. But the possibility of relending through the UFM at high rates would have acted as a check on investing just to use up surplus cash. Also, some of the larger firms became financial intermediaries themselves rather than simply relying on the UFM to take their surplus cash. Here again, market forces have led to institutional innovation which has probably contributed to greater efficiency.

The most glaring examples of misallocation appear to have been the cases where government was heavily involved in arranging large packages of foreign and domestic financing for projects of questionable profitability, such as the steel mills, shipyards, and petrochemical complexes. In these cases, although interest rates, cost-benefit ratios, and internal rates of return may have been given lip service at the time of project appraisal, they were actually irrelevant to the final decision, which was made by government on grounds of national defense or prestige. The Korean financial institutions have had little influence over these decisions and should not be held accountable for them.

SEVEN

Policies to Influence Resource Mobilization:

The Monetary Reform of 1965

While Korean government efforts to influence the allocation of credit were relatively continuous and formalized from 1958 on, the possibilities of influencing the mobilization of financial savings were largely ignored prior to 1965. In that year, a major interest-rate adjustment was carried out, which has received much notice and generated considerable controversy.

In September 1965, the Korean government undertook a major financial reform, highlighted by a drastic increase in the interest rates on time deposits of the deposit money banks (DMBs). The primary objective of this reform was to attract into the banking institutions private savings that had hitherto been directed to the UFM or to accumulation of inventories and other real assets as a hedge against inflation. To this end, the interest rates on one-year time deposits were doubled from

15 to 30 percent per year. Bank lending rates were also adjusted upward, but less sharply.[1]

Such a large increase in the deposit interest rates brought about a dramatic increase in the holdings of time deposits at the banks, presumably at the expense of consumption, and the holdings of money, UFM primary securities, and real assets, including inventories. But, because the holding of real cash balances was already at a low level due to the previous high inflation, it appears that the shift out of money was rather marginal and that the brunt of the substitution effect was felt in other financial markets, and in the real-asset markets.

Over the past few years, the Korean experience during the high-interest-rate period has been extensively analyzed and heralded as a successful case of financial reform. Several countries, taking their cue from Korea, implemented a similar reform; to name a few, Indonesia, Brazil, the Philippines, Colombia, and Chile.[2]

It has been argued by some that the high-interest-rate policy, through its financial deepening effect, played a crucial role in stabilizing prices, raising the propensity to save, improving the allocation of domestic financial and real resources, and reducing the size of the UFM. In short, the high-interest-rate policy tore apart the financial strait jacket and, in so doing, brought about a spurt in financial and economic development.

While all these effects did occur to some extent, it is not clear that the financial reform played the major role in the takeoff of economic development that some have ascribed to it. In fact, a close examination of the events that preceded and followed the financial reform suggest that the alleged claims for the high-interest-rate policy have been exaggerated, though one cannot present clear statistical evidence for or against these claims. The task of evaluating the effects of the high-interest-rate policy is complicated by the fact that the economic authorities undertook a host of other policy measures shortly before and after the financial reforms, such as tax administration reform, export promotion, import liberalization, adoption of a floating exchange-rate system, and the foreign-loan-guarantee scheme. All these policies contributed to the phenomenal growth of the Korean economy in the latter half of the 1960s, so that attempts to isolate the effect of a particular policy on the economy are fraught with difficulty.

BACKGROUND OF THE REFORM

For the decade prior to 1965, monetary policy in Korea had been focused on holding down the growth of the money supply (M_1) in order to reduce the rate of inflation. Interest rates had been held at conventional levels or slightly above (that is, 10–15 percent per annum) to relieve the burden on borrowers and avoid cost-push effects from financing. There was also the pious hope that, in time, inflation would diminish enough so that the interest rates would become "realistic." The Bank of Korea set the interest rates for both deposits and loans of the commercial banks, and the Ministry of Finance controlled the rates of the special banks. An anti-usury law put an overall ceiling on interest rates of 15 percent, despite which the unregulated money markets operated at three to four times that ceiling.

During the brief period of relatively low inflation from 1958 to 1962, interest rates on bank loans and deposits did become positive in real terms, and the holdings of currency plus bank deposits (M_2) increased significantly from 10.5 to 14.8 percent of GNP, but, with the renewed inflation in 1963–1964, real interest rates again became negative and M_2 dropped to 9.1 percent of GNP. Korean financial officials were increasingly aware of the paradox that accelerated growth of bank credit and money supply in nominal terms led to accelerated decline of those values in real terms.

An explanation of this paradox was presented in 1965 by Professor C. N. Lee who argued that both raising of interest rates and reduction of inflation were necessary to induce savings in financial form and to rationalize investment.[3] Shortly thereafter, Professors John Gurley and Edward Shaw of Stanford University and Hugh Patrick of Yale University collaborated on a study of the Korean financial system, commissioned by the U.S. Aid program. Their recommendations (presented below, pp. 298–303) emphasized improved techniques of monetary control and measures to increase the flow of savings into liquid assets. In connection with the former, they proposed creation of a stabilization account at the Bank of Korea (described in the next chapter) to give the monetary authorities direct control over the reserve base of the monetary system and thus over the money supply. To stimulate the flow of savings into liquid assets, they recommended elimination of legal ceilings and increase of actual rates of interest on deposits of all financial institutions to levels that would be competitive (after allowance for differential risk) with the curb(UFM)-market rates. They also made suggestions for improving the allocation of finance, the efficiency of the banking system, and the development of long-term finance.

The Gurley, Patrick, and Shaw report,[4] completed in late July 1965, led to action by the National Assembly raising interest-rate ceilings in August and implementation of many of their recommendations in a financial-reform package on September 30, 1965. One factor that contributed to this rapid implementation was a provision in the annual stabilization program for 1965, jointly agreed upon by the American and Korean governments as the basis for the annual U.S. aid program to Korea, that a financial reform would be implemented by the end of the third quarter of that year. Thus, the reform met this time schedule and the flow of aid funds was not interrupted.

ELEMENTS OF THE REFORM

The main elements of the financial reform were a substantial increase in the interest rate on bank time deposits, a smaller and selective increase in the rates on bank loans, and a partial shift from direct to indirect controls over the volume of bank credit. While the increase in deposit rates applied to various categories of time and savings deposits, the most significant one was the 2.5 percent per month or 30 percent per year rate on the new eighteen-month time deposits. This rate was not much below that being paid by the curb market and proved to be a powerful attraction for new deposits.

Although payment of interest on demand deposits had been recommended by Gurley, Patrick, and Shaw (they suggested 6 percent per annum), this was not included in the reform. Also, one of the special banks (the Korea Reconstruction Bank) did not change its rates at the time of the reform and, therefore, did not participate in the subsequent growth of deposits.

The increase in loan rates applied to only a part of total loans, and specifically did not affect the low subsidy rates for export producers, farmers, and many categories of investment loans by the special banks (see Table 39). These subsidized loans were generally rediscounted at the Bank of Korea at even lower rates, so the commercial and special banks were still able to earn a positive net interest from them. The range of lending rates on regular commercial loans, from 24 to 28 percent per annum, while higher than the average interest paid on the combination of demand and time deposits, was below the maximum rate paid on time deposits of more-than-one-year maturity. This so-called "reverse margin" on interest rates caused complaints from the banking community.

Prior to the financial reform, bank loans had been subject to ceilings imposed by the central bank, and, at the time of the reform, those ceilings were temporarily removed. Banks were allowed to expand loans within the limits of their excess reserves, and the Bank of Korea introduced the stabilization account proposed by Gurley, Patrick, and Shaw and also revived a former practice of forced sales of BOK stabilization bonds to the banks. Both these instruments gave the central bank the means to curtail unilaterally the reserves of individual banks as well as the whole banking system.

SHORT-RUN CONSEQUENCES

The most remarkable impact of the financial reform was on the growth of bank time deposits. They increased by over 40 percent within three months and then approximately doubled in each of the three succeeding years. Between the end of 1965 and the end of 1969, time and savings deposits rose from 3.9 to 21.0 percent of GNP, and M_2 went from 12.7 to 32.7 percent of GNP (see Table 45, p. 230). This dramatic increase in the holding of liquid assets reflected in the first instance a shift from other forms of asset holdings, most notably real goods and claims on the unregulated financial markets. While there is no reliable way of estimating the magnitude of these shifts, there was ample evidence at the time that individuals and businesses were adjusting their asset holdings in response to the new price ratios.

Along with the increase in bank deposits, there was a parallel expansion of bank loans. With the rapid build-up of time deposits that had a reserve requirement of only 10 percent, the banks started to expand their lending with equal speed. This led to concern among the monetary authorities about the inflationary consequences of such rapid credit expansion, so that required reserve ratios were raised steadily throughout 1966, reaching a peak of 45 and 50 percent marginal reserve requirements on time and demand deposits respectively by October 1966, one year after the interest-rate reform. In 1967, the Bank of Korea began to make use of both forced sale of stabilization bonds to the banks and required deposits to the stabilization account (as suggested by Gurley, Patrick, and Shaw). As these instruments became effective, the marginal reserve requirements were eliminated and the standard reserve ratios again applied (see the discussion of monetary policy instruments in Chapter 8).

Another consequence of the interest-rate reform was to increase the demand for foreign credit which, together with the foreign-loan repayment-guarantee scheme and the recent treaty settlement with Japan, led to a massive inflow of foreign financing. All measures relating to the foreign sector took a quantum jump in 1966: imports increased by almost two-thirds and foreign exchange reserves did also (an unusual parallel movement), while exports continued their 40 percent annual growth. Monetary expansion arising from the influx of foreign exchange contributed to apprehension about inflation and the imposition of domestic credit restraints as described above.

There were concerns, voiced before the reform, that higher interest rates would lead to both inflation (due to higher costs of production) and to recession (due to reduced investment). In the year or so after the reform, however, businesses were able to increase their borrowings, both at home and abroad; industrial production went up by 25 percent; employment increased; and inflation continued at about 10 percent. Thus, the dire predictions of imminent disaster were refuted, at least in the short run. Also, a number of significant shifts in the financial structure were brought about. But the more pervasive long-run effects on savings, investment, inflation, and financial structure require further analysis.

LONGER-RUN CONSEQUENCES
AND THEIR THEORETICAL IMPLICATIONS

The years between 1965 and 1969 witnessed the most dramatic increase of domestic savings in Korean history. Within five years after the reform, domestic savings as a proportion of GNP more than doubled—a performance that rivaled the growth of financial assets (see Table 5, p. 28, and Table 48, p. 267).

At the theoretical level, there are three competing propositions that have been applied to explain this exceptional growth of savings in Korea. One is the well-known classical view on consumers' intertemporal choice between present and future consumption in which an increase in the interest rate induces people to substitute increased savings for consumption out of current income. A second is McKinnon's hypothesis that increased holdings of private wealth, particularly in the form of real cash balances, are a necessary complement to increased investment, which will tend to raise the propensity to save when income itself is growing rapidly.[5] Therefore, monetary policy that induces individuals to increase their stock of financial assets could encourage private saving. A third argument is the asset-adjustment approach to saving in which the savings function is derived from the demand for assets. According to this view, the savings behavior is positively related to the asset-income ratio, which is dependent upon a number of variables, including the interest rates.[6] We shall examine the relevance of these theories to the Korean experience.

According to McKinnon, an increase in the interest rates raises the desired stocks of financial assets; the desire to maintain large stocks of financial assets in portfolio balance, contrary to the standard proposition of Pigou and Metzler, induces a further increment to saving once growth begins.[7] The crux of McKinnon's argument is that a higher yield on money—money being defined broadly to include savings deposits—increases the demand for both money and real assets because these two categories of assets are complements in savers' portfolios rather than substitutes as the neoclassical theory assumes.[8] In a developing economy with a simple financial structure of two assets, money and real assets, this increase in demand can be satisfied only by reducing consumption out of current income.

One serious flaw in this argument in the context of the Korean economy is the disregard of the role of the UFM in the saving-investment process. Even if money and capital were complements to each other, these assets would, to some extent, be substitutes for the UFM securities savers could hold in their portfolios.[9] Therefore, the increase in the demand for money generated by a higher rate of return on money could be at the expense of the holdings of the UFM securities and hence would not necessarily represent a corresponding increase in savings.[10] This conclusion follows independently from the complementarity relation between money and capital. Moreover, it is not clear whether money and capital can be treated as complements in LDCs.[11]

Two recent studies suggest that they are not complementary

in a number of Asian countries, including Korea, and thus question the validity of McKinnon's hypothesis.[12] Even if they were, McKinnon's argument might not be relevant to an open economy like Korea, where firms and households could borrow from abroad to increase their stock of domestic financial assets. If an increase in interest rates creates a positive discrepancy between interest rates in the domestic and foreign financial markets, other things being equal, this discrepancy will induce foreign capital inflows in various forms, such as cash loans, suppliers' credit, commercial bank loans, and direct investment. Whichever form foreign capital inflows may take, these inflows would allow individuals to increase their holdings of money and other financial assets without necessarily reducing their consumption. This possibility, which does not exist in a closed economy, also implies that the high-interest-rate policy may not increase domestic savings, even under McKinnon's hypothesis of complementarity.

Shaw has suggested an alternative explanation for the sudden shift in the propensity to save and the sustained expansion of domestic savings that is compatible with the classical framework of consumers' intertemporal choice between present and future consumption. He argues that, in a developing economy with low levels of per capita income and wealth, a large increase in interest rates could produce powerful effects on saving over and above the influence of time preference.[13] He suggests that the high-interest-rate policy could augment the supply of output directly as it tends (1) to improve the productivity of a given stock of real assets and (2) to expand the real supply of money which is claimed to be a vital input into productive processes. This effect, together with an increase in domestic savings directly associated with high interest rates, could also reduce inflationary pressures or expectations and thereby raise real interest rates on financial savings even higher.

The question of whether the stock of real cash balances can be regarded as an input of production has been and still remains a controversial issue. Although a number of economists have discussed the implications of production functions with real cash balances and even estimated such functions, the theoretical basis for these functions is still debated.

As compared with a barter economy, it can be seen that, given the medium-of-exchange function of money, the use of money and a higher real quantity of money could respectively increase the available amount of the factors of production, labor and capital. This consideration implies that real cash balances could be treated as a third factor of production, as Mundell and Bailey have argued, ascribing to money a "direct" productivity.[14] It would be more accurate to say, however, that real cash balances have only an indirect productivity, as Claassen shows, in a well-defined sense that money switches real resources—both labor and capital—from the exchange activity to the production activity.[15] The use of money would lead to a discrete increase in real output as it reduces the amounts of resources employed in the trading activity. An increase in real money holdings would release further amounts of labor and capital which could be employed for direct production activity. The extent to which a higher real quantity of money increases real output would then depend upon the capital-labor ratio in the trading activity and the relative scarcity of these two factors of production in a given economy. Sinai and Stokes show that the presence of money is highly labor-saving, suggesting that the amount of capital employed in the exchange activity is of a rather low magnitude.[16] This would be particularly true in capital-scarce and labor-surplus LDCs like Korea. An increase in the real stock of money would then most likely release only labor. In Korea in the late 1960s, any released labor was absorbed by the rapidly growing export sector of labor-intensive manufacturers, and thus the real growth of the stock of money, through its supply-augmenting effect, may have contributed to slowing down the rate of inflation which had averaged more than 20 percent per year before the reform. A similar influence may have arisen from the demand-reducing effects of the higher interest rates.

One of the specified objectives of the 1965 reform was to draw private savings away from the UFM and into the organized financial system. In this regard, however, the Korean experience suggests that the reform was less than successful. One reason for this may be related to the hypothesis on the complementarity between bank loans and UFM credit, discussed in Chapter 5. There was, however, another equally important reason associated with the explosive capital inflows induced by the interest-rate differential between the home and foreign capital markets.

After the reform, foreign leaders were attracted by the interest-rate differentials and the loan-guarantee system which eliminated the risks of default and foreign-exchange depreciation. Korean borrowers were encouraged by the cost differentials between the domestic and foreign interest rates and a mistaken expectation that the exchange rate would remain stable.

Short-term foreign debt with an original maturity of less than three years increased from virtually nothing in 1962 to $70 million by the end of 1968, close to 40 percent of the value of Korean foreign-exchange earnings in that year. In the face of this massive inflow of foreign capital, which caused a large increase in the domestic money supply, the Korean authorities had the following options.

They could let the exchange rate float and appreciate until the appreciation narrowed the interest-rate gap between home and abroad. Although the wŏn was floating within a limited range, this option was not acceptable for fear that such an action would slow down the growth of export earnings.

Another option was import liberalization, which would soak up the excess liquidity of the economy. This alternative was again seriously considered; however, there was intense opposition from protected domestic manufacturers and the fear that any further liberalization would reduce the profits on sales in the domestic market, which was where many of the manufacturers were recouping their losses on exports.

The third option was to impose direct controls or an interest-equalization tax on capital inflows, but it was only recently that the guarantee scheme to induce foreign investment had been introduced, and there was a reluctance to shut off this inflow of foreign credit and foreign exchange.

The fourth policy alternative, adopted and carried out throughout the period 1966–1970, was to accumulate foreign reserves, squeeze the supply of some kinds of domestic credit, and in time reduce the deposit interest rates. Once this option was taken, the monetary authorities had an up-hill battle to control liquidity within the economy, as they continued to purchase foreign exchange in the market. To offset the expansion of the supply of money originating in the reserve accumulations, they attempted, therefore, to squeeze the other source of the supply of money—domestic credit—by means of raising the reserve requirements of the banking sector, as discussed on page 203.

Thus, the monetary authorities found themselves simultaneously pursuing two contradictory policies. On the one hand, they raised the deposit interest rates to expand the demand for bank liabilities and with these resources to augment the supply of loans. Because of the unexpected large increase in the foreign supply of loans, however, they had to squeeze the supply of domestic credit. In fact, they were mobilizing domestic financial savings at a high rate of interest, converting them into foreign reserve assets, and in so doing lending to foreign borrowers at a low interest rate.

As the monetary authorities continued to squeeze the supply of domestic credit—a source of liquidity created by the central bank—to moderate monetary expansion, this led to a relative reduction of credit available to some sectors of the economy. Not every Korean enterprise could borrow from abroad; to qualify for foreign loans, one had to have proper political connections and be engaged in favored industries, especially exports. The tightening of domestic credit supply and the inflow of foreign capital therefore led to an uncomfortable situation in some sectors that were faced with a relative credit squeeze, whereas others, notably exporters and those who had access to foreign loans and could bring in cash loans, had a large amount of liquidity.

This situation would not pose serious problems in an economy with a sophisticated financial structure. If there had been organized short-term credit markets in Korea at that time, the excess liquidity of the export sector would have been channeled to those who were in need of credit the banking system could not supply. Within the RFM, there were no such secondary credit markets to take up this role, and the UFM had to enter into the intermediation scene. Those who had excessive holdings of liquidity in the forms of money and savings deposits were lured into the UFM as suppliers of funds, and also to take advantage of the tax system, which discriminated against equity financing and encouraged channeling equity through the UFM. Those in need of funds were forced to enter the UFM for credit in the face of the credit squeeze in the RFM.

The demand for and supply of loanable funds in the UFM were probably reduced initially as a result of the high official interest rates. However, the massive inflow of foreign capital and the subsequent domestic credit squeeze increased both the demand for and the supply of credit in the UFM. The net effect of the interest-rate reform on the size of the UFM was thus, at best, ambiguous.

The financial reform of 1965 was intended to stimulate the growth of the organized financial system by raising the rate of savings, the share of savings held in the form of financial assets, and particularly the assets issued by the banking institutions. It was also supposed to give the banks greater autonomy and incentive to respond to market forces, and give the Bank of Korea improved means of financial control.

The reform did result in a very large increase in the deposit liabilities of the banking system and a similar rise in bank lending, so that the financial system grew substantially as did the relative share of the banking sector. Initially, there was some shift of financial intermediation from the UFM to the banking sector, but, in time, as the supply of finance increased, and then as the high-interest policy was abandoned and growth of the banking system slowed, the UFM revived as an important intermediary. The reform, the foreign-loan guarantee scheme, and the successful export strategy, also contributed to a massive inflow of finance from abroad which relieved the savings and balance-of-payments constraints on economic growth and shifted the economy onto a high growth path. The effect of the financial reform on domestic savings is ambiguous, because it was only one of many changes that contributed to the upward shift in the savings function. Finally, the effects on the autonomy of the financial system were more negative than positive, as the increased availability of resources invited greater direct government involvement in their allocation.

EIGHT

Price-Stabilization Problems and Policies

Korea's financial history has been marked by erratic instability of prices. The country experienced several bouts of severe inflation in the 1860s and 1870s due to overexpansion of the currency.[1] During the Japanese colonial period, there were some long swings both up and down in the price index, culminating in suppressed inflation during World War II that broke out into open hyperinflation in 1945. This was gradually being brought under control in 1949–1950, but then the Korean War precipitated a new round of hyperinflation.

Since the mid-1950s, there have been alternating periods of relatively moderate—less than 10 percent—annual rates of inflation in the latter part of the 1950s and of the 1960s and relatively high rates in the early 1960s and throughout most of the 1970s. Each of these periods had quite distinct characteristics that can be described in simple terms:

1) The relative stability of prices from 1957–1961 was attributable mainly to a massive inflow of foreign aid and restrictive monetary and fiscal measures. It was accompanied by slow growth and generally depressed conditions in the economy.

2) The resurgence of inflation in the early 1960s resulted from numerous governmental measures to stimulate economic growth and was exacerbated by poor agricultural harvests in 1962 and 1963.

3) The second period of less than 10 percent inflation, from 1965–1971, was a kind of Golden Age, characterized by very high growth of output, exports, imports, inflow of foreign capital, and accumulation of domestic financial savings. There were no serious balance-of-payments problems or gaps between expected saving and investment.

4) From 1972–1978, abrupt swings in the external sector severely buffeted a much more open Korean economy, and successful attempts to maintain high rates of growth in spite of these external pressures resulted in monetary expansion and price inflation as part of the adjustment process. The high rate of inflation, triggered by the oil crisis, was brought under control in 1976 and 1977, only to accelerate again in the following year.

THE HISTORY OF INFLATION

The experience of moderate to high inflation over the past forty years has undoubtedly imparted an inflationary bias to expectations. Inflation and stabilization have been constant topics of discussion in the press, the government, business, and academic circles. While all groups have professed the desire for price stability, they have seldom been willing to put up with the financial and fiscal constraints and possible retardation of growth that really low rates of inflation might require. The government has, over the past two decades, claimed to be pursuing the two objectives of stability and growth, and frequent shifts in the ordering of these two muses have been intended to indicate subtle shifts in emphasis. In fact, the emphasis on output, export, and investment targets has almost continuously placed the growth objective in the superior position.

Most businessmen seem to find mildly inflationary conditions favorable to their interests, especially when accompanied by easier availability of credit. Much of the pressure to curtail inflation has come from foreign agencies, particularly the United States government and the International Monetary Fund, both of which often contended that price stability was a necessary condition for economic growth, despite Korean performance to the contrary. The divergence of views about the effects of inflation frequently resulted in a kind of cat-and-mouse game, where the foreigners tried to force anti-inflation policies on the Korean government, which, in turn, devised ingenious ways to circumvent them. Recently, in the absence of any other serious economic problems, inflation has become *the* most important issue in Korea, and there is some indication that both the government and the general public would be willing to trade 1 or 2 percent of growth for greater stability of prices.

The role of the financial system over the years has shifted from the active source of both inflationary and contractionary pressure to passive acceptor and absorber of the consequences of fiscal or external forces. Because the financial system has been consistently treated as an instrument of broader government economic policy, the monetary authorities have not been in a position to pursue their own independent objectives. The priorities of the government have been overriding.

INFLATION DURING THE COLONIAL PERIOD

During the early years of Japanese occupation, prices, as measured by a Seoul wholesale price index, were quite stable until the inflationary effects of World War I reached Korea and precipitated a 150 percent increase in prices between 1916 and 1920, followed by a sharp recession in 1921. Thereafter, Korea had a decade of steady to gradually declining prices until the world Depression brought a 30 percent decline in the index between 1929 and 1932. Over the next twelve years, through 1944, Korea experienced rising prices at a trend rate of 10.1 percent per year. These were years in which the economy was growing steadily and industrializing.[2] They were also the years that the post-independence Korean leadership remembered most clearly, thus perhaps giving a sense of normalcy or even desirability to a 10 percent inflation rate (see Table 40).

POST-WAR HYPERINFLATION AND INFLATION

The moderate inflation rates during the war years were the results of strong repression of inflationary forces. When the repression was removed in July and August 1945, the price index jumped 24-fold. It receded by about a third over the next few months, but still ended up the year with nearly a 20-fold price rise. As shown in Table 41, there was only a tripling of the note issue during 1945, so the flight out of currency into goods was of the sort that characterizes hyperinflation. In 1946, the hyperinflation continued with a 370 percent increase in prices and only 127 percent increase in money.

Hyperinflation appears to have ended after the first quarter of 1946, according to material presented by Bloomfield and Jensen (see Table 42). In the fourth quarter of that year, prices actually dropped as the fall harvest became available. Over the next two years, prices moved up more or less in tandem with money supply, and, from the fourth quarter of 1949, they dropped below the money-supply growth.

Bloomfield and Jensen express some surprise that the Korean inflation after early 1946 did not revert to hyperinflation. They note that, "despite the large and persisting price increases over the period (from September 1945 to March 1950), there were no signs that the inflation was moving into the stage of hyperinflation." They go on to say:

> In view of the magnitude and continuance of the inflation, following upon the huge price increases in the two months preceding the liber-

TABLE 40 Seoul Wholesale Price Index, 1910–1944
(1936=100)

Year	Index	% Change	Year	Index	% Change
1910	54		1929	109	-3.5
1911	59	9.3	1930	95	-12.8
1912	62	5.1	1931	77	-18.9
1913	64	3.2	1932	76	-1.3
1914	60	-6.3	1933	84	10.5
1915	56	-6.7	1934	85	1.2
1916	65	16.1	1935	94	10.6
1917	92	41.5	1936	100	6.4
1918	123	33.7	1937	121	21.0
1919	155	26.0	1938	139	15.8
1920	161	3.9	1939	164	18.0
1921	121	-24.8	1940	180	9.8
1922	119	-1.7	1941	187	3.9
1923	128	7.6	1942	196	4.8
1924	136	6.3	1943	215	9.7
1925	123	-9.6	1944	241	12.1
1926	115	-6.5			
1927	113	-1.7			

Source: BOK, *Review on Price Index* (1949).

tion, this can be accounted for only in terms of a failure on the part of the bulk of the population fully to grasp what was happening to the purchasing power of their money, or of a belief that the rise in prices would soon come to an end. Since the transition from inflation to hyperinflation is, however, essentially a reflection of a change in the state of mind, that transition could have occurred suddenly at any time during the period under consideration once the public became fully aware of what was taking place and began to act accordingly. It is unlikely, moreover, that the inflation could have continued much further without such a change occurring.[3]

This evaluation is somewhat surprising in light of their previous description of how the Korean financial system had adjusted to the high inflation. Their statement deserves to be quoted at

TABLE 41   Bank of Chōsen Notes Issued and Seoul Wholesale
Price Index, 1939-1945

	Bank of Chōsen Notes Issued	Seoul WPI	Change over Previous Period	
			Bank Notes (%)	WPI (%)
	million wŏn[a]	*1947=100*		
Dec. 1939	0.44	0.40	–	–
Dec. 1940	0.58	0.45	31.8	12.5
Dec. 1941	0.74	0.46	27.6	2.2
Dec. 1942	0.91	0.48	23.0	4.4
Dec. 1943	1.47	0.54	61.5	12.5
Dec. 1944	3.14	0.60	113.6	11.1
July 1945	4.70	0.69	49.7	15.0
Aug. 15, 1945	4.98	17.0[b]	6.0	2,363.8
Sept. 8, 1945	8.50	11.2[b]	70.7	-34.1
Dec. 31, 1945	8.76	11.8[b]	3.1	5.4

Source: BOK, *Annual Economic Review* (1949).

Notes: [a]The amount of bank notes issued in old wŏn denomination is converted into the presently used wŏn denomination, dividing by 1,000.
[b]Monthly average.

some length because it is one of the early assessments by foreign observers, and it illustrates their failure to grasp the true significance of the unorganized financial markets, which are vaguely perceived to be lurking in the background, but are obscured by the lack of hard data:

> There is evidence, statistical and otherwise, that in 1945-50 few Koreans, whether private individuals or businessmen, held notes or deposits idle for any length of time in view of the persisting rise in prices, which made them anxious to dispose of their money receipts more quickly than usual. Cash balances were held overwhelmingly for transactions purpose and in anticipation of early disbursements, and even the size of those balances relative to transactions may have been economized to a greater degree than usual. Hoarding of goods and purchases of dollar notes on the black market* tended to replace

*Available statistics indicate that the black market rate for "greenbacks" rose from

TABLE 42 Indexes of Money Supply and Retail Prices,
1945-1950
(1947=100)

End of quarter		Money Supply		Retail Prices on Open Market in Seoul	
		Index	% Change	Index	% Change
1945	3	30		12.4	
	4	33	10.0	15.9	28.2
1946	1	36	9.1	49.5	211.3
	2	41	13.9	51.7	4.4
	3	53	29.3	81.7	58.0
	4	77	45.3	68.7	-15.9
1947	1	81	5.2	95.0	38.3
	2	88	8.6	89.8	-5.4
	3	102	15.9	100.8	12.2
	4	151	48.0	140.3	39.2
1948	1	152	0.7	149.3	6.4
	2	162	6.6	174.2	-2.3
	3	179	10.5	166.4	19.4
	4	208	16.2	167.1	-4.5
1949	1	219	5.3	178.1	0.4
	2	231	5.5	206.3	6.6
	3	307	32.9	257.2	15.8
	4	360	17.3	315.0	24.7
1950	1	336	-6.7	385.9	22.5

Source: Bloomfield and Jensen, p. 29.

domestic money as a means of satisfying the "speculative" and "precautionary" motives. To some extent, moreover, barter dealings and payments in kind tended to take the place of monetary transactions. The inflation was also reflected to some degree in the abnormally high rates of interest on the open market, ranging from 5 to 15 percent

---

450 wŏn to the dollar at the beginning of 1948 to a peak of 4,500 wŏn in January 1950. By May 1950 the rate had receded to 2,200 wŏn.

per month.** Those rates were considerably higher than might normally have been expected even in an underdeveloped country such as Korea, and in part reflected the fact that open-market lenders always had as an alternative the purchase of goods to profit by the rising prices; consequently, open-market interest rates tended to bear at least some approximation to the rate of price increases.[4]

This discussion points up the facts that Korean money was used largely for transactions purposes, that goods and foreign currency were major forms of inflation-proof assets, and that the unorganized financial markets were operating at competitive interest rates to intermediate between borrowers and those savers willing to hold some financial claims at the prevailing interest rates. We have doubts, based on later experiences, about Bloomfield and Jensen's assessment of the size of the curb market or of the limited sources of its funds (see Chapter 4).

The rate of inflation was undoubtedly closely linked to the rate of monetary expansion between 1946 and 1950, but a somewhat higher rate of monetary expansion and price increase would have undoubtedly raised UFM interest rates and possibly caused some limited conservation of transactions balances without precipitating a major flight from money. This seems to have been borne out during the Korean War.

The main cause of monetary expansion, and thus of inflation, during the 1945 to 1950 period was the lending by the Bank of Chosun to the government. From 1948 on, this accounted for about half the money-supply increase. Also beginning in 1947, there were proceeds from the sale of aid goods which were deposited in the banks as an offset to the credit expansion. This was the first of the "counterpart" accounts that were to play an

---

**Practically nothing is known about the behavior of open-market rates over the period as a whole, nor even of the participants in that market. The borrowers appear to have consisted largely of speculators in commodities and necessitous merchants or consumers who were unable to get the necessary accommodation from banks, while the lenders chiefly comprised landlords and wealthy businessmen. The market was believed to be a very narrow one and the total amount of loans was estimated to be insignificant relative to the volume of bank loans. Needless to say, open-market rates ruled far in excess of the legal maximum fixed rates charged by banks.

important and often misunderstood role in Korea's stabilization and aid relations—the major issue being whether the counterpart funds were usable to meet current operating and investment expenditures, or whether they were an offset to credit that had already been extended and therefore should be held as idle balances to neutralize the expansionary effects of the credits.[5] Because the inflow of aid goods was approximately equal to the difference between imports and exports, Bloomfield and Jensen described the causes of monetary expansion in the following terms:

> The net increase in money supply was a reflection of the fact that the Government budget deficit plus the increase in bank loans to parties other than the Government and other banks exceeded the balance of payments deficit.[6]

They noted further:

> Although most of the bank loans to private parties and to Government Agencies were ostensibly granted only for periods of up to one year, an apparently large fraction of them remained outstanding for longer periods, and in effect because long-term loans, in view of lax attempts at loan collection and easy renewal policies on the part of the banks. (The "rice loans" were a conspicuous exception.) Despite a formal prohibition on loans for speculative purposes, moreover, a large part of the bank loans, especially those to private individuals and enterprises, is believed to have been used to finance the hoarding of commodities.[7]

There were indications that restraints on credit expansion and increased generation of counterpart funds were beginning to slow the rate of monetary expansion in the first half of 1950. Money supply actually declined by 7 percent during the first quarter, and the Pusan price index declined during the second quarter by 5 percent (Table 43). Whether these trends would have continued can only be matters of speculation, because the Korean War, which began in late June, threw the economy and the financial system back into a condition of near chaos.

TABLE 43   Indexes of Money Supply and Retail Prices,
1950–1953

End of quarter		Money Supply		Pusan Retail Price Index	
		Index	% Change	Index	% Change
1950	1	15.2		10.6	
	2	15.9	4.7	9.9	–4.9
	3	19.4	22.0	20.5	107.0
	4	37.0	91.0	29.7	44.9
1951	1	54.0	46.0	32.2	8.4
	2	68.0	26.0	64.2	99.4
	3	81.2	19.0	97.0	51.1
	4	100.0	23.0	100.0	3.1
1952	1	115.0	15.0	151.0	51.0
	2	133.0	16.0	185.0	22.5
	3	154.0	16.0	239.0	29.2
	4	199.0	29.0	204.0	–14.6
1953	1	212.0	7.0	250.0	22.5
	2	268.0	27.0	236.0	–5.6
	3	366.0	37.0	268.0	13.6
	4	445.0	23.0	292.0	9.0

Source: BOK, Economic Statistics Yearbook, various issues.

INFLATION DURING THE KOREAN WAR

The potentional for hyperinflation clearly existed during the Korean War but it did not really materialize. Money supply expanded by 90 percent in the last quarter of 1950 and 46 percent in the first quarter of 1951. Over the next two years, it increased by about 20 percent per quarter but moved up nearer a 30 percent rate in 1953 (see Table 43).

Prices[8] shot up by more than 100 percent in the quarter immediately following the outbreak of hostilities, then slowed down over the next two quarters as the influx of the fall harvest offset the increases in money supply. There was a renewed surge of prices in the second and third quarters of 1951, but, for the next six quarters, prices moved in parallel with money supply and, by mid-1953, dropped well below the rate of monetary expansion.

The relative movements of prices and money supply from mid-1950 to mid-1953 support the proposition that money was used mainly for transactions purposes and that, while there were brief periods in 1950 and 1951 when prices increased significantly more rapidly than money, indicating a flight from money into goods, there was a strong underlying tendency to back away from that kind of hyperinflationary behavior.

Throughout these years, the banking system was mainly engaged in supplying funds to the Korean government and to the United Nations Forces,[9] while the unorganized financial markets continued to provide credit to private business and to trade in U.S. dollars and U.S. military payment certificates (MPCs), which were the main forms of financial asset holdings. These foreign monies also served as important transactions media, as they were used largely in lieu of local currency by the several hundred thousand foreign soldiers stationed in Korea.[10]

There was a significant flow of goods through the U.S. military PXs and commissaries out into the open market, partly as barter transactions, but also in exchange for MPCs. Because the MPC was a usable medium of exchange in both the military and open markets in Korea and Japan, it was an important supplement to the national currency in each country, but, because the same MPCs were used in both countries, it is not possible to determine how significant they were in either country in terms of augmenting the money supply.

Thus, the statistics on both the financial and real side are misleading during this period. The supply of Korean money was substantially augmented by foreign currencies, the circulation of which was illegal but ubiquitous. The supply of commodities in the country from domestic production and legal imports was also augmented by a flow of commodities through military channels that was also illegal but nonetheless significant. The least distorted indicator is the price index which, as noted above, was leveling off during the last year of the war, 1953.

CONTROLLING INFLATION 1954–1960

In the immediate post-war years, high rates of monetary expansion continued to impart a strong inflationary bias that erupted in 1955. Efforts to control the growth of money were applied from 1956 through 1960, resulting in an average rate of increase of 22 percent for the five years. Foreign-aid levels also were relatively high from 1955 through 1958, averaging about 11 percent of GNP. The impact of these two forces on the rate of inflation was offset by a poor grain harvest in 1956; but favorable harvests in 1957 and 1958 brought the rate of inflation down to a negative level in 1958 for the only such experience in Korea since 1932.

Between 1957 and 1960, a new policy mechanism was introduced to try to control inflation. This was the annual financial stabilization program, prepared for and approved by the Combined Economic Board, consisting of senior Korean economic ministers and United States aid officials. The stabilization programs set quarterly ceilings for expansion of money supply, bank credit, government borrowings from the central bank, and other key financial variables. The role of the stabilization programs is described by B. K. Kim, who attributes the attainment of price stability from 1957 through 1961 to a strengthened budgetary position and rigorous enforcement of the stabilization programs.[11]

Unfortunately, the stable prices and related tight credit policies were associated with a significant slowdown in the rate of economic growth. While gross fixed investment continued at roughly 10 percent of GNP, non-agricultural output grew at a relatively low rate of 5.5 percent, due, in part, to lack of demand. This was also a period of primary-import substitution (using Ranis's terminology),[12] which required substantial imports of capital goods to establish the new industries and intermediate goods to keep them running. Declining aid levels after the peak in 1957 (and negligible exports) tended to limit the supply of intermediate goods and curtail output.[13]

During this stabilization period, the organized financial system grew significantly in real terms as shown by the ratios of M_1, quasi money, and M_2 to GNP (see Table 44). Real interest rates on bank time deposits in 1958 were positive for the first time in Korea's post-World War II history, as a nominal rate of 12 percent per annum (on one-year deposits) combined with a negative price change (of 6.5 percent in the wholesale price index) to give an effective real rate of nearly 20 percent. In mid-1959, the nominal interest rate was reduced to 10 percent, which, together with a 2.6 percent price rise, gave a real rate of 8.4 percent. In these two years (1958-1959) quasi money, consisting mainly of time and savings deposits, tripled as a share of GNP and the ratio of M_1 to GNP also rose by 44 percent. The resumption of 10 percent inflation in 1960 and the decline in the real time deposit rate to zero brought this brief period of financial growth to an end. (The apparent recovery indicated in Table 44 during 1961-1962 will be discussed subsequently.)

Little is known about the volume of financing in the unorganized financial markets during this period. It seems likely that they lost some ground relative to the organized sector, which was growing quite rapidly and, thus, was able to supply more credit.[14] Also, the importance of foreign currency dealings may have diminished somewhat as the value of Korean currency became more stable.

RETURN TO INFLATION 1961-1964

One of the reasons given by the military leaders for their overthrow of the Chang Myon Government in 1961 was the slow growth of the economy. It is not surprising, therefore, that the Military Government initiated a number of new programs to stimulate the economy, or that these eventually led to renewed inflation. One of the Military Government's early actions was to instruct the National Agricultural Cooperatives Federation (NACF) to take over, and pay off, the debts of the poor farmers to the private money lenders (see Chapter 3, p. 56).

The government also ran substantial deficits beginning in 1961 and became a heavy borrower from the Bank of Korea. These

TABLE 44 Ratios of M_1, M_2, and Quasi Money to GNP, 1953–1964

	M_1/GNP	M_2/GNP	QM/GNP	% Interest Rate on One-Year Time Deposits	% Change in Wholesale Price Index	% Real Deposit Interest Rate
1953	6.3	7.3	1.0	4.8	25.3	-20.5
1954	8.8	9.5	0.8	9.3	28.2	-18.9
1955	8.2	9.0	0.9	12.0	81.1	-69.1
1956	8.0	9.1	1.1	12.0	34.8	-22.8
1957	7.3	8.2	0.9	12.0	16.0	-4.0
1958	9.3	10.5	1.2	12.0	-6.5	18.5
1959	10.5	13.3	2.8	11.0	2.6	8.4
1960	9.9	12.5	2.6	10.0	10.7	-0.7
1961	12.1	13.9	1.8	12.5	13.2	-0.7
1962	11.3	14.8	3.5	15.0	9.4	5.1
1963	8.6	11.3	2.7	15.0	20.6	-4.6
1964	7.0	9.1	2.1	15.0	34.6	-15.6

Source: Derived from BOK *Economic Statistics Yearbook*, various issues.

expansionary pressures were offset in part by a relaxation of import controls and a drawing down of foreign-exchange reserves in 1962 and 1963. Also, food-grain production in 1961 was 13 percent above the 1960 level, thus assuring a better food supply in 1962.

But concern over the very large monetary expansion in 1961 and also the belief that moneylenders and unscrupulous businessmen were hoarding their profits in large currency holdings, which could be thrown on the economy at any time with disastrous effects, led the government to carry out a currency reform in June 1962 (see Chapter 3).

While this reform caused a temporary forced increase in time deposits, its more pervasive effect was to undermine people's confidence in the organized financial institutions and their financial instruments, and to encourage the holdings of real assets, foreign exchange, or claims on the UFM.

This financial debacle was exacerbated by a severe decline in the rice harvest in the fall of 1962 and the barley harvest in the spring of 1963, starting an inflationary surge that carried through the summer of 1964. The resumption of joint U.S.-Korean government stabilization agreements in 1963 focused on eliminating the government fiscal deficit and controlling lending to the private sector. Increased inflows of foreign aid and foreign capital in 1962 and 1963 relieved somewhat the inflationary pressure and contributed to rapid growth of non-agricultural output by relaxing the supply constraint on imported raw materials and intermediate goods.

The year 1964 proved to be one of very difficult transition. The United States government practically forced the Korean government to put through a 50 percent devaluation by holding up on PL 480 agreements until it was carried out. Open discussion of these negotiations in the press contributed to speculative increases in food and import prices. Once agreement was reached and the devaluation carried out, the inflation practically stopped. A combination of improving food supplies and extremely tight ceilings on bank credit kept prices from rising later in the year.

But the bank-credit constraint and a sharp decline in imports, especially of non-food items, along with higher import prices, put a severe squeeze on the industrial sectors. Non-agricultural output grew by only 3.9 percent from 1963 to 1964.

Throughout 1964, the UFM played a very active role in reallocating the very limited supply of loanable funds. After the devaluation, increased earnings from exports gave some relief to those enterprises engaged in exporting, but at that time they were a very small part of total manufacturing. At the end of the year, the scramble to settle outstanding debts and bring bank balance sheets within prescribed loan ceilings brought the velocity of currency circulation nearly to infinity within the Seoul financial district.

STABLE HIGH GROWTH, 1965–1971

Relaxation of this credit squeeze and a reorientation in monetary policies during 1965 brought a substantial change thereafter, and the next six years were a period of outstanding performance for the Korean economy. Non-agricultural production grew at an average annual rate of 15 percent. Price increases, as measured by the wholesale price index, averaged 8 percent per year (13 percent on the GNP deflator). The financial sector grew at an unprecedented rate as the ratio of M_2 rose from 9 percent of GNP at the end of 1964 to 34.4 percent at the end of 1971. The inflow of capital from abroad was substantial and, together with increased domestic savings, supported very high levels of investment. The one weak point in the economy was food-grain production, which hardly grew at all over the period, but there was some increase in the non-food-grain sectors, such as vegetables and fruits.

The stimulus for industrial growth came largely from the export sector and the government's campaign to promote exports. Korea's remarkable export performance and the effect that it has had on many aspects of the economy is described in many sources.[15] But some of the important links between exports and finance have been less fully explored. Since 1965, the commercial banks have given loans at very favorable interest rates to all export producers. These loans are granted automatically on the basis of valid export letters of credit or similar evidence of export orders, as discussed in Chapter 6.

This system of automatic loans undoubtedly spread the lending activity of the commercial banks more broadly throughout the manufacturing sector than would have been the case if the loans had been discretionary. It also eliminated much of the extra cost involved in obtaining the rationed loans of the banking system.

The main defect of the automatic export-credit system was that it resulted in some loss of control over credit expansion by the monetary authorities. This was not a serious problem in the mid-1960s, when exports were a small fraction (5–7 percent) of GNP, but, as they moved up to over 20 percent of GNP by the 1970s, the importance of this continuing outflow of credit became more serious. The monetary authorities attempted, initially, to compensate for the expansion of export credit by imposing restrictive ceilings on other types of bank lending, but, when exports exceeded the expected levels, as they frequently did, there was a double expansionary effect on the money supply. Not only was there an automatic increase in bank credit, but also an unexpected increase in foreign-exchange reserves that further added to the money supply. The substantial inflow of foreign credits was still another factor adding to the build-up of foreign reserves.

In the face of these expansionary pressures, the monetary authorities raised reserve requirements to unprecedented levels, that is, a marginal rate of 50 percent on increases in demand deposits from October 1966 through March 1967, but the credit expansion continued unabated. That it was possible to have such a rapid expansion of credit (for example, an 8-fold increase in bank loans between 1965 and 1970) without causing severe inflation is attributable mainly to the matching growth in demand for bank deposits. This, in turn, was mainly due to the rise in real interest rates paid on time deposits beginning in the fourth quarter of 1965. As shown in Table 45, the nominal deposit rate was increased from 15 to 30 percent per year on time deposits, but the concurrent decline in the rate of inflation between 1964 and 1965 boosted the real interest rate from –20 percent to +20 percent, and time deposits began their dramatic increase from 2.1 percent of GNP at the end of 1964 to 21.7 percent at the end of 1969. There has been some debate over the extent to which the rise in interest rates in 1965 contributed to the rise in the rate of domestic saving. We dealt with this issue in Chapter 6. But it is clear, regardless of the conclusion on the savings rate, that the higher deposit rates increased the demand for deposits as compared to other forms of saving, and this, in turn, made it possible for the banks to expand their lending without serious inflationary consequences.

The change in the deposit rate was the main element of the monetary reform of 1965. Other steps to increase loan interest rates were of limited effect because they applied to only a fraction of total lending. As shown in Chapter 3, the domestic monetary reform was paralleled by the measures to encourage the inflow of foreign capital, which resulted in rapid build-up of foreign-exchange reserves and foreign-loan guarantees by the banks. The monetary authorities' efforts to restrict domestic credit expansion by raising reserve requirements in 1966 and 1967 were an alternative to reducing deposit rates and thereby curtailing the growth of deposits, or slowing down foreign borrowing.

It is not particularly clear, even retrospectively, what would have been the best mix of policies. If there had been more rapid growth of domestic credit, it might have raised the inflation rate slightly or gone into more imports and thus slowed the accumulation of foreign reserves. A reduction in foreign borrowing, which was used mainly for investment in infrastructure and export industries, would probably have lowered the high rate of output growth.

Clearly, the real deposit rate in excess of 20 percent per annum led to extremely rapid build-up of time deposits, perhaps

TABLE 45 Financial and Real Growth and Interest Rates, 1964–1978

Year	M₁/GNP	Quasi Money/ GNP	M₂/GNP	Percentage Change in Real GNP	Percentage Change in Wholesale Prices	Percentage Change in Consumer Prices	Nominal Interest Rate on 1-Year Time Deposits	Real Deposit Interest Rate[a]
1964	6.8	2.1	8.9	9.6	35.1	—	15.0	−20.1
1965	8.1	3.9	12.1	5.8	9.9	—	30.0	+20.1
1966	8.2	6.9	15.1	12.7	9.0	11.6	30.0	+21.0
1967	9.6	10.2	19.8	6.6	6.4	10.4	30.0	+23.6
1968	10.8	15.7	26.4	11.3	8.6	10.9	26.0	+17.4
1969	11.7	21.0	32.7	13.8	6.4	12.5	24.0	+17.6
1970	11.5	22.1	33.6	7.4	9.1	16.1	22.8	+13.7
1971	10.9	22.2	33.1	8.8	8.8	13.4	22.0	+13.2
1972	13.0	23.3	36.3	5.7	13.8	11.7	15.0	+1.2
1973	14.3	24.3	38.6	14.7	6.9	3.2	12.6	+5.7
1974	13.0	20.5	33.5	7.5	42.1	24.3	15.0	−27.1
1975	12.3	20.1	32.3	7.0	26.6	25.3	15.0	−11.6
1976	11.8	19.8	31.7	14.2	12.1	15.3	15.6	+3.5
1977	13.0	21.5	34.6	10.5	9.0	10.1	15.8	+6.8
1978	12.2	22.6	34.8	12.5	11.7	14.4	16.9	+5.2

Sources: BOK, *National Income in Korea,* 1978; BOK, *Monthly Economic Statistics,* 1979. 1,3.

Note: [a]Adjusted for the rate of change of wholesale prices.

more rapid than the banks could wisely lend. An earlier beginning of the downward adjustments of the nominal deposit rate probably would have slowed the growth of time deposits and given better overall balance to the financial scene. One reason why this was not done was that American and IMF financial advisors were arguing against reducing the deposit rate so long as there were inflationary pressures and excess demand for loans within the economy. [16] Since they were unable to convince the Korean authorities to raise the lending rates, they seemed to prefer a second-best solution of raising reserve requirements and hanging on to the high deposit rates.

During the period of stable high growth, and high deposit rates, the huge build-up of time deposits in the commercial banks drew resources away from the UFM. The tremendous growth in the number of small savers in time deposits and installment deposits must have reduced the contributions to *kye* and similar savings activities.

At the same time, the increased availability of bank financing for business, especially through the export-credit program, undoubtedly resulted in a substantial flow of funds into the UFM. As we have suggested previously, business fed such funds into the UFM on a short-term basis to earn the difference between the 6 percent per year bank loan rate on exports and the UFM deposit rate, which may have been only moderately above the bank's one-year deposit rate at this time. The most that could be earned on short-term notice deposits with the banks, however, was 5 percent per year. Thus, the UFM probably intermediated more between the export industries and the non-exporting sectors during this period than it did between households and business. Lending interest rates in the UFM moved down from the high levels of the previous high inflationary years.

RETURN OF INSTABILITY, 1971–1975

The configuration of policies that resulted in high growth, low inflation, and balance-of-payments surpluses began to come apart in 1970–1971. Exporters were having increasing difficulty

TABLE 46 Relation of Automatic Loans to Total Loans of
Deposit Money Banks, 1967–1978
(billion wŏn)

	Export Loans		Loans Against Installment Deposits		
	Amount	%	Amount	%	Total Loans
1967	16.7	9.3	32.4	18.2	178.0
1968	24.5	7.4	57.1	17.2	331.2
1969	35.1	6.2	112.4	20.0	563.0
1970	55.9	7.7	84.4	11.7	722.4
1971	80.1	8.7	81.2	8.8	919.5
1972	108.4	9.0	91.8	7.6	1,198.0
1973	221.6	14.0	179.2	11.3	1,587.5
1974	359.5	14.8	319.5	13.2	2,427.8
1975	338.9	11.7	479.5	16.5	2,905.5
1976	461.8	12.4	524.9	14.1	3,724.9
1977	567.1	12.0	637.1	13.5	4,709.0
1978	883.2	13.4	859.4	13.0	6,609.0

Sources: BOK, Economic Statistics Yearbook, 1976; BOK, Monthly Economic Statistics, 1973.

meeting the ever-rising export targets. In part, this was because costs were rising faster than the exchange rate was depreciating. Also, there was growing resistance abroad to some export products, such as textiles (and a slowing down of demand from the two main importing countries—Japan and the U.S.—due to anti-inflation programs).

The Korean government initially resorted to increased export subsidies, but in 1971, despite strong opposition from the business community, shifted over to devaluation (by nearly 20 percent) as a means of improving export earnings. The devaluation, however, also caused a corresponding increase in the cost of servicing foreign loans that had grown so dramatically since 1963. In the scramble for funds to meet the foreign obligations, the businesses had three major potential sources—domestic banks, foreign lenders, and the unregulated financial markets.

Unfortunately, the growth of time deposits slowed markedly after 1969 and, therefore, the growth of bank loans followed suit. Foreign-loan guarantees went up sharply in 1971, but about 20 of the 45 percent increase was simply a reflection of the devaluation. In 1972, the loan guarantees actually declined and businesses were forced to turn to the UFM.

After considering various means to relieve the financial pressure on business, the government finally implemented its August 3, 1972 measures, which essentially turned all the curb-market high-interest, short-term loans into low-interest, long-term loans with several years of grace period. These measures did solve the immediate problems of those firms with large foreign borrowings, but they also eliminated the UFM as a significant source of funds for several years (see Chapter 5).

The financial difficulties leading up to the recession of 1971–1972 are consistent with the financial instability model of Hyman Minsky.[17] According to Minsky, economies in which debt is an important source of financing for investment are prone to financial instability. During periods when the economy is functioning well, the easy repayment of existing debt, and the high profits being earned from past debt-financed capital, encourage new borrowing and investment, leading to an investment boom that becomes increasingly speculative. Eventually, some borrowers become overextended, some of the more speculative loans fail, and panic may ensue as pressure to lower debt ratios increases. Then new financing dries up, expectations turn pessimistic, and investment drops, thus accelerating a downward spiral.

Korea differs from Minsky's typical capitalist market economy in that the government owns and controls most of the sources of debt financing so that it can prevent adverse developments from drying up the flow of finance; entrepreneurs face a less demanding creditor. But, still, the period of high growth and investment from 1965 to 1970 did turn into a speculative boom, and, when the devaluation raised the costs of foreign debt, while at the same time the growth of domestic credit and foreign demand for exports were slowing down, business prospects deteriorated appreciably. Enterprises resorted to very speculative high-cost financing from the curb market, and many of them were on the verge of bankruptcy when the government intervened and relieved their most acute debt problems.

The recession and financial distress of 1972 were also partially curbed by the export and investment boom of 1973. Korea's devaluation in 1971 followed by Japan's appreciation of the yen in late 1972 resulted in a tripling of Korea's exports to Japan between 1972 and 1973, and a doubling of Korea's total exports, from $1.6 billion to $3.2 billion. GNP grew by 16.5 percent, the balance of payments had a large surplus, and wholesale prices rose only 7 percent. It was clearly a spectacular year and seemed to be the beginning of another extended period of stable high growth.

The oil price increases of late 1973, however, caused a sudden dampening of Korea's prospects. Because of its very limited natural resource base, Korea was heavily dependent on imported oil. In the previous five years, many oil-fired thermal power plants had been constructed, and some new petrochemical producing units were just coming on stream. The oil price increases caused a 20 percent deterioration in Korea's net barter terms of trade.[18] The related world recession caused a weakening in world demand for Korea's exports.

Korea's response to the oil crisis was rapid and substantial. A set of policies was implemented in January 1974 designed to mitigate the worst effects of the price increases and maintain overall growth. The two main policy measures were to impose heavy taxes on oil products to discourage their use, and to borrow heavily abroad to finance the imports needed to sustain production and investment. Little effort was made to hold down domestic price increases—they were accepted as inevitable—and bank credit was expanded by nearly 50 percent to help finance the needed imports.

What was the outcome of these policy measures? On the negative side, wholesale prices rose by 42 percent in 1974 and another 26 percent in 1975. The current account deficit went from about half a billion dollars in 1972 and 1973 to about 2.2 billion in both 1974 and 1975. On the positive side, GNP continued to rise by 8 percent in real terms during each of the latter two years. Unemployment did not increase significantly. The overall balance-of-payments position was in substantial surplus by 1975, as foreign borrowing exceeded the current account deficit by roughly one-half billion dollars.

This gambler's approach to the externally generated instability seemed, by 1976, to have paid off handsomely. The upturn in the world economy contributed to another boom year for Korea's exports, so that the vociferous concerns of 1975 about excessive foreign debt-servicing burdens were clearly unfounded. By relying heavily on external financing to overcome the trade-balance crisis, Korea managed to limit the effects on the domestic economy mainly to the price increases. If external demand had been slower to recover, some debt-servicing problems could have arisen, but as it worked out, these problems were minimal.

SUPPRESSED INFLATION, 1976-1978

Following the two years of rapid price increases caused by the quadrupling of oil prices, inflation measured by both WPI and CPI showed a sharp deceleration in 1976 and 1977 (see Table 45), due in part to the tightening of the supply of domestic credit and imposition of strong price-control measures covering a wide range of consumer and producer goods. Beginning in 1978, however, prices began to soar again and had risen by almost 20 percent at the end of the year. The sudden upsurge of prices was not expected and caught the government authorities off guard, but several inflationary factors had been lurking behind the scene for some time.

The monetary authorities shifted to a contractionary policy in the middle of 1976 by imposing quotas and ceilings on central bank credit to the DMBs and introducing a marginal reserve system in the stabilization account (see p. 203). As a consequence, the total of central bank general loans and bills discounted rose by only 3 percent, and DMBs' deposits in the stabilization account registered a 10-fold increase from 35 billion wŏn to 373.6 billion wŏn during the 1976–1977 period.

The monetary authorities' efforts to restrain liquidity expansion were, however, more than offset by a large increase in net foreign assets of banking institutions which was, in turn, caused by growing overall balance-of-payments surpluses. Because of the interest-rate differential between the domestic and foreign capital markets and easy availability of foreign credit, business firms continued to rely on foreign sources for the financing of their imports. Denied short-term working capital at the banks, some of these firms, in particular the large ones, borrowed more from abroad in the form of the prepayment of exports. These inflows of short- and long-term capital together with a small surplus in the current account led to overall balance-of-payments surpluses amounting to $1,174 million and $1,313 million in 1976 and 1977 and inevitably to domestic liquidity expansion.

The monetary authorities also found it difficult to control the supply of domestic credit. During and right after the oil crisis, the government was very much concerned about the sluggish demand for business fixed investment. In order to revive such investment, therefore, it was decided to enlarge the availability of long-term loans earmarked for fixed investment with the resources of the National Investment Fund, and to expand foreign currency loans both to discourage direct foreign borrowing and to encourage investment. For short-run stability of the economy, however, the monetary authorities felt the need to restrain the expansion of total domestic credit, which they did by squeezing the supply of short-term working-capital loans that are as important an input as labor and capital in production processes. Thus, the monetary authorities were expanding long-term credit and at the same time reducing the rate of increase of general short-term loans. Because of an inadequate supply of short-term loans, it was claimed, an increasing number of business firms were not able to operate newly constructed factories and, in some cases, had to shut down their operation altogether. Previously, this need for short-term funds would have been met by the UFM, but those institutions were still recovering from the August 1972 measures. Under strong business pressure, the monetary authorities in the end had to relax their policy and to accommodate the short-term credit needs of business, thereby offsetting the contractionary policy. As a result, the supply of M_1 grew by 30.7 percent in 1976, to be followed by another expansion of 41 percent in 1977 and 25 percent in 1978. The expansion of M_2 was equally large: it rose by 33, 39, and 35 percent during the same periods.

Household savers, in the meantime, had very little incentive to hold bank deposits because of the low real interest rates on these assets and a high expected rate of inflation. Much of the excessive liquidity has therefore been poured into the markets for land, residential houses and apartments, jewelry, and even antiques for speculation.This speculation in real assets provoked further acceleration of inflation and made it more difficult to control prices.

The government's direct price-control measures may have succeeded in suppressing some price increases in recent years, but they have inevitably created black markets for a large number of commodities where the prices were much higher than the official ones. This discrepancy not only made the public distrust the official price statistics but also caused formation of a distorted and higher expectation of future prices on the basis of black-market prices.

It was alleged at the time that the introduction of the value-added-tax (VAT) system in 1976 worsened the inflationary problem. Although there is no reliable empirical evidence, the VAT system could have contributed to accelerating inflation for the following two reasons. Replacement of the excise taxes with the VAT was expected to bring about a restructuring of prices. Some prices were supposed to go up and others to fall or remain unchanged. Given the downward rigidity of prices, however, those prices that were expected to decline did not and most others went up. Because of the unfamiliarity and accounting problems of the system, which were expected in the early stage of implementation, most retailers simply added the taxes on to their prices as if they were additional taxes. Also, some businesses undoubtedly took advantage of the opportunity to raise prices at the time of imposition of the new tax in hopes that it would be less noticed by both consumers and government price-control officials or could at any rate be blamed on the tax. This is another manifestation of suppressed inflation.

In comparison to the past experience of inflation, recent instability may not appear too serious, but it has generated more concern and criticism than in the past. There appear to be several reasons for this change in attitude.

After nearly fifteen years of double-digit growth, the Korean people became confident that it would continue and they no longer saw the trade-off between growth and stability as inevitable. On the other hand, as the society has become more stable and incomes as well as wealth have increased, the people have become more concerned about the erosion of their real incomes and the value of their financial asset holdings than before. Unemployment, or underemployment, which used to be one of the most serious problems, by 1978 no longer appeared to be a pressing issue. The balance of payments in the current account improved to the point of accumulating surpluses unless significant import liberalization measures were taken. There was general consensus that Korea's balance-of-payments position was healthy and no longer a constraint to growth. Distributional equity, though far from ideal, was regarded as one of the best among the developing countries. In short, unlike the 1950s and 1960s, Korea in the late 1970s had not been beset by any serious economic problems other than inflation. Naturally, the inflation problem received much more attention than it would have otherwise.

There was also concern expressed in some quarters that continuing inflation would, in the long run, undermine Korea's capacity to grow. Price inflation is likely to be accompanied by comparable, if not higher, wage increases as the labor market tightens up further. This development would weaken Korea's international competitiveness in world markets. Inflation may also make it increasingly difficult to mobilize domestic savings and may cause deterioration in the distribution of income if necessary countermeasures are not taken. Insofar as public opinion was unwilling to accept considerable inflation, the government came under increasing pressure to alter the ordering of its economic objectives.

THE DECISION-MAKING PROCESS AND INSTRUMENTS OF MONETARY POLICY

When the Bank of Korea was established in 1950, the founders of the central bank clearly specified that decisions and implementation of monetary policy were vested in the BOK in reflection of the prevailing concept of financial autonomy and neutrality. While there was a continuing struggle between the Ministry of Finance (MOF) and the BOK over the control of monetary policy during the 1950s, with the inauguration of a new government after the military revolution in 1961, much of the power assigned to the BOK in the original charter was transferred to the government. This was done on the grounds that final responsibility for the conduct of monetary policy rests with the government and that the transfer would promote a better coordination between monetary and fiscal, exchange rate and other related policies. Since then, the BOK has had only nominal independence, and it is the Ministry of Finance that determines the direction and implementation of monetary policy. The Minister of Finance serves as chairman of the Monetary Board, the highest decision-making organ of the monetary system, and he has the power of requesting reconsideration of the Board's resolutions (a de facto veto power), auditing the bank books, and approving the bank budget. In addition to the MOF and BOK, the Economic Planning Board (EPB), which is in charge of budgetary operations and short- and long-term planning, exerts a strong influence on the direction of monetary policy. The Ministry of Commerce and Industry (MCI) is also involved indirectly in implementing monetary policy, since the Ministry's responsibilities include trade promotion and industrial development.

Throughout the period under discussion, the monetary authorities (MOF and BOK) in seeking to control such monetary aggregates as M_1, M_2, and domestic credit have relied mainly on required reserve policy and two powerful central bank direct control measures: the BOK's discount and loan policy and direct control of DMBs' loans and investment. Heavy reliance on direct control measures has been justified (rationalized) by the underdeveloped money and capital markets that preclude open-market operations and the low-interest-rate policy which produces a chronic excess demand for bank credit and makes the discount-rate policy ineffectual.

RESERVE POLICY

Control of the required reserve ratio has been the most frequently utilized indirect monetary policy instrument. Since 1957, the required reserve ratio against demand deposits has been adjusted twenty-one times and that against saving and time deposits twelve times. Throughout the period, the required reserve ratios have been set at relatively high levels. The ratio of required reserve against demand deposits ranged from 10 percent to as high as 35 percent and that against time deposits varied between 10 and 25 percent. The reliance on this instrument was most pronounced during the high-interest-rate period between 1965 and 1970. Although the required ratio on demand deposits was raised to 35 percent in February 1966 and remained at that level for the next three years, the increase was not sufficient to mop up the excess liquidity caused by foreign capital inflows. To cope with the situation, the BOK invoked a marginal required reserve system which had been established earlier in 1952. During the period from October 1966 to March 1967, increments of demand deposits over the average balance of the first half of 1966 were subject to 50 percent additional reserve holdings and those of savings and time deposits to 45 percent.

High levels of required reserve ratios have reduced the capacity of credit expansion of DMBs and frequent changes in them have made the M_1 and M_2 supply multipliers relatively unstable. Even large changes in the volume of reserves permit small changes in deposits, given the high reserve ratios and relatively high currency demand in Korea. The high ratios also reduce the profitability of banks and have often been alleged to be one of the causes of the chronic failure of DMBs to maintain required reserves. In order to shore up the DMBs' income, the BOK has paid interest on required reserves ranging from 3 to 15 percent per annum, and, in many cases when DMBs were not able to meet the required reserves and had to pay penalties, the BOK extended them general loans so that the DMBs could make up the reserve deficiency, thereby weakening the effectiveness of the instrument. Given these problems associated with the high ratios, one wonders why the monetary authorities have not kept them fixed and at lower levels in the first place. It might be argued that high ratios are motivated by a desire to protect depositors, but bank failures in Korea cannot be easily imagined. The only plausible reason seems to be the government's desire to keep DMBs under very tight control. By setting the ratios at high levels, the monetary authorities in fact reduce the liabilities of DMBs and increase those of the BOK. Thus, the BOK has a larger role in the allocation of credit than it would have otherwise.

STABLIZATION ACCOUNT

By 1967, it was becoming clear that changes in required reserve ratios and sale of stabilization bonds by the BOK to the DMBs were less effective in controlling liquidity than expected, largely because the DMBs simply failed to hold required reserves or invented accounting manipulations concealing their reserve deficiency. In an effort to reinforce reserve policy and also to develop a new instrument similar to open-market operations, the Stabilization Account System was established upon the recommendation of Gurley, Patrick, and Shaw in 1967. According to this system, the BOK is empowered to require DMBs to deposit a certain fraction of their loanable funds into a special stabilization account of the BOK. As far as the mechanism is concerned, the system is identical to a required-reserves system, but it can exert effects similar to open-market operation. Stabilization-account deposits initially earned an interest of 15 percent per year, until the rate was raised to 17 percent in 1977. In 1975, the system was divided into A and B accounts. A account is the same as the original stabilization account, but B was established to absorb the liquidity arising from the sale of foreign exchange to the BOK by the DMBs.

DISCOUNT AND LOAN POLICY OF THE BOK

The BOK supplies credit to the banking system, either by rediscounting commercial bills or by extending general loans on the collateral of selected bank assets of the DMBs. General loans have been supplied to DMBs mostly to support their reserve positions at the BOK. The bills eligible for rediscount consist of commercial bills, which are divided into those of prime and ordinary enterprises, and the bills for export promotion and the development of agriculture and fishery sectors. Rediscounts of the bills for export promotion and other designated sectors are preferential loans that are rediscounted automatically and thus are outside the BOK's control. In essence, they are direct central bank credit to exporters and other preferred borrowers distributed via DMBs.

In a financial environment where the interest rates are controlled and maintained at a level lower than what would have prevailed in competitive markets, variations in the discount rate and the rate of interest on general loans have little practical importance. In Korea, they do not have even symbolic significance. DMBs have always been confronted with an insatiable demand for loans by their customers, and, to satisfy them, banks are willing to borrow as much as they can from the central bank. The cost of borrowing is irrelevant; the availability of credit is all that matters.

Under these circumstances, the monetary authorities are forced to regulate the volume of their lending by non-price direct measures such as (1) outright rejection of rediscounting or loan applications, (2) setting quotas or ceilings on rediscounts and loans, and (3) restricting the bills eligible for rediscounting. These measures have been the most effective and constantly used instruments of monetary control in Korea. Since 1968, the BOK has every year set the ceiling on the availability of general loans and, within this limit, loans have been distributed among DMBs with due consideration of each bank's reserve as well as loanable funds positions.

OPEN-MARKET OPERATIONS

Capital markets have grown rapidly in terms of their depth, breadth, and resilience since the late 1960s, when the monetary authorities began implementing a wide range of far-reaching policy measures to foster bond and equity markets. Before then, there had effectively been no open market for government or government-guaranteed bonds. Even after nearly a decade of rapid development of capital markets, however, only modest amounts of such securities are held outside the financial system. The scope and effectiveness of open-market operations still remain very much limited.

The first serious effort at facilitating open-market operations was made early in the 1960s when the Stabilization Bonds Act was promulgated. According to the Act, the BOK was authorized to issue short-term stabilization bonds with ninety-day maturity within the limit of 10 percent of the money supply at the time of issuance. These bonds carried an interest of 10 percent or less and were thus hardly attractive securities, either for savers or financial institutions. In the absence of any demand, sales of these bonds were allocated among the banks in specified amounts in an administrative fashion that attempted to provide reasonable equity among competing institutions. Although the sale or purchase of these bonds preserved the facade of open market operations, they were, in effect, compensated either by compulsory changes in required reserves or, later, in stabilization account deposits. Since 1973, these bonds have been made publicly subscribable through auctions and have carried more realistic interest rates in accordance with market conditions. Yet, most of these bonds have been purchased by DMBs and other non-bank financial institutions. For about four years, the BOK conducted open-market operations of government or government-guaranteed bonds, such as highway, housing, electricity, and industry-development debentures with DMBs before the operation stopped in 1972. The operation resumed in 1977 with an overall amendment of the Treasury Bills Act and its operational guidelines. At present, the government can issue short-term treasury bills with the terms reflecting bond-market conditions. The BOK is allowed to conduct its open-market operations, not only with financial institutions but also the general public.

DIRECT CONTROL OF DMBs' LOAN
AND INVESTMENT

Article 66 of the Bank of Korea Act empowers the Monetary Board to set the ceiling on DMBs' loans and securities investments and also to limit the rate of expansion of these bank assets when the liquidity situation requires such an action. This is the most direct means of controlling domestic credit expansion. In some cases, the BOK, acting in behalf of the government, determines the priority and borrowers of bank loans and also specific uses of DMBs' loanable funds. While the BOK claims that this measure was seldom used between 1965 and 1977, it is generally believed that the BOK and the MOF have maintained some form of credit ceiling and direct control over the lending of all banks throughout this period. It has been an acknowledged instrument of control since 1977, when monetary expansion became excessive and could not be slowed down by other indirect means.

THE IMPACT OF MONETARY POLICY
ON STABILITY

Growth and stability of the economy have always been proclaimed as the two most important economic policy objectives in Korea. While, for the past decade and a half, growth has been remarkable by any international standards, the same can hardly be said about the stability record. The rate of inflation has been close to 15 percent a year on average, almost three times as high as the rates of Korea's major trading partners, the United States and Japan, and has ranged from a low of 6 percent to a high of 42 percent, as measured by the wholesale price index.

Monetary policy cannot be blamed entirely for the poor record. After all, it is no more than one of several anticyclical policies which must be coordinated in any serious effort to maintain price stability. Monetary policy alone can not be expected to eliminate short-run fluctuations or prevent secular inflation in the face of highly expansionary fiscal policy or large foreign capital inflows. The annual stabilization programs were intended to achieve such coordination among the various short-run stabilization policies, but in fact they often failed. Monetary policy measures and year-end money-supply targets were often the most publicized aspects of the stabilization programs, but they were frequently sacrificed to the cause of growth or overwhelmed by changes in other variables, as discussed below. Although monetary policy may be relatively more flexible than other tools, its effect on, and the channels through which it influences, the level of economic activity and prices remain controversial.

On the institutional side, some of the traditional instruments of monetary policy, such as open-market operations and the discount-rate policy, can be effective only if there are developed money and capital markets where the price mechanism functions. Such a financial system has not existed in Korea. In the absence of well-developed money and capital markets, as we have earlier shown, the monetary authorities have had to rely mostly upon direct control measures—direct control of central bank credit to the DMBs, imposition of ceilings and quotas on the DMBs' loan expansion and allocation, changes in required reserve ratios, and manipulation of the DMBs' stabilization accounts with the central bank.

While Korea has lacked the modern accoutrements of monetary policy in the form of money and capital markets, it has had the more traditional unregulated markets and growing access to international financial markets, and these have affected the impact of the direct credit controls over the banking system.

The role of the unregulated financial markets has probably been two-sided. On the one hand, it has served to receive the signals of financial ease or constraint fairly quickly from both the business community and the financial community and to transmit those signals to the business community, either in the form of changes in interest rates or credit availabilities. On the other hand, the UFM has tended to disperse rapidly any new or excess liquidity so that it would flow quickly into new production or real-asset accumulation and, under the opposite circumstances, to disperse and mitigate the effects of a credit squeeze by reallocating the available liquidity to those who needed it most urgently. Thus, the monetary authorities and the DMBs could lumber along with their direct controls and arbitrary credit allocations, while the UFM danced around the edges picking up the temporary cash surpluses and transferring them to those with temporary deficiencies. In essence, the UFM facilitated the working of monetary policy by transmitting signals and funds quickly and mitigating the more arbitrary and disruptive consequences that might have arisen from actions in the managed part of the system. The fact that it may have, at the same time, weakened the impact of some of the monetary measures was a small price to pay for keeping the economy functioning.

Growing access to international capital markets also tended to moderate the effects of domestic monetary policy in a way that served broader national interests. Foreign borrowing has become a ready substitute for domestic borrowing, especially for the larger Korean enterprises. At times of financial constraint at home, those enterprises have obtained financing abroad, thereby easing short-run balance-of-payments pressures and eventually increasing the supply of domestic goods. Thus, domestic monetary adjustments would be translated quickly into balance-of-payments adjustments that contributed to stability of prices and of output.

Some of the existing pieces of empirical evidence bear out the short impact lag and moderate potency of monetary policy. In general, the available empirical studies show that the effects of changes in the supply of M_1 exert a quick influence on the level of real GNP in the short run, whereas the effects on the price level are spread over a longer period. One simulation study shows that a 10 percent increase in M_1 for one period over the actual level results in 1.07 percent increase in real GNP within the first three quarters after the action is taken. After that, the increase in M_1 has a negative effect on real GNP, due to the subsequent price and wage increases. The effect of the increase in M_1 on the price level has a longer duration and in general lasts over the next two years.[19] Another recent study suggests that a similar simulation exercise produces an equally quick but more powerful effect on real GNP and a somewhat less pronounced impact on prices, but these effects are drawn out over a relatively longer period than the previous study indicates.[20] According to this study, the initial shock raises real GNP by 3.6 percent after six months over the baseline and by 1.9 percent after one year. The initial expansion raises prices by 1.5, 2.1, and 1.6 percent over the base after six, twelve, and eighteen months, respectively.

The above-mentioned studies rely on a simple two-equation model, which places emphasis on the demand for money, assumes money supply or base money determined exogenously, and concentrates on the interaction between real GNP and the supply of money. In this sense, the structure of the models may be characterized as a variant of the monetarist model of income determination.

In a more elaborate study relying on a somewhat more complicated structural model, in which the supply of money is determined endogenously, monetary policy is shown to be less powerful than other policy instruments.[21] According to the simulation results of this study, a "sustained" decrease of 10 percent in central bank credit to the government, which leads to a reduction in the stock of money in the subsequent periods, reduces real GNP by 0.16 percent and 0.19 percent and the level of prices by 0.24 and 0.25 after one and two years, respectively. This less significant impact is attributable to the subsequent changes in the external sector, which tend to improve the overall balance-of-payments position and thus offset the initial contraction in base money. This study also draws the conclusion that the exchange-rate and interest-rate policies are as effective in influencing some of the major macro variables as monetary policy, which operates through changes in central bank credit.

MONETARY POLICY
AND THE BUSINESS CYCLE

We shall attempt an overall assessment of the role of monetary policy as a major stabilization tool for the past twenty years in a simple, but not simplistic, framework. For this purpose, we shall first discuss cyclical fluctuations of the economy and, on the basis of this discussion, shall proceed to evaluate the extent to which the conduct of monetary policy has contributed to moderating cyclical movements.

According to the official BOK estimation based on a diffusion index, the Korean economy went through five business cycles between 1954 and the middle of 1975.[22] Since then, the economy has been in the sixth cycle. Although the BOK has not yet published an official date for it, it appears that the most recent business cycle peak was likely to have been reached in the fourth quarter of 1978. The dates of peaks and troughs as well as cyclical durations are reproduced in Table 47.

TABLE 47 Dates and Duration of Business Cycles in Korea,
1945–1978

| | | | Duration (in months) of | |
| | | | Expansion Ending at Peak | Contraction Ending at Trough |
Cycle	Business Cycle Peaks	Business Cycle Troughs		
1	1957.1	1957.11		10
2	1959.10	60.6	23	8
3	63.7	64.6	37	11
4	71.8	72.6	86	10
5	74.5	75.7	23	14
6	78.9[a]	–	38[a]	–

Source: BOK, *Han'guk ŭi kŭmyung chŏngch'aek* (December 1977), p. 230.

Note: [a]Unofficial estimate.

The official dates and general profiles of the business cycles reveal the following characteristics of the post-war short-run fluctuations:

1) The duration of expansions varied from two years in the second and fifth cycles to seven years and two months in the fourth, whereas contractions lasted less than a year, except for the fifth cycle.

2) Total real output continued to grow even during the contraction periods. Thus the business cycles essentially display fluctuations around a rapidly growing trend of real GNP.

3) Expansions and contractions in the first two post-war cycles were generated by such exogenous factors as reductions of foreign aid, which limited the volume of imports (essential for business fixed investment), and the conditions of grain crops—rice and barley. These cycles reflect the predominance of the agricultural sector in the economy at that time and, therefore, do not conform to the concept of the business cycle as it is commonly used.

4) Since the middle of 1960s, when the expansion phase of the third cycle began, exports and the level of output in the

manufacturing sector have emerged as the major factors leading to either expansion or contraction. This phenomenon has become more pronounced with the rapid growth of the external sector.[23]

5) Finally, there is no evidence that business cycles have been generated or induced by monetary-policy actions. Monetary authorities have, however, exacerbated cyclical fluctuations by implementing the wrong measures at the wrong time.

In order to examine the ways in which the monetary authorities conducted monetary policy in response to observed economic events and future economic changes forecast within a policy-makers' framework explaining the interaction among these events and expected changes, we have estimated monetary-policy phases. These phases are then compared with the phases of the business cycle to see whether the stance of monetary policy has been procyclical or anticyclical (see Figure 6).

In describing the monetary-policy phases and terms used to describe the posture of monetary policy as well as the dating of the phases, we have relied upon *Annual Reports* of the Bank of Korea and also a historical description of policy actions taken by the BOK in *Financial Policy in Korea,* another official publication of the Bank. Nevertheless, it is not expected that the dating of the phases would be accepted universally, since different people would have different interpretations of monetary-policy developments. As we have stated previously, monetary policy is only one of several tools of short-run stabilization, and monetary-policy actions are often taken for considerations other than short-run stabilization. This has been particularly true in the context of the Korean economy, as the discussions in other chapters make clear. The monetary authorities do not have perfect foresight. Nor do they have a perfect understanding of the causes underlying observed economic events. For these reasons, it is often difficult to discern the objectives of any particular policy action. To make things worse, *Annual Reports* of the BOK are often ambivalent about the direction of monetary policy. The dating is therefore subject, to some

FIGURE 6 Business Cycle and Monetary-Policy Phase

		Business Cycle Phase	Policy Phase		
1st cycle	January	1957		1957	
	November	contraction trough	restraint		
	1958			January	1958
2nd cycle	1959	expansion	ease	1959	
	October	peak		December	
	1960	contraction trough		1960	
	June	1961	restraint	1961	
3rd cycle	1962	expansion		July	1962
	1963	ease	September	1963	
	peak				
	July	1964	contraction	restraint	1964
	June	1965	trough	September	1965
	1966	ease	December	1966	
4th cycle	1967	expansion	neutral and moderate restraint	1967	
	1968		1968		
	1969		1969		
	1970		restraint	1970	
	August	1971	peak	1971	
	1972	contraction trough		January	1972
	June	1973	ease	1973	
5th cycle	expansion	June			
	April	1974	peak	restraint	1974
	1975	contraction	December	1975	
	July	1976	trough	ease	1976
	1977	expansion	September	1977	
6th cycle	1978	restraint	1978		
	peak				

Source: BOK, *Han'guk ŭi kŭmyung chŏngch'aek*; and *Annual Report,* various issues.

extent, to our personal judgment, though it reflects the views of the BOK to the fullest possible extent. The relation of phases in monetary policy and business cycles for the past twenty years is presented in Figure 6, which clearly shows that, except for a few phases, monetary policy has been procyclical rather than anticyclical as it should have been. Perhaps one could go so far as to say that monetary policy has accentuated rather than moderated cyclical movements.[24] Figure 6 shows the following relationships:

1) Since 1960, every contraction, except the 1975 recession, was preceded by a period of monetary restraint. Although the 1974 recession followed tight monetary policy, it would be correct to say that that was generated by the oil-crisis-induced worldwide recession and had little to do with domestic policy actions.

2) In every cycle, the monetary authorities continued to tighten credit when the diffusion index indicated a clear downturn and even when the economy was deep into a contractionary period.

3) Since 1960, the start of each period of business expansion has been preceded by a period of easy money.

4) During the long expansion period in the fourth cycle, the monetary authorities had taken contractionary as well as expansionary measures. On the one hand, they raised the required reserve ratios to high levels, made use of a marginal reserve system, conducted open-market purchases of stabilization bonds, and took other restraining measures to curb excessive expansion of credit. On the other hand, they raised the official interest rates which augmented the volume of loanable funds of DMBs through the increase of deposits and foreign capital inflows caused by higher interest rates, although the expansion was noninflationary.

The preceding observations suggest that monetary policy has not been effective in dampening short-run cyclical fluctuations. This does not mean, however, that changes in monetary policy have been random or arbitrary. On the contrary these observations show that the monetary authorities have, in fact, responded in a regular and positive manner to observed economic events and new developments that they consider to be threatening an overheating or a slowdown of the economy. The main thing that has gone wrong has been the timing of their actions.

THE TRADE-OFF BETWEEN STABILITY AND GROWTH

As discussed by Kim and Roemer,[25] the Korean economy has undergone rapid and dramatic structural changes from an agrarian economy to an economy with export orientation of labor-intensive manufactures and, in recent years, to export orientation of capital- and skill-intensive manufactures. The rapid structural changes inevitably make it difficult to diagnose correctly the implications of current economic events for policy actions and to forecast the future. The rapid growth of the external sector has also weakened the effectiveness of monetary policy. Furthermore, despite supposedly strict government control of capital movements, businesses somehow have managed to borrow from abroad when domestic financial markets have become tight, though the reverse phenomenon has yet to be observed. These and other factors are certainly important causes for the procyclical features of monetary policy, but we believe there are other equally, if not more, important institutional constraints and biases embedded in the growth-first policy at the expense of stability that have restricted the scope as well as effectiveness of monetary policy.

One such constraint has been the repressive financial system itself, which can be attributed to a development strategy in which financial policies have been used predominantly as a means of mobilizing and allocating domestic and foreign resources. As pointed out in Chapter 3, large government deficits financed by the central bank, government loans through the

DMBs, control over the interest rates, and attendant repression of financial institutions all reflect this growth-oriented role of financial policy in Korea and have contributed to weakening the use of monetary policy for stabilization.

Insofar as the government deficits and subsidies to preferred industries were financed by borrowing from the central bank, it was inevitable that the share of credit to the government and preferred industries in total central bank credit would increase and, as a result, the scope of the direct control of the central bank over credit to the DMBs would be limited. This phenomenon was most pronounced during the 1950s and until the middle of the 1960s.

The control over the nominal interest rates of the RFM, which has kept these rates in real terms below the market level, even during the high-interest-rate period of 1965–1971, has, over the years, resulted in fragmented and artificially segmented markets for a large number of financial assets and uneven flow of funds among these markets. As long as the prices of these assets are not determined by the free play of the market, equilibrium in these markets can be maintained only through quantity rather than price adjustments. As a result, exogenous changes in the rate of return to any assets, including real assets, or the expectation of change, bring about sizable asset substitutions in the aggregate-wealth portfolios, thereby making financial-asset markets highly unstable and the effects of monetary policy unpredictable.

To the extent that the government attempts to mobilize domestic resources by means of excessive credit expansion and inflation, and banking institutions are the major source of business financing, it would be quite logical as well as unavoidable to allow—at least implicitly—continuous roll-overs of short-term loans and accumulation of overdue loans when DMBs are confronted with a huge excess demand for loans. This is precisely what has taken place in Korea. This practice of roll-overs and making implicit long-term loans for fixed business investment by the DMBs has made their asset portfolios extremely illiquid.

This illiquidity makes it difficult for the DMBs to adjust their asset portfolios in response to any changes in financial-market conditions or monetary policy. When the banks were forced to reduce credit, they could do so only after a long delay. Thus, expansionary monetary policy could be easily implemented, but any tightening of the availability of credit brought about no measurable response from these institutions in the short run. If the tightening was vigorously enforced, everyone believed it would produce serious disruptive effects on the level of output and employment, because business firms are highly dependent on bank loans, and so no one was willing to take the consequences of the contraction.

So long as rapid growth is the prime economic objective, contractionary credit policy runs very quickly into strong resistance from the business community—usually the favored and influential borrowers—and is soon reversed, even if the prevailing economic conditions call for a continuation of credit squeeze. Thus, when the economy was sluggish, the monetary authorities implemented an expansionary credit policy, and the supply of money increased; when the economy was overheated, they were not able to reduce domestic credit as much as they should have, thereby permitting a continuous and excessive expansion of domestic credit. And, when there was a large inflow of foreign exchange or foreign credit, the monetary authorities found it impossible to enforce an offsetting contraction of domestic credit.

The government control of financial institutions has also added to the problems of short-run management of monetary policy. Most of the financial institutions, except for the branch offices of foreign banks, are under strict government supervision and control. In fact, the DMBs are no more than a banking bureau of the government, whose main role is to mobilize deposits and allocate these resources and new credit supplied to them by the BOK to the sectors and industries and sometimes even the borrowers the government designates. The government has the power of appointing practically all the bank officers above the level of department heads, approves the budgets, and interferes with minor details of operation of these institutions. What the government demands from bank managers and rates highly is their ability to follow instructions.

Managerial efficiency and profitability of these institutions have often been of secondary importance. A large percentage of banks' loanable funds has been appropriated for preferential loans and the allocation of the remainder has, again, very often been dictated by government policy. Bank managers, therefore, have had very little to do with the actual management of their assets and, consequently, seldom felt accountable about either the profitability or liquidity of their loan portfolios.

These institutions have always been fully loaned up, and the bulk of their resources committed to de facto long-term lending. When a credit squeeze was imposed, therefore, they were not able to recall their loans and could only slow down the extension of new credit. They often failed to meet their required reserves or borrowed from the central bank to make up their reserve deficiencies. Since the failure to maintain reserves was not entirely their fault, the government usually bailed them out, thereby offsetting in part the effect of contractionary policy.

The passivity and lack of self-discipline of banking institutions in bank loan management may have, in turn, provided the justification for the government's tighter grip on these institutions and their loan allocation in recent years, but, then, the tighter the control, the less motivated and responsible the bank managers and officers became. So the vicious circle continued.

Finally, the process through which, and the framework in which, monetary-policy decisions have been made and policy measures implemented was in part responsible for the unsatisfactory record of monetary policy. The framework that provided the basis for the conduct of monetary policy in Korea was the annual Financial Stabilization Program (FSP), first introduced in the 1950s.

The FSP, prepared by the MOF at the end of each year, was, in a narrow sense, a national financial budget and provided general guidelines for monetary and credit policy of the government in the following year. Ostensibly, the FSP took into consideration government budgetary operations, the annual development plan or overall resource budget, and the prospects of the economy for the coming year. The basic guiding spirit of the Stabilization Program, however, generally seemed to be a crude quantity-theory equation. The FSP planners first estimated the real demand functions for M_1 and M_2, whose independent variables were often limited to real income without any regard for a lag structure. Given the target rates of growth and increase of prices, which were policy objectives, the estimated income elasticities of the demand for M_1 and M_2 then provided estimates of an acceptable level of nominal stocks of M_1 and M_2—consistent with the target rates of growth and inflation. The "theoretical" framework ignored not only the lag structure but also the interaction among real income, prices, interest rates, and the balance of payments. Whether such a simplistic framework was appropriate for an increasingly complicated and open economy may be subject to debate, but the problem was not so much the lack of sophistication as it was the way in which the program has been implemented.

Once an "acceptable" level of M_2 was determined, then an "acceptable" level of domestic credit was calculated, using the consolidated balance sheet of the banking system including the BOK, with some assumptions on changes in DMBs' foreign and other asset holdings. Having calculated the amount of financial resources available, the FSP decided how these resources should be allocated among competing uses. Of course, much of the domestic credit was first allocated to predesignated sectors, uses, and borrowers all for particular objectives. The 1977 FSP had over fifty different types of preferential loans—preferential in terms of the cost and availability. These loans were often immune to monetary control for purposes of stabilization.

The remainder was then allocated to meet the demands for overdrafts, discounted bills, and general loans. The volume of these non-preferential loans accounted for less than 30 percent of the total loans of DMBs outstanding at the end of 1977. These short-term loans were mostly what the monetary authorities controlled for stabilizing the economy. Thus, the FSP was extremely rigid and did not leave much room for flexible implementation of monetary policy, especially in response to changes in the original assumptions of the program. For example, if exports rose above the target, there followed an automatic expansion of credit through the export-promotion loan system. In order to maintain the acceptable rate of expansion of domestic credit, therefore, the monetary authorities should have been forced to contract the supply of general loans. Since many of these loans were used for business working-capital financing for other (that is, non-export) sectors, the curtailment of these loans had the same effect as cutting down the supplies of electricity, water, replacement parts, and other inputs.

There was clearly a limit to which the monetary authorities could squeeze short-term loans. Business firms could utilize long-term loans for short-term purposes, which they often did, or turn to the UFM, which was busy reallocating the expanded export loans. As we have pointed out, however, businesses financed much of their fixed investment through banking institutions. Given the close relationship between the government and business, and the government's commitment to maintaining high growth, most businessmen would assume that the government would in the end accommodate their short-term credit needs as well, whatever the liquidity situation of the economy might be, since it had done so often before.

The Korean government would often blame the excessive credit expansion on the unexpected developments in the economy but would seldom acknowledge that it could or should have taken corrective action to offset those developments. The FSP was a kind of treaty negotiated with the IMF that authorized a certain amount of expansion of credit in a given time period. If the targets were exceeded, it was often possible to claim that this was "due to circumstances outside the control of the Korean authorities," and, so long as real economic growth continued at 8–10 percent, it was hard to fault them for serious mismanagement of the economy.

Thus, over the past three decades, Korea has experienced moderately high and erratic inflation. For the first half of that period, the inflation was attributable to war, political instability, and periodic mismanagement of a very shallow and small financial system. In the latter half, the financial system has been considerably enlarged and diversified, but has still been operated through direct governmental controls to serve the interests of investment and growth more than price stability. In the early stages, the UFM often softened the effects of restrictive monetary-policy measures by reallocating the scarce supply of liquidity, but, in more recent years, external financing has been a more important source of relief as well as instability. Management of the conventional instruments of monetary policy for purposes of stabilization has been neither an esteemed art nor a practical political objective.

On the other hand, there is little evidence that growth has been adversely affected by either secular or cyclical inflation. Rather, the growth performance has been dominated by external trade relations and the policies relating thereto. And, recently, the greatly expanded external trade and financial flows have become important sources of internal instability. In the one period when the government did agree to a single-minded pursuit of stability, during the latter half of the 1950s, the contractionary financial policies, in conjunction with the waning incentives of excessive import substitution, led to reduced growth. Consequently, it is not surprising that, despite the frequent references of politicians to "growth and stability" or "growth with stability," there remains some question whether the two objectives are compatible, much less complementary, in the Korean context.

NINE

Financial Development and Economic Development

In the preceding chapters, we have analyzed in some detail the structure, size, and historic evolution of the Korea's financial system and the effects of major financial policies. Now we shall attempt to evaluate the role of finance in the process of economic development over the past three decades, focusing on the extent to which finance has contributed to saving, investment, and growth.

As suggested in Chapter 1, there are several hypotheses concerning the causal nexus between finance on the one hand and economic development on the other. None of these, however, is universally accepted. Our discussion in the preceding chapters also shows that the pattern of financial development and the interaction between the financial and real sectors of the economy varied from period to period. Consequently, the Korean experience over the past thirty years cannot be explained by any single theory; rather, different hypotheses seem to be relevant to different periods. For this reason, we have divided the post-war era into three periods on the basis of the distinctive characteristics of development in each period. The first period covers the twenty years after independence in 1945; the second from 1965 to 1971; and the third from then to the present.

FINANCIAL STAGNATION, 1945–1964

For almost two decades after independence in 1945, the formal or regulated financial sector displayed no significant growth, and the direction of financial policy was one of continued repression. The size of the regulated financial system was relatively small in comparison to the real sector, the variety of its financial assets and liabilities was very much limited, and money and capital markets were moribund. The unregulated money markets, on the other hand, were very active in mobilizing and reallocating the limited stock of financial assets.

This period encompassed three distinctive sub-periods of economic development: the period of economic devastation and social and political turmoil resulting from the two wars; the primary import-substitution sub-phase from the end of the Korean War to the early 1960s; and the early years of export orientation, when export-promotion policy was established. Although the real sector of the Korean economy underwent such diverse structural changes, finance remained stagnant and was neither leading nor accommodating to economic development.

World War II and the Korean War seriously damaged the infrastructure of the financial system and a banking tradition that had developed during the colonial period. Economic dislocation and political and social turmoil in the 1950s and early 1960s were hardly conducive to normal growth of finance. Throughout the period, deposit money banks (with a nationwide network of branch offices) and a handful of life insurance companies were the only modern financial intermediaries serving the nation's financial needs. For all practical purposes, currency, demand, and time deposits were the only claims on the modern financial system available to the public. Foreign currency and claims on the unregulated money markets offered more attractive alternatives for those wishing to hold financial assets. Domestic money provided a minimal medium of exchange, with the high proportion of currency suggesting it was used mainly for small transactions. Foreign currency was often used for larger transactions and as a store of value, especially during the war and high-inflation years.

As shown in Table 44, the stock of M_2 as a proportion of GNP, the best available measure of the size of the regulated financial system during the period, remained on average at about 10 percent, except for the 1961–1962 period, when the ratio rose to 14.8 percent, due largely to the excessive expansion of M_1 following the Military Revolution in 1961 and the currency reform in 1962. The nominal rates of interest on bank time deposits with maturity over one year were kept at 12 percent per year throughout the 1950s. Although these rates were raised to 15 percent in 1962, they were still very low compared with the rates prevailing in informal credit markets. When these bank deposit rates were adjusted for inflation, they were either negative or close to zero and provided little incentive for savers to hold their wealth in the form of bank deposits. Much of the limited supply of bank credit was rationed and channeled to preferred import-substituting industries and large borrowers who could provide real asset collateral. In all, the regulated financial system during the period could be characterized as a repressive regime in the Shavian sense.

In analyzing the causes underlying the financial stagnation during this period, there appear to be three alternative hypotheses. One could argue, as Shaw does, that the financial repression reflected both a lack of confidence on the part of policymakers in the market system and a lack of appreciation of the need for price stability to encourage the holding of financial assets. A second hypothesis, which Bloomfield seemed to support, was that per capita incomes in Korea were so low that there was little hope of trying to mobilize domestic financial savings, even under the most favorable policies. Therefore, the main aims of financial policy should be to attract foreign saving and to allocate it efficiently.[1] A third line of argument is in terms of an appropriate role of financial institutions and policy as identified in the Ranis typology of phases of economic development. The repressive regime represented a system that was appropriate, if not ideal, for a successful implementation of the primary-import-substitution phase of development in Korea.

After the Korean War, the prime economic objective of the government was to reconstruct and expand the industrial sector, in particular those industries that could replace imported consumer goods. The objective thus called for channeling resources, particularly imported equipment and intermediate goods, to the new highly protected industries. The Korean government could have relied more than it did upon the market mechanism and incentives to mobilize domestic saving and to bring about the desired allocation of resources. With little public confidence in the financial system, however, and a strong preference for real assets as opposed to financial assets, financial institutions were in no position to carry out either task. Neither could the tax system, with its inefficient administration and widespread tax evasion, mobilize sizable blocks of domestic capital resources. It was believed that nothing short of harsh involuntary measures could mobilize much domestic savings. As a result, the government directed its efforts on one side towards bringing in as much foreign assistance as it could. It also resorted to deficit spending financed by central bank credit, and the granting of low-interest-rate loans to preferred government and private enterprises through government-controlled banking institutions as the predominant means for allocating resources.

A liberalized financial regime of privately owned banks and an independent monetary authority could, in theory, have been as effective as the repressed, government-controlled one in achieving the objective of the primary-import-substitution phase. In retrospect, however, given the lack of entrepreneurial capacity and adequate infrastructure, including that in the financial sector, such a system probably would not have been very successful. As pointed out in Chapter 5, in an economy characterized by labor surplus, the predominance of the primary sector, and a small light-manufacturing base, the majority of borrowers as well as lenders would have consisted of agriculturalists, small firms, and small retailers and wholesalers, who would require financial resources for short-term periods distributed in very small blocks, as compared with an economy dominated by the non-primary sectors. Consequently, in a competitive situation without government intervention, these characteristics of lenders and borrowers would have been conducive to the development of regionally based and atomistic money and capital markets consisting of many small-sized and specialized financial institutions. This, in fact, was a role played by the unregulated money markets in Korea.

The atomistic pattern might have been superior to one dominated by a few large government institutions in mobilizing financial savings. Many regionally based smaller institutions would have been likely to develop a stronger customer relationship and thereby able to provide financial services tailored to the needs of borrowers and lenders, but they would have been mainly accommodating in nature. Unless market forces or other governmental interventions had encouraged investment in the major industries and infrastructure of the primary-import-substitution phase, these atomistic financial institutions would not have been able either to lead the development, or to accommodate the financial requirements of the industrial sector. In retrospect, therefore, it was perhaps inevitable for the government to have assumed the leading role of propelling economic development by channeling aid-generated counterpart funds through its own financial institutions at low interest rates to bring about the structural changes required during the primary-import-substitution period.

The UFM filled in around the edges of the government-regulated institutions by holding the savings of the small savers, providing a market for the major forms of cash holdings (foreign exchange and U.S. military payment certificates), and making short-term loans to the small-scale and low-priority borrowers. The UFM also provided short-term loans to the priority industries when bank loans were insufficient or slow to materialize. Thus, the UFM was very important in keeping the economy functioning *and* assuring that the non-priority, but still essential, parts of the economy had some access to financial services. The UFM also enhanced the value of the loans received by the priority industries by providing them with a high-yielding, short-term repository for their low-cost bank funds when these were not needed for current operations.

RAPID FINANCIAL GROWTH, 1965–1971

After two decades of stagnation and underdevelopment, the regulated financial sector suddenly took off on a rapid growth path beginning in 1965. Over the next five years, the aggregate stock of its financial assets as a proportion of nominal GNP more than doubled, and the stock of M_2 relative to the GNP shot up from less than 10 percent in the early 1960s to almost 33 percent in 1969 (see Table 45). The spectacular growth was sparked by the monetary reform undertaken in September 1965, in which the ceiling on the interest rates on bank time deposits was raised from 15 percent to 30 percent. This readjustment had, in turn, increased the real interest rates on those deposits to +20 percent in 1965 from a –20 percent in the preceding year and maintained them at a level +17 to +24 percent for the following four years.

The interest-rate differential between the home and foreign capital markets together with the government repayment guarantee which eliminated any risk of default and foreign-exchange depreciation on foreign loans induced a massive inflow of foreign capital in the form of trade credit, cash loans, and direct investment. Due largely to these inflows, the supply of money (M_1) expanded by 39 percent a year on average and the stock of M_2 by 62 percent between 1965 and 1969. Such a rapid expansion of M_1 would normally generate strong inflationary pressures, but, during this period, the rate of increase in the wholesale price index (WPI) was below 10 percent per annum (see Table 45).

On the real side of the economy, domestic savings relative to GNP more than doubled from 7.5 percent in 1964 to 17.5 percent in 1969. This increase in domestic savings, together with massive inflows of foreign capital, fueled a high rate of investment that sustained a rate of growth of over 10 percent a year on average during the years between 1965 and 1969 (see Table 48).

The expansion of exports was equally remarkable. Exports registered more than a 5-fold increase over the five-year period, thereby pushing up the export-to-GNP ratio from 7 percent in 1964 to 15 percent in 1969, as shown in Table 48. Imports of goods and services grew at a slower pace than exports, but, because of the relative decline in the U.S. aid transfers, the current account recorded a growing deficit, which was more than offset by long- and short-term capital inflows.

Overall, the economic performance of Korea during this period was impressive. Finance played an important role in the rapid growth process; however, the pattern of financial growth and its interaction with the real sector of the economy during the period were unique in many respects, and do not render support to any of the existing theories of finance and development.

The period covers five years of the export-promotion phase which began early in the 1960s and in which development strategy placed emphasis on exports of labor-intensive manufacturers. As Ranis predicts, the period witnessed a monetary reform which reduced the interest-rate differential between the regulated and unregulated financial markets, an expanding and increasingly specialized financial intermediation network, and most of all, rapid financial growth.

TABLE 48 Investment, Savings, and Exports as Percent of GNP, 1960-1978

	Investment	Domestic Savings	Foreign Savings	Exports
1960	10.86	0.82	8.57	4.12
1961	13.16	2.86	8.60	6.32
1962	12.80	3.26	10.69	5.96
1963	18.11	8.69	10.42	5.43
1964	14.04	8.74	6.85	6.69
1965	15.01	7.37	6.39	9.54
1966	21.59	11.84	8.45	11.90
1967	21.91	11.38	8.81	13.58
1968	25.88	15.08	11.15	14.73
1969	28.83	18.83	10.63	15.39
1970	26.88	17.43	9.33	16.03
1971	25.38	15.47	10.78	17.21
1972	21.85	15.83	5.28	21.94
1973	26.22	24.11	3.89	32.05
1974	31.27	20.67	12.51	29.72
1975	29.85	18.85	10.61	29.53
1976	25.83	23.33	2.46	35.07
1977	27.90	25.60	0.61	38.00
1978	31.68	27.20	3.27	36.69

Source: BOK, *National Income in Korea* (1978).

It is not correct to claim, however, as Shaw and McKinnon have done, that the interest-rate reform and the structural policy of creating new financial institutions and expanding the network of the existing ones were part of a government program to liberalize a number of markets previously controlled by government—a package, according to Ranis, required to shift from import substitution to export orientation. The reform took place several years after the economy had begun the transition to export orientation, though any clear demarcation between the two phases is difficult and subject to personal judgment. Although a number of commercial and specialized banks were established in the latter part of the 1960s, a significant degree of specialization of financial intermediaries materialized only in the 1970s.

The main changes that occurred during the latter half of the 1960s were the substantial increase in the official deposit interest rates, the resultant build-up of deposits, and the massive inflow of foreign loans which the banks were required to guarantee. The monetary reform of September 1965 was a very small step in the direction of financial liberalization (defined as money and capital markets where the price mechanism reigns); it was, rather, a controlled restructuring of interest rates aimed at both increasing private savings and drawing private capital from the UFM into the RFM. Even this limited reform was largely rescinded by 1970.

The Korean experience during the 1960s was one in which the transition from import substitution to export orientation and sustained export growth was made possible by active government intervention capitalizing on existing comparative advantage. Once internal and external prices were readjusted through devaluation, finance was used as one of the more important instruments of government for expanding the production of exportables and providing a direct subsidy to exporters.

An export drive in a resource-poor country such as Korea, which is very dependent on imported intermediate and capital goods, can be easily undercut by domestic inflation or a balance-of-payments squeeze, unless accompanied by corresponding increases in domestic savings or foreign capital inflows which give some latitude for short-run imbalances. Without these parallel developments in resource mobilization, the export expansion can be easily choked off by rising prices and wages. The financial reform of 1965 contributed to domestic stability by raising domestic savings, much of which were held in financial assets, and by facilitating foreign-capital inflows, thereby alleviating the inflationary pressure generated by the export expansion. These financial flows also made possible the import of needed raw materials and the build-up of productive capacity to feed the export boom.

Although the available data suggest that a growing share of the nation's capital was being allocated to export industries,[2] there is no way of determining the extent to which financial subsidies to export industries in the form of short-term, low-interest export loans and other long-term loans facilitated such a reallocation. In the early 1960s, both short- and long-term loans for export promotion had accounted for less than 5 percent of total bank loans. During the Second Five-Year Development Plan period (1967-1971), the share went up to 10 percent. Since then, export loans have risen in step with the growing volume of exports.

Export industries have received many other forms of subsidies, and it is not possible to determine the relative impact of the financial or the other subsidies in promoting exports. It is clear, however, that, *in toto,* they contributed to a spectacular expansion of exports over the years from 1963 to 1978. This expansion, more than anything else, contributed to sustained rapid growth of GNP, which, in turn, more than offset the possible loss of output resulting from any inefficiencies in the allocation of resources that mismanagement of the financial system might have caused.

One may argue that exports could have risen as fast as they did under a liberalized financial system and free financial markets if all the relative prices, including the exchange rate, had been maintained at a market level. Again, this is a proposition no one can prove or disprove. What Korean experience does show is that the emphasis of financial policy on savings mobilization and export promotion was not inappropriate in view of the successful expansion of exports and healthy growth of the whole economy. During the high-interest-rate period, the government was able to supply abundant low-cost credit to exporters without generating serious inflation, because savers were willing to hold larger deposit balances than they would have otherwise.

DECELERATION OF FINANCIAL GROWTH, 1971–1978

After 1970, the DMBs grew less rapidly in terms of both their assets and network of operation. On the other hand, a variety of new financial intermediaries came into existence, and along with them new types of financial assets multiplied. The regulated financial sector by 1978 included, in addition to the DMBs and insurance companies, short-term financing companies, mutual credit companies, various credit cooperatives, financial lease firms, a land bank, merchant banks, securities trust companies, and a securities finance company. An issues market for equities and bonds was established in 1968, and, thereafter, the government waged a vigorous campaign to develop capital markets. Due in part to this effort, the capital market no longer occupied a fringe of the financial sector. In 1977, the corporate sector financed almost half its investment through these markets.

Despite some expansion and increased specialization of the financial intermediary network, the pace of financial growth only slightly exceeded the rate of economic growth. After the period of remarkable upsurge in the latter part of the 1960s, financial growth slowed down and showed considerable fluctuation in the 1970s, while the economy continued to grow at more than 10 percent a year on average. The real stock of financial assets grew at an annual rate of 14.7 percent, as compared with 25 percent during the 1965–1969 period. The stock of domestic financial assets relative to GNP, which had risen from 0.81 in 1965 to 1.49 in 1970, moved up more slowly to 1.86 in 1978 after a setback during the oil crisis (see Table 5, p. 28).

Both the cross-section and time-series studies of the interaction between financial development and growth suggest that financial intermediation will increase more rapidly than GNP until it levels off at a ratio of 3:1 or 4:1. Korea is still well below that level, so that the slowdown in the 1970s is not likely to reflect a stage of financial maturity or overdevelopment of the financial sector. On the other hand, it could have been a time of breath-catching, to absorb the effects of the very rapid financial growth in the preceding five years. But that seems unlikely to have taken more than a few years. Thus the slowdown of financial growth in the face of continued output growth suggests both that the policy environment was not conducive to financial development, and that some alternative and unrecorded channels emerged to serve the financing needs of a rapidly growing economy.

The period under discussion contained a number of serious internal and external disturbances such as the August 3, 1972 measures, which severely disrupted the working of the unregulated money markets, and the oil crisis in 1973–1974, which precipitated an enormous balance-of-payments deficit, rampant inflation, and a temporary slowdown in growth. Because of these disturbances and their subsequent effects on the economy, the pattern of financial evolution was more erratic in this period. However, as shown by the movements of various financial-asset-to-GNP ratios, it is unmistakable that financial growth slowed down after 1970.

One of the causative factors was undoubtedly that the rate of interest on time and savings deposits adjusted for inflation declined continuously and was negative or close to zero from 1973 to 1978. At the same time, however, the effective rate of return to equities (including capital gains) went up to as high as 124 percent per annum, due largely to government's deliberate efforts to attract savers into capital markets; the curb loan rates consistently carried interest rates over 40 percent on average; and the land-value index for Seoul almost doubled between 1970 and 1975 (see Table 49). This type of yield structure was not conducive to sustained financial growth for a number of reasons.

First, the reduction in the real interest rates on bank deposits drove savers away from the banking institutions to the markets for equities and real assets—in particular, land, apartments, and houses—for speculation, and to the informal credit institutions. Second, the high rate of return to equities that was maintained

TABLE 49 Trend of Interest Rates and Equity Yields, 1960–1978 (%)

	Nominal Interest Rate on Time and Savings Deposits	Wholesale Price Index (1970=100)[a]	Real Interest Rate (A)[b]	Real Interest Rate (B)[c]	Curb-Market Interest Rate[d]	Dividend Yield + Capital Gains[e]	Rate of Return on Public Debentures[e]	Land Value Index for Seoul (1963=100)[f]	Rate of Change in Seoul Land Value Index
1960		13.0				—			
1961		14.8				—			
1962	15.0	16.1	5.7	-2.9		—			
1963	15.0	19.4	-4.6	-11.1	52.4	—		100	
1964	15.0	26.2	-14.9	-11.6	61.4	—		168	68.0
1965	18.8	28.8	8.1	11.9	58.8	9.7	29.4	225	33.9
1966	30.0	31.4	19.2	13.5	58.7	23.5	36.6	—	—
1967	30.0	33.4	22.2	12.4	56.4	139.1	44.2	495	—
1968	27.6	36.2	17.7	9.9	55.9	33.0	—	755	52.5
1969	24.0	38.5	16.6	8.0	51.2	—	—	1,390	84.1
1970	22.8	42.0	12.6	6.5	50.8	23.8	34.9	1,445	4.0
1971	22.2	45.7	12.3	8.5	46.3	53.8	28.4	1,860	28.7
1972	15.7	52.0	1.7	0.1	38.9	124.5	19.2	1,966	5.7
1973	12.6	55.6	5.3	-0.7	39.2	50.2	17.0	1,997	1.6

TABLE 49 (continued)

	Nominal Interest Rate on Time and Savings Deposits	Wholesale Price Index (1970=100)[a]	Real Interest Rate (A)[b]	Real Interest Rate (B)[c]	Curb-Market Interest Rate[d]	Dividend Yield + Capital Gains[e]	Rate of Return on Public Debentures[e]	Land Value Index for Seoul (1963=100)[f]	Rate of Change in Seoul Land Value Index
1974	14.8	79.0	-19.3	-11.8	37.6	4.1	21.3	2,610	30.7
1975	15.0	100.0	-9.2	-7.1	41.3	45.9	21.4		
1976	15.5	112.1	3.0	-2.6	40.5	12.8			
1977	16.2	122.2	6.6	0.7	38.1				
1978	16.7	136.5	4.5	-1.8	41.7				

Notes: [a]BOK, *Economic Statistics Yearbook.*

$$[b] (1 + \text{Col. I}) \cdot \frac{\text{WPI}_{t-1}}{\text{WPI}_t}$$

$$[c] (1 + \text{Col. I}) \cdot \frac{\text{GNP Deflator}_{t-1}}{\text{GNP Deflator}_t}$$

[d]BOK, *Kiŏp kŭmyung mit Sagŭmyung silt'ae chosa.*

[e]S. W. Nam, "Financial Structure, Corporate Investment and Financing Behavior in Korea" (Ph.D. dissertation, MIT, 1977), p. 17.

[f]E. S. Mills and B. K. Song, *Urbanization and Urban Problems* (Cambridge, Mass., 1979).

by the government in order to cultivate capital markets succeeded in bringing a large number of savers in the urban areas into those markets. But few firms were willing to raise funds through the equity markets beyond the amounts required by government, because of the low fixed selling price and high financing cost on new issues. As a result, there was a large excess demand from buyers for new issues of equities, but only limited mobilization of new equity capital from them. Third, because the banking institutions were not able to mobilize adequate financial savings to meet the growing demand for bank loans, small and medium firms had to turn to the informal credit markets or large exporters who, along with their export business, increasingly combined the role of unofficial financial intermediary. Fourth, large corporations with access to international money and capital markets continued to borrow heavily from abroad, even though they were the relatively favored borrowers at domestic financial institutions. Excessive foreign-capital inflows played havoc with short-run monetary management and accelerated inflation, which, in turn, depressed the real interest rate further and consequently heated up real-estate speculation.

From 1972, a variety of new financial assets were offered to the public by both existing and new financial institutions. However, those with low fixed interest rates or artificially determined yield structures were ineffective in attracting domestic savings. For example, certificates of deposit, introduced in 1974, may be a convenient instrument of saving compared with other financial assets to some savers, but, as long as their interest rates are depressed, as they have been, the creation of CDs may cause a substitution of this for other low-yielding financial assets but is not likely to generate new savings. Indeed, the Korean experience indicates that creation of a large number of different assets may have only subdivided the financial sector into a larger number of inefficient small sub-markets. The resource costs of enlarging the menu of financial assets might have been higher than the benefits of new savings it may have generated, and also less productive than simply raising the returns on existing types of financial assets.

In the 1970s, the government reverted to the pre-1965 style of financial repression, not only by lowering the official interest rates, but also by intensifying the controls over credit allocation by the financial institutions—all symptoms of financial repression common in the earlier import-substitution period. There was a growing feeling in the early 1970s among policy-makers that saver confidence in the organized institutions had been established and that, therefore, the relationship between interest and saving rates was less significant. Instead, savings were likely to depend mainly on changes in real income, so that the interest rate could safely be reduced.[3] This argument, together with the ever-present business pressure for lower interest rates and a mild recession in 1970 and 1971, led to a substantial reduction in both deposit and lending rates in 1972. The rate of interest on bank time deposits was reduced to 12.6 percent in 1973 from 23 percent in 1970. This readjustment lowered the real deposit interest rate to 3 percent per year in 1973 and to negative levels thereafter.

Another reason for the resumption of financial repression was related to the paradox that the rapid opening up of the Korean economy had been achieved in large measure by private enterprise operating under highly centralized government guidance. Over time, there emerged several dozen so-called *chaebŏl*—a form of business conglomerate—which accounted for a large share of Korean exports and was also heavily involved in the development of heavy, chemical, and defense industries.[4] In the process of rapid business expansion, these conglomerates had amassed considerable wealth and increasing economic and financial power, which they hoped to use to exert greater influence on government policy. In order to prevent any further concentration of economic power, the government felt the need to keep these groups under control. It was considered infeasible, however, for the government to maintain its hold on these groups and at the same time to liberalize previously controlled markets and relax import restrictions and foreign-exchange regulations in a manner consistent with Ranis's model of export-led industrialization. The government, under these circumstances, attempted to exercise its power over the groups by retaining control of the financial institutions that still supplied a significant share of their domestic credit needs. The government also refused to let these conglomerates set up their own banking institutions, as they had in Japan, because this would further dilute government power.

Along with the rapid opening up of the economy, Korea had become more exposed to changes in world market conditions and economic fluctuations in Korea's major trading partners. This, in turn, magnified the problems of maintaining internal and external balance of the economy. Given the limitations of the traditional, market-oriented, short-run stabilization-policy instruments, the economic authorities relied upon direct control measures of domestic credit, such as ceilings on both central bank credit to the DMBs and on the loans of the DMBs. Resort to these multi-layered, direct monetary-policy instruments was a major facet of government's continuing domination over financial institutions.

From a longer-run perspective, however, the renewed financial repression may be linked to the shift in the export-led industrialization strategy from emphasis on labor-intensive manufactures to promotion of capital- and skill-intensive heavy industrial products that has taken place with government intervention and encouragement since the early 1970s. In the preparation stage of the Third Five-Year Plan (1972–1976), it was decided that the high-growth objective would be better served by major shifts in production and exports through the expansion of heavy and chemical industries. This change in strategy was premised on the belief that Korea was bound to lose its comparative advantage in labor-intensive exports in the world markets because of a rapid increase in wages at home and growing competition from latecomers among the LDCs following on the path of export-led industrial growth. The new Korean strategy was made public in 1972 and pursued vigorously thereafter.

The new strategy meant, however, that a secondary-import substitution of selected heavy and chemical industries, such as steel, machinery, shipbuilding, and petrochemicals, had to be accomplished first so that these industries could supply and support the existing export industries and then, in due course, could be developed into major exporters. Thus, the period under discussion may be characterized as a secondary-import-substitution-cum-export-promotion phase.

The development of these new industries required enormous investment in fixed capital and technology with a long gestation period and uncertain rate of return, not to mention the difficulties of cultivating new foreign markets for the products. Understandably, even the large business firms were somewhat reluctant to take on the risks inherent in the development of heavy and chemical industries, and the government had to provide a combination of guarantees, equity participation, and increasingly distorted incentives in the form of tax concessions and preferential low-interest credit to get these new industries started.

While financial growth, as measured by various standard ratios, slowed down considerably between 1970 and 1978, this leveling off had no apparent adverse effects on either overall economic growth or saving. In spite of the renewed financial repression, the Korean economy managed to grow at a rate in excess of 10 percent per annum on average through 1978. Although domestic saving in relation to GNP fell off sharply in the first three years of the 1970s, it rebounded in 1973 and showed a rising trend through 1978. Domestic saving rose to 27 percent of GNP in 1978 from 19 percent in 1969, and, as compared with the financial sector, its growth was impressive despite continuing inflation. Therefore, there was a noticeable divergence between the growth of the real economy and domestic saving on the one hand and that of the financial sector for the years 1970–1978. What were the factors that underlay this divergence? What was the role of finance during the period? Several considerations are relevant.

It should be emphasized that, in the development of the real economy, the heavy and chemical industries were promoted, not only for import substitution, but also for export expansion, and that some of these industries, such as shipbuilding and machinery, managed to achieve significant levels of exports within a short period of time. The real cost to the Korean economy of these achievements is still unknown, because they were subsidized in many ways, and their returns will depend on both world prices and the rates at which these new facilities are used over time. Nevertheless, the Korean economy through 1978 had not suffered from the symptoms of inefficiency that frequently arise from a secondary-import-substitution regime.

It also appears that the savings incentives of the latter half of the 1960s, such as favorable real-interest rates and availability of attractive financial instruments, had been replaced by other powerful savings-inducing factors, such as the growth of per capita income and exports of both goods and services. For example, many overseas workers in the Middle East and Southeast Asia transferred home sizable remittances which were saved and often subsequently invested in houses or businesses.

The availability of foreign financing was another important factor. Korea's access to international capital markets steadily improved due to its continuous strong balance-of-payments position and rapid growth of exports and income. An increasing number of business firms, especially large ones, established viable credit ratings in the international capital market and were able to mobilize foreign resources on favorable terms, sometimes without government or bank guarantee. Whenever the economy could not generate sufficient domestic savings to finance the level of investment required for a target rate of growth, the government did not hesitate to borrow directly from abroad, or to encourage private businesses to borrow on their own account, as evidenced by the experience during the oil crisis of 1973–1974.

Because of the insufficient finance generated by a government-controlled financial system, the large industrial groups (*chaebŏl*) increasingly combined their production and sales activities with those of financial institutions in the 1970s. These groups utilized non-bank financial institutions, such as life-insurance companies, merchant banks, and securities brokerage houses they controlled, as their financial arms to mobilize and distribute financial resources among the business firms they owned or controlled. Although these non-bank institutions were subject to some forms of government control and regulation, ways were found to circumvent these restrictions and to provide the desired financial services.

Another development that was important for our discussion was the authorization by government of large trading companies fashioned after Japanese *sōgo shōsha* in 1975. Although these trading companies were seen by the government as instruments of export promotion through development of new export markets, achieving greater efficiency by vertical integration and division of labor between the sales and production of export goods, they have also come to function as financial intermediaries in Korea, as they do in Japan. A major difference, however, is that, in Korea, this financial role is informal, because the trading companies have not been permitted to establish their own banks as they have in Japan. The Korean companies have gotten around this restriction by borrowing large amounts from domestic and foreign money and capital markets and relending to the small firms they deal with. The trading companies have knowledge of the credit-worthiness of the small firms, and, thus, are in a position to provide small loans at relatively low cost, which banks are unwilling, or find it difficult, to do. The loans are, in general, tied to specific purposes and often take the form of providing imported raw materials on credit, financing new equipment or other fixed capital investment, or prepayment of export sales before delivery to the foreign buyer.[5] Even before the establishment of these trading companies, the industrial groups and large business firms had departments specializing in the financial intermediary function of the trading company, which contributed to vertical and horizontal integration among export-oriented firms. These groups and large individual corporations supplied financing to small and medium manufacturing companies they controlled through equity participation or by providing long-term funds. Thus, the creation of trading companies in some ways legitimatized and institutionalized informal financing practices that had been going on for some time.

Finally, one must not overlook the role of the UFM, which again became active as the growth of the organized financial system slackened. Non-export-oriented small firms, when denied credit by the banking institutions, continued to go to the UFM, as they had been doing all along, mainly for the financing of their working capital. In fact, informal credit markets have become so well integrated with the formal system that changes in the interest rates in these unregulated markets are often regarded as the most reliable gauge of the credit conditions in the economy as a whole. If the credit volume of the UFM and the finance generated by inter-firm lending could be added to the total assets of the regulated financial system, it would not be surprising to find that financial growth in Korea from 1970 to 1978 was much greater than the flow-of-funds accounts and the financial ratios suggest.

Thus, it would be incorrect to conclude, on the basis of the divergence between the statistical growth of the real and financial sectors, that finance has not mattered very much in Korea in the 1970s. Rather, it has played an important accommodating role. This recent Korean experience suggests that, if the formal financial system cannot provide adequate financial services, it can be supplemented by foreign finance, by the UFM, and by internal finance generated by the businesses themselves, provided that the government does not manage to obstruct this process, and provided, also, that powerful forces driving economic expansion are present. Here again it is misleading to judge the role of the financial system only in terms of regulated financial institutions' assets and liabilities.

TEN

Lessons from the Korean Experience

The purpose of this study has been to analyze the path and characteristics of financial development in Korea, especially since 1945, with a view to evaluating the interrelationship between finance on the one hand and economic growth and internal and external balance of the economy on the other.

As the previous chapters have shown, financial development in Korea in this century occurred in two spurts, with an intervening period of implosion and repression and a recent period of slower growth with some diversification. The size of the organized financial system relative to the level of economic activity achieved similar proportions at the end of the 1930s and the 1960s. In between it diminished in size to levels comparable to the early stages of colonial modernization in 1910. By the 1970s, the overall ratios of financial assets to GNP of approximately 2.2 to 1 were comparable to the ratios Gurley and

Goldsmith have found in other countries at similar levels of development. Thus, in this sense, it appears that the size of the Korean organized financial system in the 1970s was roughly consistent with its level of development.

The structure of the system, however, exhibits a number of unusual characteristics. Korean businesses rely heavily on external finance, in a manner similar to Japanese businesses. As a consequence, direct securities (stocks and bonds) have been relatively unimportant but recently growing, while the intermediation of financial institutions has been relatively large. Reliance on foreign financing is also large but not unusual for a small, open, developing country. The mechanism for channeling foreign finance through the domestic banking system (via the loan-guarantee system) is more unusual, though it was necessitated by the weak credit standing of Korean businesses in international capital markets. Finally, Korea has had a dualistic financial structure, one part regulated and recorded, the other part unregulated and ill-defined in quantitative terms. The unregulated part of the system has continued to play a major role, despite the growth of the regulated sectors and repeated efforts of government to suppress the unregulated sectors. This persistence is evidence that the unregulated institutions have been meeting a demand unsatisfied by the more modern institutions.

In evaluating the performance of the Korean financial system, it is not appropriate to use micro-economic efficiency criteria of prices and profits. Such an approach is misleading, because many prices in the Korean economy are controlled or distorted, and, in particular, interest rates have seldom been allowed to clear financial markets or allocate resources. As in the case of Japan during the post-war period, and also in many other developing countries, the regulated part of the Korean financial system may be characterized as a "disequilibrium system," in which institutional controls have taken away from interest rates much of the function of allocating resources.[1] The Korean government eschewed financial policies oriented towards achieving competition and leaving the results to the market system. Instead, the government has been actively involved in managing the system, using it to mobilize financial resources from abroad and at home, and to allocate those resources in ways that supported its high-growth policies. To the extent that there has been probing of alternative financial technologies, it has been within the limits of a centrally managed system. In retrospect, it appears that this approach was based upon a desire for rapid growth and industrialization, and also a lack of confidence in the efficacy of Western free-market systems. To judge from the remarkable performance of the economy over the past decade and a half, the total mix of policies has been effective in transforming Korea from a poor agricultural to a newly industrialized middle-income country.

The financial system has not always been managed effectively. In the 1950s and early 1960s, there were violent swings from inflationary excess to severe constraint, from public to private and then back to public ownership of the commercial banks. In that era of financial turbulence, the informal money markets flourished, as they were the most stable and reliable aspect of the financial system. But, as the government put together a more coherent set of financial policies for channeling domestic and foreign savings through the banking institutions, the unregulated institutions receded in importance and assumed their more customary role of supplementing the regulated financial institutions.

Because most of the regular bank loans and foreign-loan guarantees were, in fact, long term, there was an important need for the unregulated institutions to meet urgent short-term requirements. The combination of the government-imposed capital levy on the unregulated money markets in 1972 and the subsequent creation of financing companies that issue short-term bills and provide short-term financing to business, and mutual credit companies and various credit cooperatives, which cater to the credit needs of small households, took some activity away from the unregulated lenders, and induced some of the larger ones to set up new finance companies and become a part of the modern sector, but it clearly did not eliminate them altogether.

Government control of the banking institutions has been a principal means for guiding and regulating private enterprise. Most businesses of any size have been continuously and heavily indebted to one or more of the government-owned banks. While some of the bank loans are for long term, many are nominally short term and their renewal is subject to bank or government discretion. Those larger businesses that conformed to government policies and were responsive to government suggestions could count on automatic renewal of their lines of credit, but those that did not could expect difficulty. Also, approval of new investment financing, either through domestic bank loans or guarantee of foreign loans, gave the banks and the government a periodic opportunity to evaluate business performance and apply pressure for conformity. The government has not flaunted these powers openly, but they have been perceived clearly by all businessmen and have been an important dimension of government business relations (as described by Jones and SaKong).[2]

The relationship of finance to risk in Korea also cannot be viewed in the same terms that would apply to a free-market, private-enterprise system. Government ownership and control of most banking institutions has meant that deposits were guaranteed in nominal terms, but subject to the erratic erosion of inflation. Borrowers from these institutions have experienced considerable risk that their de facto long-term loans might be called on short notice. The fact that this risk was linked as much to political performance as to economic prospects did not make it any easier to live with. Because of its active role in the promotion of the securities markets, the government was considered likely to assure that security values would not diminish significantly. This could be accomplished either by arranging financing for any firms with marketed securities that were experiencing financial difficulties, or by supporting the security prices directly.

At the other extreme, the repeated government efforts to eliminate the unregulated financial institutions made the deposits in those institutions extremely risky. This undoubtedly raised the risk premium on such deposits and thus increased the cost of credit from the informal money markets. An announced policy of benign neglect would probably reduce costs and increase the volume of their activities substantially. A further step in that direction would result from giving them access to legal authority to enforce their loan contracts. On the other hand, such moves would also expose them to taxing and similar constraints that would raise costs.

In its search for more effective means of mobilizing financial savings, the Korean government's experiments with high deposit interest rates in the latter half of the 1960s seemed to confirm the efficacy of such policies. The move from a negative to a positive real rate of interest on longer-term time deposits in September 1965 led to a dramatic and continuous rise in such deposits for the next five years. When nominal deposit rates were lowered and real rates became negative in the 1970s, growth of time deposits practically stopped. While many would argue that the rise in time deposits was, in part, a substitution for other forms of financial and real assets, there are, on the other hand, few who deny that the higher interest rate probably had a significant effect on the savings rate. The rise in private savings from 4 to 10 percent of GNP between 1964 and 1966 and the fact that the private savings rate stayed above 10 percent of GNP for the next five years give support to this argument. With the decline in the real interest rate after 1970, the savings rate remained at the new higher level and savings were channeled into other types of assets, which accounts for the high correlation between private savings and interest rates in one period and the low correlation over the longer run.

Domestic lending rates of the banking institutions were not raised to the same levels as the longer-term deposit rates in 1965, and many observers have criticized the government for the so-called inversion of the normal interest-rate relationships. Some have suggested that loan rates should have been "freed up" to reach an equilibrium level that would have effectively rationed bank credit and allocated it to those who could pay its true value.

It is our view that the markets for bank loans are very imperfect, especially when there are few banks and they are all either government-owned or -controlled. It is unrealistic to expect meaningful, competitive interest rates to emerge in such markets if they were to be decontrolled. In a managed financial system such as Korea's, where the free market system does not reign, interest rates on loans and deposits are instruments of government policy that should be evaluated in terms of their relative efficiency when compared with other instruments for achieving particular objectives. The Korean government wished to encourage exports, and it used a combination of fiscal, credit, and import policies to achieve that objective. The amount of credit to exporters was increased and the interest rate reduced in 1965 when the IMF insisted, as a condition for a stand-by agreement, that direct export subsidies be discontinued. It is unclear whether the generalized low-interest-rate subsidy on export loans was less efficient than a selective system of direct export subsidies, but the latter instrument was not available, and it would have been very difficult to administer a selective pattern of interest-rate subsidies. Thus, the low interest rate on all export loans was selected, and appears to have been an effective, although not demonstrably the most efficient, instrument.

Similarly, the low interest rates on medium- and long-term loans from the special domestic banks in Korea were a conscious subsidy to investment that gave the government a strong hand in allocating investment. The chronic excess demand for such loans obviously created opportunities for corruption and could have led to inefficient allocation of resources. The government has sought to reduce these problems by increasing the supply of loanable funds from both foreign and domestic sources and keeping the pressure on for rapid implementation rather than by raising the interest rates.

In the course of pursuing the export-led industrialization strategy, the problems of maintaining internal and external stability of the economy have been magnified. Government restraints over financial institutions and interest rates have left the economic authorities with limited anticyclical policy instruments. Along with the rapid expansion of the export sector, which has accounted for an increasingly large share of output, domestic business fluctuations have been very much influenced, and often led, by changes in world market conditions. In such an environment with a fixed exchange-rate system, monetary policy as an anticyclical weapon loses much of its effectiveness, even if the economy has a sophisticated financial system. Institutional controls, rationing, and financial subsidies have inevitably resulted in an increasingly rigid financial system and artificially segmented financial markets, which have simply not been amenable to monetary control for short-run stability of the economy. Most of the traditional instruments of monetary policy have been largely inoperative because of underdeveloped money and capital markets and, in recent years, the easy access to foreign funds. The more effective instruments of direct credit controls have not been fully utilized when control over domestic liquidity has clashed with the growth objective. Also, the monetary authorities have not tried to vary deposit interest rates as an instrument of short-run monetary policy, despite the demonstrated effectiveness of this instrument in affecting the demand for deposits on a longer-term basis in the 1965–1970 period.

The prevailing highly managed financial system may interfere in the future with successful implementation of Korea's outward-looking strategy. Financial institutions, though they have grown in number and variety, have had little incentive to expand their intermediation capacity or improve financial technology, and have been unresponsive to changing financial market conditions and needs of the economy. They have, until recently, been cut off from the international financial community, and have continued outdated financial practices suitable only to a closed economy that is unable to meet international competition. In contrast, private businesses, in particular export-oriented ones, have aggressively penetrated into, and succeeded in enlarging their share in world markets. They have modernized their production processes and management and adopted sophisticated marketing strategies. The domestic financial institutions, however, have been ill-equipped to provide adequate and efficient international financial services to these world-market-oriented businesses. So long as it remains a lagging sector unable to meet the financial needs of an economy that is rapidly opening up, the financial sector may indeed restrict the growth of the economy itself in the long run or force businesses to seek better services abroad.

At times, the Korean government has professed a desire to step back and leave greater room for the free functioning of the domestic money and capital markets, but it has in fact found this a very difficult path to follow. An early example was the transfer of commercial banks to private ownership in the late 1950s, which led to a decline in their access to the rationed supply of credit, and eventually to repossession by the government on grounds of both equity and effectiveness of government control. Another example was the policy to encourage the sale of corporate stock and broaden public ownership of the larger business enterprises. A number of favorable tax and other incentives were offered to businesses that "went public," but most of them were reluctant to do so for obvious reasons. The government's response of requiring corporations to go public and then setting very low prices for their shares kept the government very much at the center of the securities market and the whole range of business financial decisions. It also may have committed the government to a long-term role of assuring financial support to any of the "public" corporations that get into difficulty. Here again the Japanese provide a model.

This pattern of government manipulation or utilization of the financial system to support and guide the private and public enterprises in carrying out the government's development program has meant that finance has been neither supply-leading nor demand-following in Korea. Instead, it has been one of the several instruments, including fiscal, trade, price policies, and direct commands, that the government has drawn upon to promote high rates of economic growth. The government has tried, at least since the mid-1960s, to see that the needed financial resources were available to carry out the investment, production, and export plans. If critical financial shortages arose, the government took steps to relieve them—as with the loans for export production in 1965, guarantees of suppliers' credits for new investment after 1963, refinancing of guaranteed foreign loans in 1972, and providing credit for purchase of oil and other imports during the oil crisis in 1974. In each instance, the government took action to remove financial constraints and to see that the economy could move ahead at high speed. Also, in most instances, the unregulated money markets helped accommodate the short-run needs and reallocate the available funds to their most urgent uses. In fact, this is what the unregulated markets were doing so effectively in 1972 when the government decapitalized them.

While the government, in that instance, used what seemed to be an easy means of relieving the financial pressure on large corporations, it did so in part out of a lack of appreciation of the complementary role of the unregulated institutions and in total disregard of the welfare of their depositors. Probably the aspect of the unregulated money markets that has been most disturbing to the Korean government over the years is that they do operate outside the sphere of government regulation, whereas all other financial institutions are clearly within that sphere. Although the government did succeed in forcing a one-time registration and revision of terms of most informal-money-market loans, it did not try to impose a continuing system of regulation, but chose instead, and wisely, to try to create some competitive, regulated institutions.

We believe that the unregulated money markets have been a major factor during the high-growth period in giving the Korean financial system flexibility to respond to the needs of a high-pressure, tightly managed, and tightly financed economy. The government has attempted to mobilize and allocate—mainly through the commercial banking system—the large blocks of finance needed for high growth. The unregulated money markets have provided the flexibility and the lubrication to keep the engine running as smoothly and rapidly as it has. These markets may have reached levels of operation and sophistication in Korea that exceed those found in most countries. International comparisons of this gray area of finance are very difficult. But the long tradition of private savings associations and moneylenders in Korea, plus the effects of financial repression and the emergent needs for institutions that could mobilize large amounts of funds for short periods of time to fill the gaps arising from the often slow-moving, government-run banking institutions, created a favorable climate for the unregulated money markets throughout the period under consideration. This interaction between the regulated and unregulated financial sectors in Korea is one form of integration, which does not depend upon the existence of formal money or capital markets, but rather on the fact that both households and enterprises were both borrowers and lenders in both financial sectors.

In the latter half of the 1970s, conditions appeared to be changing, as the financial constraints for Korea were more relaxed (due to a rise in the domestic savings rate, a narrowing of the foreign trade gap, and increased access to world capital markets), the range of domestic financial institutions was broadening, and large industrial and commercial enterprises were themselves engaging in financial intermediation. In time, the unregulated institutions may recede to a peripheral role as some of them shift over to new parts of the regulated markets and others go out of operation. But it is unlikely that they will disappear altogether, and we suggest that any further attempts, similar to the August 1972 measures, to force them out of existence would be contrary to the broader public interest.

On the other hand, government efforts to foster the primary securities markets and broader ownership of private corporations have been costly undertakings. So long as the government retains a dominant role in corporate policy-making, controlling the flow of finance to the corporate sector as well as their dividend and reinvestment decisions, the opportunities for shareholders to participate either in decision-making or in high yields on their investment are limited. There may be little advantage other than short-term speculative gains to be derived from investing in stocks rather than real assets, or bank deposits or the informal money markets. The government practice of grossly underpricing new stock issues generates little new capital for the corporations and gives a windfall to those lucky enough to get some of the new shares when their prices rise, as they generally do. This, in turn, creates overly optimistic expectations among investors. While this approach may be considered a long-term investment in developing a capital market, there is still a long way to go before this market will be worth its cost, and it may not progress beyond the state of a government-controlled and contrived artifact so long as government-business relations continue as they are.

One lesson to be learned from Korean experience with both the unregulated money markets and the capital markets is that it is costly and difficult for government to destroy a financial institution that is fulfilling a useful role, and it is equally difficult to create a viable institution before its time. Developing countries are cluttered with grossly inefficient financial institutions—development banks, agricultural banks, and even central banks—that operate in a protected, "hot-house" environment, making practically no effort to mobilize financial resources and squandering in an unproductive manner the resources "given" them. Commercial banks and unregulated money markets are often ignored or suppressed as non-developmental. In Korea, those "non-developmental" institutions have had the major responsibility for channeling financial resources to the high-growth sectors of the economy and, *at times,* the Korean government has had the wisdom to facilitate and support their effort.

Another lesson to be drawn from the Korean experience is

that the real sector variables, such as investment, government expenditures, exports, and imports, are likely to be more important than finance in explaining growth and development in highly managed economies. This does not mean that finance is not important. What it does mean is that the Shavian system of finance, where prices clear markets and allocate resources, may not be relevant to the economies in which the government is forced, or chooses, to control many facets of economic activity. Nor would such a system necessarily prove efficient. In these economies, the financial system is likely to be managed and financial policies to be used as major instruments of achieving concrete objectives such as rapid growth.

The managed system, although it may be part of a repressive political system, need not lead to a repressive financial environment. So long as policies affecting savings, investment, imports, and exports are "right" and the financial system accommodates credit-worthy borrowers, such a system may well contribute to both economic and financial development.

On the other hand, it does run some real long-term risks in terms of both equity and efficiency. A managed system can lead to concentration of lending and of economic power in the hands of a few enterprises which are then able to dominate their industries or allied subsidiary firms. If, instead, a conscious effort is made under a managed system to disperse credit widely among many smaller enterprises, it becomes more difficult to make efficient choices without greater reliance on market prices and diffusion of control. In the first instance, with concentration of economic power, the large enterprises are likely to demand the right to create their own financial institutions as well as a lessening of governmental control. This could lead to a shift in the current balance of power in Korea between government and big business. Movement in the other direction, towards greater dispersion of finance and economic power, is also likely to generate demands for local control of institutions and financial resources.

Thus, the current, managed financial system in Korea inevitably must change to meet the needs of a growing and increasingly complex economy. The choices appear to be among more pervasive and detailed central management with a probable rise in inefficiency, a shift of authority and decision-making responsibility to large enterprises and their captive financial institutions, or, conversely, a diffusion of power to smaller enterprises and financial institutions. The last two choices have uncertain implications for both efficiency and equity; but they do bear upon, or are inextricably caught up with, the broader political choices currently being worked out in Korea.

Epilogue

The period of systematic analysis covered in this study ends with the year 1978. The lengthy period of writing, reviewing, and editing, however, extended through mid-1982, long enough to witness a much-publicized financial scandal that rocked the Korean government in May 1982. While the full consequences of this financial crisis are still unfolding, its origins and early manifestations conform to and confirm many of the themes of this study.

In its barest essentials, the scandal arose when a man and wife with important political connections became involved in money-lending to several large Korean businesses.[1] This couple followed practices differing from those of most large money-lenders in Korea in several respects. First, they obtained promissory notes from the borrowers that were much larger than the actual amounts of the loans. Second, they rediscounted the notes without the knowledge or agreement of the borrowers. Third, they rediscounted some of the notes or otherwise borrowed money from several of the government-owned commercial banks, largely on the basis of their political influence. When the notes came due and the people or institutions holding them tried to collect, the borrowers were unable to pay. When this became known in Seoul financial circles, all lenders tried to redeem their claims and the whole scheme collapsed.

Newspaper accounts were quick to blame the curb, or unregulated money markets, for the scandal,[2] but such accusations hardly seem warranted. The money-broker couple were not bona fide money-market dealers, and they did not observe the standard rules of the game. Most such dealers do not have strong political ties, are not in a position to rediscount their paper at the commercial banks, do not demand claims in excess of the amount loaned, and do not rediscount such paper without notifying the borrowers.

The firms that obtained the loans from the couple under relatively unfavorable terms were obviously unable to obtain bank financing under any better terms. Whether they could have been accommodated by other moneylenders under similar terms is unclear. But it was the inadequacy or high cost of bank financing or the firms' poor financial condition that led them into the unfortunate set of arrangements with the couple.

One of the most interesting aspects of the scandal occurred when the government began arresting people connected with the improper loans and related bribery payments. Most private moneylenders immediately stopped operations in anticipation of further government crackdowns on the unregulated money markets. A relatively large industrial firm, the Sam Jin Aluminum Company, which was listed on the Seoul Stock Exchange and had outstanding bank loans of $80 million, was, according to newspaper accounts, plunged into insolvency because local banks dishonored promissory notes valued at $640,000. The company was reportedly operating profitably but had a cash-flow problem. The company's president claimed that, "had the curb market been operating normally, (the company) wouldn't have had problems in securing a loan."[3] He reportedly approached a commercial bank "for a loan to cover funds that couldn't be raised in the curb market. But . . . the bank denied the request because Sam Jin didn't have any collateral" (that wasn't already pledged to cover existing bank loans). The company was, therefore, "seeking one or two investors who would be able to put up (some additional) collateral." One foreign banker in Seoul was reported to have said that, "if the curb market doesn't get back to normal soon . . . there are going to be wholesale bankruptcies of small companies."[4]

The Korean government's response to this situation was initially to arrest and prosecute the principal participants, then to replace the "responsible" cabinet ministers, and finally to adopt some "corrective" measures. These measures consisted, on the one hand, of attempts to restrict the operations of the unregulated markets and, on the other, the encouragement of the regulated short-term money markets so that they could become more competitive with the unregulated moneylenders.[5] There were also renewed calls for turning the commercial banks over to private ownership to make them more competitive and independent of government direction. The government announced a lowering of interest rates and relaxation of ceilings on bank credit.[6]

While these measures were expected to make more money available at lower cost for the business community in the short run, they were likely to result before long in rising prices, negative real interest rates, a decline in the real financial resources of the banking institutions, and ultimately the restoration of conditions conducive to recovery of the unregulated financial institutions. This suggests that the mixed public-private, regulated-unregulated, directed-nondirected financial system will be continued without much change.

Appendix A

Farmers' and Fishermen's
Usurious Debts Resettlement Order

Supreme Council for National
Reconstruction Order No. 12
Made public on May 25, 1961

This order, designed to resettle the farmers' and fishermen's usurious debts, shall be effective beginning at 12 o'clock, May 25, 1961.

1. All credits and debts, in cash or in kind, with annual interest rate exceeding 20%, are defined as usurious, and shall be resettled subject to this order.
2. The rights of creditors for the debts defined herein as usurious shall be suspended, and the term of repayment shall be stipulated explicitly in separate regulations.
3. Both creditors and debtors shall report their credits and debts to the authorities concerned.
4. The rights of creditors to claim their credits which are not reported shall be considered as terminated.
5. The reported credits or debts shall be duly considered, and those debts determined as usurious shall be substituted for government-guaranteed loans to be annually repaid by the debtors.
6. Those who violate this order shall be subject to strict punishment.
7. Other particulars needed for implementation of this order shall be prescribed in separate orders or regulations.

Appendix B

Summary of Principal Recommendations

Made by Gurley, Patrick, and Shaw

The following constitute the main recommendations in our report. Specific proposals are intended as a limited, rather than exhaustive, list to clarify the principles that are involved.

ALTERNATIVE DOMESTIC MECHANISMS FOR FINANCING INVESTMENT

1. Adequate mobilization of capital in Korea will require a major overhaul of the financial system. Although self-finance has an important role in Korea's decentralized market economy, major reliance needs to be placed on financial and fiscal methods. Certain improvements in self-finance are also desirable; for example, relative prices for output of government business enterprises should be raised to increase profits and government saving.

2. While financial reform is crucial to achieve the Korean objective of stable growth, our judgment is that tax reform will have to shoulder an even larger burden than financial reform to raise the ratio of domestic saving to national income within the coming few years. The financial system will need a significant period of recuperation from past repression and abuse. This is no excuse for delay in financial reform. Indeed it only makes more necessary the need for financial reform now.

PREREQUISITES TO FINANCIAL REFORM AND DEVELOPMENT

1. Persuade savers that they will not be taxed by inflation.

2. Maintain the equilibrium value of the foreign exchange rate of the wŏn; do not allow it again to become overvalued.

3. Release domestic interest rates on deposits and loans from their current ceilings so that savers are induced to save and in financial form, and so that funds can be allocated to investment on a more rational basis.

TECHNIQUES OF MONETARY CONTROL

1. We recommend the establishment of a Stabilization Account at the Bank of Korea to serve as the major instrument of control over the reserve base, in a manner resembling open-market operations. The monetary authority would initiate transfers between the Stabilization Account and reserve deposits of banks as required to maintain the appropriate supply of nominal money and liquidity.

2. If the Stabilization Account is adopted, the use of other techniques would be modified or discarded.

a. We recommend that legal reserve requirements be fixed, not varied as a means of control over liquidity. Uniform reserve requirements should be established on all forms of bank deposits in order to reduce variance in the relationship between the reserve base and liquid claims on banks.

b. Rediscounting by commercial banks should be in small amounts and at a rate higher than the standard commercial bank lending rate. This single penalty rate should replace the present multiplicity of Bank of Korea rediscount and loan rates. The same penalty rate should be imposed on deficiencies in bank required reserves.

c. Aggregate loan ceilings at the banks should be discarded since they will be unnecessary. Ceilings restrain interbank competition for deposits and loans, damping bank initiative in mobilizing saving.

d. Interest could be paid on commercial bank reserve deposits at the Bank of Korea where needed for incentives and to ensure adequate levels of bank profitability.

e. Severe constraints on rediscounts need not eliminate credit subsidies where they are desirable. Banks can be compensated for making approved loans by a proportionately larger share of debits to the Stabilization Account and credits to their bank reserves, or by interest payments on reserve balances.

3. In formulating policy for stabilization and finance in development, we

consider it essential to begin by clarifying precisely the determinants of a) demand for real money and other real liquid assets and b) the actual supply of money and other liquid assets in current prices. We have estimated illustrative functions; it is obvious that further research is required.

MEASURES TO INCREASE THE FLOW OF SAVINGS INTO LIQUID ASSETS

1. The measure of first priority is to eliminate legal ceilings and raise actual rates of interest on deposits at all financial institutions. Timid and tentative increases in interest rates are likely to be futile, or worse. We recommend that deposit rates be put on a level with rates to be expected in the curb market following reform less a reasonable differential in recognition of relative risks. Actual rates should have a degree of flexibility to continue to be competitive.

2. We recommend a substantial reduction in the variety of deposit forms, and that an explicit rate of interest be paid on all demand deposits to encourage the "banking habit." Quite arbitrarily, we suggest a rate of 5 per cent on checking accounts, as a minimal inducement to increase real demand for money under even optimistic expectations about price stabilization.

3. We advise against measures of compulsion to increase popular demand for financial claims in any form, as less efficient in increasing saving than inducements predicated upon a voluntary response.

4. We advise against erratic policy in attracting savings to liquid assets. In finance, continuity of policy is one of the most important requirements. In the past, good savings measures have been shorted by renewed inflation and new controls.

5. To help overcome lingering skepticism regarding sustained price stability, Korea might consider a limited experiment with escalator clauses for one or more deposit types, so long as corresponding bank loans and other assets can be escalated.

6. Government lending institutions (KRB, NACF, MIB, CNB) should become financial intermediaries, attracting their own sources of private savings with competitive interest rates on their deposits.

7. We suggest that the government guarantee against default risk deposits of farmers and fishermen in those cooperatives which meet appropriate quality standards.

MEASURES TO IMPROVE ALLOCATION OF SAVINGS BY THE MONETARY SYSTEM

1. In principle loan rates should be freed from their present ceilings, and raised to the level at which they would balance the demand for and supply of available loan funds.

2. In order to mitigate short-run adjustment problems, it may be desirable to raise, temporarily only, rates on overdue and renewed loans by less than those on net new loans, with the average of loan rates raised cautiously, perhaps with the weighted average of new time and savings deposit rates as its target.

3. The present intricate structure of interest rates on loans is inefficient and should be simplified.

4. Steps should be taken to ensure gradual collection of overdue (*de facto* long-term) commercial bank loans. We suggest progressive penalty rates and/or progressive compensatory demand deposit balances on overdue loans.

5. The present system of subsidized loans, of which export credit is one example, is inefficient and has undesirable side effects. Given the policy of subsidy, more efficient alternative techniques should be found.

MEASURES TO IMPROVE THE OPERATING EFFICIENCY OF THE BANKING SYSTEM

High unit costs in banking will fall as savings in deposit form rise and deposit turnover declines in response to price stabilization and to the interest rate reforms recommended. Additional inducements to greater efficiency in the transmission of savings to desired investment should be devised. We suggest only a "few."

1. The Bank of Korea could design incentives to bank efficiency, possibly through a rate of interest paid on bank reserve deposits.

2. A competitive stimulus to efficiency could be obtained by admitting to Korea branches of a few foreign banks that are outstanding for progressive practices.

3. The Finance Bureau of the Ministry of Finance, or the US aid program, could undertake technological instruction of bank management.

DEVELOPMENT IN LONG-TERM FINANCE

We expect that for some time the major financial means of mobilizing private saving will be through the bank system. Even so, much can be done now to increase the relative flow of long-term finance.

1. We urge reconsideration of the policy of early sale of government-held shares in government-controlled corporations and commercial banks. Its holdings are so large, current prices of listed equities so low, and the market so thin, that any significant sale would mean low returns to the government and a slump in prices that would undermine investor demand for stocks indefinitely. We caution against the use of compulsion in sales of these securities, as an inefficient means of mobilizing savings and as undermining any development of the stock market. We also caution against the direct or indirect provision of central bank credit to finance sales, since it would not mobilize private savings but would instead undercut the price stabilization program. We strongly advise against a program to fix levels of stock prices.

2. We recommend that government-owned shares serve as the nucleus of a mutual fund under KRB or other appropriate supervision to encourage development of long-term financing.

3. Once stabilization succeeds and interest rates are free there will be investors who will desire debentures. KRB could then appropriately issue its own debentures and initially guarantee issues of carefully selected private corporations, with the right to intervene quickly if any default is threatened.

4. We suggest that the Korea Stock Exchange be reorganized as a government or independent, non-profit corporation managed by a stock exchange commission.

5. We recommend some mechanism of government guarantee of individual life insurance contracts against default risk to some suitable maximum amount, but tied to improvement in life insurance company practices and higher minimum paid-in capital requirements.

THE UNORGANIZED SECTOR

1. Penalites and direct controls to repress the unorganized sector are unlikely to be effective. We recommend that organized finance be enabled to compete effectively with the unorganized sector, and that ways be devised to draw the human and other important resources in unorganized markets into organized finance.

UNITED STATES ECONOMIC ASSISTANCE

1. We suggest that there may be opportunities to employ assistance funds in developing areas of Korean finance that are especially backward. Aid for rural finance is a case in point as is aid for fishery cooperatives. Assistance funds may be used experimentally in the insurance industry to guarantee insurance commitments of some kinds and to underwrite a purchasing-power clause in insurance contracts. It would be unfortunate to use assistance funds in any way that delays financial reform.

Appendix C

Readjustment of Curb-Market Borrowings

Article 10 (Definition of Curb-Market Borrowings)

1) For the purpose of this Decree, "curb-market borrowings of loans" shall be defined as all debts borne by enterprises raised directly or indirectly from sources other than banking institutions according to the loan-for-consumption contract as of August 2, 1972 (hereinafter referred to as the "basic date").

2) The loan-for-consumption contract of Paragraph 1 shall comprise contracts for the purpose of the loan-for-consumption of such objectives as cash or other substitutes in case the obligation to pay cash or its substitutes exists, contracts to receive valuable securities or other substitutes in lieu of cash in case of loan in cash, and other similar contracts for the purpose of lending money to enterprises including held money and suspense receipts, regardless of the name, kind, and method of contracts.

3) Cases in which transfers or promises to transfer property rights in lieu of cash were made as an act to redeem a debt in cash shall be regarded as cash borrowing under Paragraph 1.

4) Cases in which checks (excluding certified checks issued by banks or treated the same as bank checks in applying the Check Transaction Act and treasury checks, the same definition is applied hereinafter), promissory notes, and other means of payment (hereinafter referred to as "means of payment") issued by enterprises are not cleared as of the basic date shall be regarded as curb-market borrowings by enterprises as of the basic date, even if the payment date has expired.

5) The following debts borne by enterprises shall not be regarded as curb-market borrowings:

   a) Liabilities borne as the price of goods and labor (including services) purchased by enterprises.

   b) Liabilities incurred in the form of security money and advance receipts by enterprises, repayable in cash, in connection with business transactions.

c) Liabilities related to corporate bonds issued by enterprises to raise required funds according to the Commercial Code or other laws and decrees and security money of other payments made in connection with the bond floating.

d) Liabilities borne by enterprises which have been permitted and approved by the government in accordance with the Foreign Capital Inducement Law, the Foreign Exchange Control Law, and other laws and decrees.

e) Liabilities rescheduled by the approved schedule for readjusting a company in accordance with the Company Readjustment Law.

f) Liabilities incurred through the contracts of mutual credit *kye* and mutual credit installments by mutual credit companies which conduct the business organically and continuously to gain profits according to Items a) and b), Paragraph 1, Article 11 of the Mutual Credit Company Act, or other liabilities incurred through contracts in the same method.

g) Other liabilities the Minister of Finance separately specifies.

Article 11 (Definition of Enterprises)

1) For the purpose of this chapter, the term "enterprise" shall be defined as any business having a business license according to Article 1 of the Business Tax Law and conducting business prescribed in Article 1 of the Business Tax Law as of the basic date (including those temporarily out of business). However, banking, insurance, and other businesses designated separately by the Minister of Finance shall be excluded.

2) Entities which conduct the businesses prescribed in Article 1 of the Business Tax Law but do not hold business licenses as a result of being exempted from the business tax according to the Tax Exemption Regulation Act and other laws and decrees shall be regarded as enterprises.

3) Entities engaged in agriculture, livestock breeding, forestry, and fishery, which pay income and corporate taxes shall be regarded as enterprises as stipulated in Paragraph 1. Of those engaged in livestock breeding, those who are exempted from the duty to pay the income tax in accordance with Paragraph 2, Article 8 of the Income Tax Law and Paragraph 2, Article 24 of the Corporate Tax Law shall be regarded as enterprises.

Article 12 (Definition of Banking Institutions)

1) For the purpose of this chapter, "banking institutions" shall be defined as comprising the following institutions:

a) The Korea Development Bank
b) The Medium Industry Bank
c) The Citizens' National Bank
d) The Korea Exchange Bank
e) The Korea Housing Bank
f) The Korea Trust Bank (including trust accounts)

g) The National Agricultural Cooperatives Federation and its members
h) The Central Federation of Fisheries Cooperatives and its members
i) Banking institutions established under the General Banking Act.

2) The following juridical persons and persons designated separately by the Minister of Finance who conduct financing business according to the approved methods of business or the methods of business provided separately by the Minister of Finance, shall be regarded as banking institutions:

a) Ri. Dong Agricultural Cooperatives
b) Cooperative Fishing Village *kye*
c) Korea Development Financing Company
d) Korea Investment Financing Company
e) Korea Investment Development Corporation
f) Korea Securities Financing Company
g) Agricultural and Fishery Development Corporation
h) Korea Mining Promotion Corporation
i) The Readjustment Corporation
j) Insurance companies established under the Insurance Law
k) Korea Reinsurance Corporation
l) Korea Stock Exchange and securities companies established under the Stock Exchange Law

Article 13 (Suspension of Repayment of Curb-Market Borrowing)

1) For all curb-market loans, any conduct on the part of either the creditor or the debtor intended to result in the repayment of loans or to make them null and void (exemption of the debt shall be excluded) shall be prohibited from the enforcement date of the Decree except in accordance with the provisions of the Decree.

2) Compulsory execution of property rights, provisional seizure, provisional disposition and auction, and auction procedures based on the Auction Act (return of a substitute and registration necessary for the transfer of ownership following provisional registration shall be included) aimed at securing the repayment of the curb-market loan shall be prohibited and the procedures already in progress shall be stopped, except that the creditor in the curb market exercises his rights in accordance with the provisions of the Decree.

Article 14 (Payment Suspension of Checking Accounts)

1) Payments of checking accounts opened in banking institutions, (cases in which the government and financial institutions are depositors shall be excluded) and clearing of the means of payment to be settled through checking accounts in the Clearing House shall be suspended during the period from the enforcement date of the Decree until August 5, 1972,

except for the repayment of debts prescribed in Item d of Paragraph 5, Article 10 and checking accounts depositors of which are foreign institutions specified by the Minister of Finance.

2) In case of the provision mentioned in the preceding paragraph, the payer or bank in charge of payment (those who are regarded as banks in the application of the Check Transaction Act are included and hereinafter it is the same) shall settle the means of payment on the condition that it is confirmed through the depositor that the means of payment is not provided for the purpose of taking the place of or in relation to repayment of the curb-market loans.

3) Enterprises must report by using the report form of the means of payment within the period specified in Paragraph 1 to the payer or bank in charge of payment (hereinafter referred to as "paying banks") regarding the important purpose of the means of payment provided to the creditor in the curb market but not settled by the basic date. In this case, the paying bank that receives the report form of the means of payment must issue a certificate of completion of the report to the reporting enterprise.

4) The paying bank to which the report stipulated in the preceding paragraph has been made must refuse to pay the means of payment after explaining the reason for prohibiting repayment in accordance with the provisions in the preceding article.

5) The paying bank which has settled or paid in violation of the prescriptions of Paragraph 2 and the preceding paragraph shall be responsible for compensating the enterprise for the loss brought about by the settlement or the payment.

6) For the means of payment, the extinctive prescriptions shall not be completed during the period specified in Paragraph 2.

Article 15 (Report of Curb-Market Loans or Borrowings)

1) Creditors in the curb market and debtor enterprise must report lending and borrowing in the curb market by using the report form provided by the government to the chief of the tax office where they are obliged to pay their corporate taxes or the classified income taxes (hereinafter referred to as the "chief of the jurisdictional tax office") or to the head of the banking institution which is located in the same area as its jurisdictional tax office. In this case, the creditors in the curb market may report lending to the heads of banking institutions of the city, county (gun), Seoul Special City or Pusan City where they reside.

2) One who either acted for, arranged, or intermediated the loan transaction in the curb market (hereinafter referred to as "intermediator") must advise the creditor in the curb market who is the real owner of the money or the substitute (hereinafter referred to as "real owner of curb-

market fund") to report the curb-market loan in accordance with the prescription of the preceding paragraph. In cases where he is unable to notify the real owner of the money or the substitute, he himself must report the loan on behalf of the creditor in the curb market in accordance with the preceding paragraph.

3) Upon receipt of the report in accordance with the preceding Paragraphs 1 and 2, the chief of the jurisdictional tax office or the head of the banking institution shall issue to the reporter a certificate of completion of the report of the curb-market loan.

4) In case of Paragraphs 1 and 2, the head of banking institution must transmit those reports to the chief of the jurisdictional tax office immediately after the period stipulated in Article 16.

5) When the enterprise and the creditor in the curb market (including the intermediator) report the loan in accordance with Paragraphs 1 and 2, they are obliged to notify each other concerning the purport of the report immediately.

6) The scope of the offices of banking institutions that appear in Paragraph 1 shall be determined separately by the Minister of Finance.

Article 16 (Period of Report)

1) Reports defined in the preceding article should be made during the period from the enforcement date of the Decree until August 9, 1972, except that it is possible to make additional reports on the basis of special measures the Minister of Finance takes for those who are traveling abroad or are compelled not to report curb-market loans.

2) For curb-market loans, the extinctive prescription shall not be completed during the period prescribed in the preceding paragraph.

Article 17 (Scope and Method of Declaration)

1) The cumulative amount of the curb-market loans should be declared when contracts of curb-market loans have been made in installments or over several times.

2) The actual creditor in the curb market when the loan was given the enterprise should be declared through the executive members of the enterprise or through a third person.

3) The total amount of the curb-market loan should be declared when the creditor gave the enterprise partly under his own name and partly under a third person's name.

4) The report form for curb-market loans under the provisions of Paragraph 1 of Article 15 should include the names and addresses of creditors and enterprises, the contents of the curb-market loan, and the collateral value (including substitute goods and temporary registrations of ownership).

5) In case any law suit involving the curb-market loan is under deliberation as of the basic date, the court, the persons concerned, and the name and number of cases must be included.

6) The means of payment or other documentary evidence of the curb-market loan or debt in the curb market should be presented, a copy of the documents being attached to the declaration.

Article 18 (Exemption of Responsibility for Undeclared Loan)

An enterprise shall be exempted from the responsibility for the repayment of the curb-market borrowing and the mortgage rights shall become null and void if the creditor or the intermediator does not declare the loan according to preceding three paragraphs.

Article 19 (Adjustment of Curb-Market Loans)

1) Curb-market loans declared by the creditor according to Articles 15 and 17 shall be repaid in equal installments every 6 months for a period of 5 years after the 3-year grace period from the basic date of this Decree. The principal of the curb market loans defined by this Decree includes the principal and unpaid interest at the basic date (prepaid interest which is not due at the basic date shall be subtracted from the principal). This adjustment of loans between creditor and borrower (hereinafter referred to as "adjusted loan") shall be effective from the date of enforcement of this Decree.

2) In cases covered by the preceding paragraph, the interest shall be paid every month from the enforcement date of this Decree of complete redemption of the curb-market loans and the monthly interest rate shall be 1.35%. In case the arbitrated interest rate is less than 1.35% the arbitrated interest shall be paid.

3) Of the loans declared by the creditor in the curb market under the provisions of Articles 15 through 17, certain loans as determined by presidential ordinance can be treated differentially from the provisions of the preceding Paragraph 2.

4) The interest rate mentioned in Paragraph 2 above shall be subject to change by presidential ordinance when policies on the official and other interest rates are changed.

Article 20 (Delivery of Adjusted Loan Certificates)

1) Enterprises shall have the obligation to draw up and deliver to the creditor in the curb market without delay adjusted loan certificates after expiration of the period specified in Article 16, which shall confirm the adjusted loans defined in the preceding article.

2) Enterprises, subject to the provision of the preceding paragraph, shall

submit a report on delivery of adjusted loan certificates to the chief of the tax office concerned within 7 days after delivery of the certificates. In such a case, the details of the adjusted loans shall be registered on the adjusted-loan ledger by the chief of the tax office concerned.

3) Concerning equal repayment of principal of the adjusted private loan as described in the preceding article, upon request of the creditor the enterprise shall issue a promissory note. However, the note is limited to installment payments for one year or less.

Article 21 (Arbitration)

1) In case any dispute arises with regard to the drawing up or delivery of adjusted loan certificates, as prescribed in Paragraph 1 of the preceding article, the creditor or enterprise may request arbitration to the provincial chief of the National Tax Office through the chief of the jurisdictional tax office concerned.

2) The provincial chief of the National Tax Office shall notify the private creditor, the enterprise, and the chief of tax office concerned of the result of the deliberation within 30 days after the receipt of the arbitration application under the provisions of the preceding paragraph.

Article 22 (Conversion of Loans to Shares)

1) In case creditor of the adjusted loan defined in Article 19 is a major shareholder of the enterprise, all the adjusted loan shall be converted to shares of the enterprise (omitting fractions in converting) within 90 days from the effective date of this Decree. The term "major shareholder" in this article shall be a large stockholder as defined in Paragraph 2 of Article 15 of the National Tax Collection Law. However, the "as of the final date for uncollected national tax payment" referred to in the same paragraph of Article 15 shall be "as of the basic date."

2) Other than major shareholders as specified in the preceding paragraph, enterprises may convert part or all of the adjusted loan as defined in Article 19 into shares upon request of the creditor.

3) Provisions of Article 334 in The Commercial Code shall not be applicable to the preceding Paragraph 2.

Article 23 (Limitations on Repayments prior to Repayment Date)

1) Prior approval of the provincial chief of National Tax Office through the chief of the jurisdictional tax office concerned shall be required in the event that, in spite of the term benefits, an enterprise, due to improvement in its liquidity or for some other reason, is willing to repay the adjusted loan defined in Article 19 prior to the repayment date.

2) In permitting such repayments, the provincial chief of the National Tax Office should confer with the debtor's major correspondent bank.

3) In case of repayment without the approval specified in Paragraph 2 above, the bank shall terminate financial support to the enterprise.

Article 24 (Forfeiture of Term Benefits)

1) In case an enterprise does not or can not repay two or more equal installments of the principal of the adjusted loans as specified in Article 19, the creditor in the curb market can cause the enterprise to forfeit the benefits pertaining to the term of the adjusted loan.

2) Except for such forfeiture of benefits as stipulated in the preceding paragraph, adjusted loans shall not be counted as liabilities upon requesting bankruptcy by the enterprise.

Article 25 (Special Tax Measures)

1) All creditors and debtor enterprises who have reported curb-market loans under Articles 15 through 17 shall be exempted from all related tax payments (excluding tax at the source) not paid by the date of report and inquiries into sources of funds, except to confirm the report submitted in accordance with the provisions of Paragraph 2 of Article 20, shall also be stopped.

2) The adjusted-loans certificates and promissory notes drawn up in accordance with Paragraphs 1 and 3 of Article 20 shall be exempted from stamp taxes.

3) Corporate enterprises shall be exempted from registration tax, in case the adjusted loans specified in Article 19 are converted to shares as prescribed in Article 22.

4) In case a creditor who is a major shareholder of the corporate enterprise does not convert his adjusted loan to shares within the period specified in Paragraph 1 of Article 22, interest payments on the loans accruing from the date after the period has ended shall not be counted as operating expenses in calculating the taxable income.

5) In the event an enterprise which is an open company according to the Corporate Tax Law does not newly meet the requirements of an open company as provided in Article 22, Paragraph 3 of the Corporate Tax Law due to the conversion of loans to shares, the enterprise shall be regarded as an open company from the date ending the period mentioned in Paragraph 1, Article 22 to the end of the business year.

6) If it is proved that, in the declarations or reports specified in Articles 15 through 17 and Paragraph 2 of Article 20, the curb-market loan has been divided or spread or has been falsely made in order to evade taxes, the

provisions of Paragraphs 1 through 3 and the preceding paragraph shall not apply.

7) In case the means of payment has cleared because of an enterprise's failure to submit a report in accordance with Paragraph 3 of Article 14 and an enterprise has paid the curb-market loan of which the enterprise has been exempted from the responsibility for repayment in accordance with the provisions of Article 18, the cleared amount or repaid amount shall be regarded as a gift, and a tax rate of 65% shall be applied. In these cases, the provisions of Paragraph 2 of Article 29–2 of the Inheritance Tax Law shall apply and the cleared or repaid amount can not be treated as operating expenses in calculating, the taxable income.

8) Interest payments on the adjusted loans in excess of the rate fixed in Article 19 shall not be considered as operating expenses in calculating the taxable income.

Article 26 (Special Provisions for Liquidating Businesses and Others)

1) Provisions of this chapter shall not be applied to the curb-market loans of these enterprises in the process of liquidation, bankruptcy, or consolidation as of the basic date.

2) When having made or approved the consolidation plan of an enterprise (excluding the plan for liquidation) according to the provisions of the Business Consolidation Law, the curb-market loan earmarked as claims or collateral for consolidation shall not be adjusted unfavorably to the enterprise, compared with the adjusted loan of the enterprise prescribed in Article 19. However, Paragraph 1 of Article 22 shall be applied there to with appropriate modifications.

3) In case an interest group cannot obtain the consent of those having more than the prescribed number or amount of voting rights, in the meeting of the persons concerned, in the consolidation plans referred to in the preceding paragraph, the court shall be able to confer approvals or to modify the consolidation plan according to the prescription of Article 19. In this case, Article 234 of the Business Consolidation Law shall not be applied.

4) When the consolidaton plan of Paragraph 2 of this article is approved or when the plan is approved according to the prescription of the preceding paragraph, the preceding article shall be applied to the curb market loans modified according to the provisions of Paragraph 2 as well as to the consolidation plan that is approved by the preceding paragraph of this article.

Article 27 (Guarantee of Secrecy)

1) Civil servants and bank officials (hereinafter referred to as "atten-

dants") who deal with the declaration sheets of curb-market loans and take charge of arbitration and other settlements of curb-market loans shall neither offer nor disclose to other persons the facts and data they obtain on duty about the curb-market loans declared or reported according to the prescriptions of Articles 15 through 17 or Paragraph 2 or Article 20. However, this paragraph shall not be applied to cases of disclosing facts for the execution of duty.

2) Except for cases when the courts issue the orders for their presentation, when the judges issue writs on them, or when the competent authorities request them by documents for tax collections, no one shall be able to ask the attendants to present information on the curb-market loans prescribed in the preceding paragraph.

3) Attendants shall be able to reject any inquiries and requests with proper explanations, except for those prescribed in the preceding paragraph.

Article 28 (Inquiry and Inspection)

1) Civil servants who deal with the declaration sheets of curb-market loans and take charge of arbitration and other settlements of curb-market loans (hereinafter referred to as "officials") shall be able to inquire of business enterprises, creditors in the curb market, and others concerned, and to inspect pertinent ledgers, documents, and other records, when deemed necessary to perform their duties.

2) Officials shall be able to ask for the presentation of the materials necessary for inspection as noted in the preceding paragraph and to take into custody the materials presented.

3) Officials shall be able to exercise the authority prescribed in other laws and decrees on taxation, in addition to those prescribed in the preceding two paragraphs, in connection with performing their duties specified in Paragraph 1 of this article.

4) Article 39 of the Tax Collection Law shall be applied, with appropriate modifications, to those cases prescribed in the preceding three paragraphs.

Article 29 (Enforcement)

1) Questions, if any, on the possible range of curb-market loans, on the procedures, including the declaration of curb-market loans, in connection with the execution of this chapter shall be settled by the decision of the Minister of Finance.

2) Forms of documents necessary to enforcing the regulations of this chapter shall be prescribed elsewhere by the Minister of Finance.

Article 30 (Punishments)

1) Any person who compels an enterprise, with violence, threats, conspiracy, or influential power, to repay adjusted loans as prescribed in Article 19 before their expiry dates or to pay the interest at a rate above the level specified in the same article shall be punished by penal servitude for not less than one year but not exceeding 10 years or by a fine of not less than 3 million wŏn but not exceeding 10 million wŏn.

2) Any person falling under one of the following items shall be punished by penal servitude for not less than 1 year but not exceeding 10 years or by a fine of not less than 1 million wŏn but not exceeding 10 million wŏn. However, any person committing an action of the following first or second items concerning the amount of curb-market loans shall be punished by both penal servitude and a fine.

a) A person who makes a false declaration in connection with the declarations prescribed in Paragraphs 1 and 2 of Article 15 and Paragraphs 1 through 3 of Article 17, or a false report in connection with the reports specified in the provisions of Paragraph 2 of Article 20.

b) A person who provokes or forces other persons to make false declarations or reports in connection with the declarations or reports specified in the preceding item.

c) A person who hinders other persons with violence, threat, conspiracy, or influential power, from making the declarations of reports under the provisions of Paragraphs 1 and 2 of Article 15, Paragraphs 1 through 3 of Article 17 and Paragraph 2 of Article 20.

3) Any person falling under one of the following items shall be punished by penal servitude not exceeding 10 years or by disqualification not exceeding 10 years.

a) A person who violates the provisions of Paragraph 1 of Article 17.

b) An attendant who receives, demands, or promises to receive a bribe in connection with his duties under the provision of this chapter.

c) An attendant who impairs, through forgery, destruction, concealment, or other methods, the effectiveness of the means of payments or documents which have been reported and declared under the provisions of this chapter.

4) Any person falling under one of the following items shall be punished by penal servitude not exceeding 5 years or by a fine of not less than the amount but not exceeding twice the amount of the curb-market loans or the means of payments to be reported, declared, or which have been nullified.

a) A person who violates the provisions of Paragraph 1 of Article 13.

b) A person who neglects to make the declaration or report under the provisions of Paragraph 3 of Article 14, Paragraph 1 of Article 15, Paragraphs 1 through 3 of Article 17, and Paragraph 2 of Article 20.

5) Any person who makes payment in violation of the provisions of Paragraph 4 of Article 14 or makes repayments in violation of the provisions of Paragraph 1 of Article 23 shall be punished by penal servitude not exceeding 3 years or by a fine of not less than half of the amount but not exceeding the amount of the repayment.

6) Any intermediator who violates the provisions of Paragraph 2 of Article 15 shall be punished by penal servitude not exceeding 2 years or by a fine not exceeding 2 million wŏn.

7) When the representative of a juridical person or an agent an employee or a hired person of a juridical or a natural person commits any of violation enumerated in the preceding six paragraphs in performing proper business on behalf of a corresponding juridical person or natural person, not only the violator shall be punished but also the juridical or the natural person shall be punished by the pertinent fines specified in the previous corresponding items.

8) In applying the provisions of this article, when the behavior also constitutes a crime under the provisions of other laws than this article, the heaviest punishment among them shall be applied.

9) Of the means of payment declared under the provisions of Paragraph 3 of Article 14, checks presented for payment after the enforcement date of this Decree shall be exempted from the provision of Paragraph 2 of Article 2 of the Illegal Cheques Control Act (including cases due to negligence).

Notes

ONE   *Theories of Financial Development and the Relevance of Korean Experience*

1. Edward S. Shaw, *Financial Deepening in Economic Development* (New York, 1973), p. 7.

2. A. I. Bloomfield, "Central Banking in Underdeveloped Countries," *Journal of Finance* (May 1957); S. Boskey, *Problems and Practices of Development Banks* (Baltimore, 1959); L. V. Chandler, *Central Banking and Economic Development* (Bombay, 1962); W. Diamond, *Development Banks* (Baltimore, 1957); Diamond, *Development Finance Companies* (Baltimore, 1968); J. Marquez, "Financial Institutions and Economic Development," in H. S. Ellis, ed., *Economic Development for Latin America* (New York, 1961); R. S. Sayers, "Central Banking in Under-Developed Countries," in *Central Banking after Bagehot* (London, 1957); S. N. Sen, *Central Banking in Under-Developed Money Markets*, 3rd ed. (Calcutta, 1961).

3. Raymond W. Goldsmith, *Financial Structure and Development* (New Haven, 1969); John G. Gurley, "Financial Structure in Developing Countries," in D. Krivine, ed., *Fiscal and Monetary Problems in Developing States* (New York, 1967).

4. Raymond W. Goldsmith, *Financial Institutions* (New York, 1968); Rondo Cameron with the collaboration of O. Crisp, H. T. Patrick, and R. Tilly, *Banking in the Early Stages of Development: A Study in Comparative Economic History* (New York, 1967) Chapter I, Introduction, pp. 1–14; *Banking and Economic Development: Some Lessons of History*, ed. R. Cameron (New York, 1972), Chapter I, Introduction, pp. 3–25. Some of the more interesting individual country case studies are: R. L. Bennett, *The Financial Sector and Economic Development: The Mexican Case* (Baltimore, 1965, 1966); P. J. Drake, *Financial Development in Malaya and Singapore* (Canberra, 1969); D. D. Psilos, *Capital Market in Greece* (Athens, 1964).

5. Raymond Firth and B. S. Yamey, eds., *Capital, Saving and Credit in Peasant Societies* (Chicago, 1964), give many examples of primitive financial systems from different parts of the world.

6. John G. Gurley and Edward S. Shaw, *Money in a Theory of Finance* (Washington, 1960).

7. See J. O. Light and William L. White, *The Financial System* (New York, 1979), Chapter 10, for a discussion of risk.

8. W. T. Newlyn, *The Financing of Economic Development* (London, 1977), Chapter 2.

9. Shaw, *Financial Deepening,* p. 118.

10. Newlyn; and David C. Cole, "Concepts, Causes and Cures of Instability in Less Developed Countries," in Ronald McKinnon, ed., *Money and Finance in Economic Growth and Development* (New York, 1976).

11. See William R. Cline and Sidney Weintraub, eds., *Economic Stablization in Developing Countries* (Washington, 1981).

12. Shaw, *Financial Deepening;* Ronald McKinnon, "Money, Growth, and the Propensity to Save: An Iconoclastic View" (Stanford University Research Center in Economic Growth, 1973); McKinnon, ed., *Money and Finance;* A. D. Chandavarkar, "Some Aspects of Interest Rate Policies in Less Developed Economies: The Experience of Selected Asian Countries," *International Monetary Fund Staff Papers* (March 1971).

13. Homer Jones, "Korean Financial Problems" (U.S. Operations Mission to Korea, June 1968); J. G. Williamson, "Why do Koreans Save 'So Little'?" *Journal of Development Economics,* 6 (1979).

14. A. I. Bloomfield and J. P. Jensen, *Banking Reform in South Korea* (New York, 1951).

15. Gilbert T. Brown, *Korean Pricing Policies and Economic Development in the 1960s* (Baltimore, 1973).

16. U Tun Wai, "Interest Rates in the Organized Money Markets of Underdeveloped Countries," *International Monetary Fund Staff Papers* 5.2:249–250, 252–253, 255, 258, 276–278 (August 1956); "Interest Rates Outside the Organized Money Markets of Underdeveloped Countries, *International Monetary Fund Staff Papers* 6.1: 80–83, 107–109, 119–125 (November 1957).

17. See Chapter 4. See also Chang-Nyol Lee, *Mobilization of Domestic Capital* (Seoul, 1965).

18. Brown, *Korean Pricing Policies;* Shaw, *Financial Deepening;* McKinnon, "Money, Growth, and the Propensity to Save."

19. Jones, "Korean Financial Problems."

20. Bloomfield and Jensen; and Bloomfield, "Monetary and Financial Development in Korea" (mimeo, 1952); Jones, "Korean Financial Problems"; Shaw, *Financial Deepening;* McKinnon, "Savings Propensities and

the Korean Monetary Reform in Retrospect," in McKinnon, *Money and Finance.*

21. Bloomfield and Jensen; Bloomfield, "Monetary and Financial Development"; Bloomfield, "A Report on Monetary Policy and Banking in Korea" (submitted to the United Nations Command Economic Coordinator and to the Governor, Bank of Korea, 30 November 1956); Jones, "Korean Financial Problems"; Brown, *Korean Pricing Policies.*

22. Shaw, *Financial Deepening.*

23. Korea Development Finance Corporation, *Money and Capital Markets in Korea and the Potential for Their Improvement: A Proposal* (Seoul, September 1970).

24. P. Hasan and D. C. Rao, *Korea: Policy Issues for Long-Term Development* (Baltimore, 1979), Chapter 12.

25. Gurley and Shaw, *Money in a Theory of Finance.*

26. Gustav Ranis, "Economic Development and Financial Institutions," in Bela Balassa and Richard Nelson, eds., *Economic Progress, Private Values and Public Policy: Essays in Honor of William Fellner* (Amsterdam, 1977).

TWO   *The Financial System: Size, Structure, and Patterns of Intermediation*

1. Kwang Suk Kim and Michael Roemer, *Growth and Structural Transformation* (Cambridge, Mass., 1979).

2. Goldsmith, *Financial Structure,* pp. 490–494.

3. Gurley, "Financial Structure."

4. Sang-Chul Suh, *Growth and Structural Changes in the Korean Economy, 1910–1940* (Cambridge, Mass., 1978).

5. Goldsmith, *Financial Structure,* p. 209.

6. Gurley, "Financial Structure."

THREE   *Korea's Regulated Financial Institutions*

1. James B. Palais, *Politics and Policy in Traditional Korea* (Cambridge, Mass., 1975).

2. Ibid., p. 99.

3. Ibid., pp. 171–172.

4. Ibid., p. 172.

5. Ibid., pp. 174–175.

6. Karl Moskowitz, "Current Assets: The Employees of Japanese Banks in Colonial Korea" (PhD dissertation, Harvard University, 1979).

7. C. D. Campbell and C. S. Ahn, "Kyes and Mujins—Financial Intermediaries in South Korea," *Economic Development and Cultural Change* (October 1962), pp. 56–68.

8. Moskowitz, "Current Assets." The KDB was something of an exception.

9. Bloomfield and Jensen, *Banking Reform.*

10. Ibid., pp. 63–64.

11. Moskowitz, "Current Assets."

12. Bloomfield and Jensen, *Banking Reform,* p. 66.

13. Ibid., p. 73.

14. Ministry of Finance, *Uri nara kŭmyung chedo mit chŏngch'aek kaegwan* (August 1966), p. 31.

15. See Chapter 6.

16. Ministry of Finance, *Uri nara kŭmyung,* p. 33.

17. B. K. Kim, *Central Banking Experiment in a Developing Economy: Case Study of Korea,* The Korean Study Series (Seoul, 1965), 12, 66.

18. See below, pp. 60–61.

19. See B. K. Kim for a detailed description of this struggle.

20. Ibid., p. 45.

21. Ibid., p. 46.

22. David C. Cole and Princeton N. Lyman, *Korean Development: The Interplay of Politics and Economics* (Cambridge, Mass., 1971), Chapter 4.

23. As pointed out in Chapter 8, it is difficult to say to what extent this reflected an increase in real savings vs. a rearrangement of asset holdings, including a shift from claims on the unorganized money markets to claims on the banks.

24. BOK, *Financial System in Korea* (1974), p. 63.

25. Jones, "Korean Financial Problems."

26. BOK, *Financial System in Korea* (1978), pp. 23–25.

27. BOK, *Financial System* (1974).

28. It was rumored at the time that Kim Chong-p'il and other political leaders had used this stock-market manipulation to raise money for the Democratic Republican Party and the forthcoming presidential election in which Park Chung Hee was elected to his first term.

29. For the evidence on the underpricing of new equity issues, see Il SaKong, "An Overview of Corporate Finance and the Long-term Securities Market," in *Planning Model and Macroeconomic Policy Issues,* Essays on the Korean Economy, Vol. 1, ed., K. C. Kim (Seoul, 1977), pp. 228–264.

30. Until 1967, personal income taxes were levied differently according to the classification of the source of income. The 7 years from 1968 to 1974 were a transitional period during which this classified income tax

system coexisted with a newly introduced global income tax. The global income tax, however, was applied only to those persons whose income from any of the classified sources exceeded a specified amount, and thus it accounted for only a minor portion of total personal income taxes. After 1975, the classified income tax system was largely eliminated and replaced by a global income tax.

FOUR   *The Unregulated Financial Institutions and Markets*

1. See U Tun Wai, "Interest Rates Outside the Organized Money Markets."

2. This, however, does not necessarily mean that the UFM is completely immune from the policy actions of the monetary authority.

3. Moneylenders include pawnshop owners. At the end of 1971, there were 940 pawnshops with total outstanding loans of 386 million wŏn. See Yi Yun-sŏk, "Sŏmin kŭmyung ŭi silche wa tayanghwa," *Kŭmyung* (November 1972), p. 23.

4. C. Geertz, "The Rotating Credit Association: A 'Middle Rung' in Development," *Economic Development and Cultural Change* (April 1962), pp. 241–263.

5. Ibid., p. 242.

6. Campbell and Ahn, "Kyes and Mujins; K. C. Oh, "The Economics of Kye: An Informal Association of Individuals for Savings and Loans" (PhD dissertation, Vanderbilt University, 1972).

7. K. C. Oh, Chapter 3.

8. Campbell and Ahn, p. 55.

9. Chung-Nyol Lee, *Mobilization of Domestic Capital*, Chapter 3.

10. K. C. Oh, Chapter 3.

11. Ibid., Chapter 4.

12. BOK, *Survey of the Savings Behavior*, 1967, 1969, 1971, 1973, and 1976 editions. The 1973 survey shows that about 50% of the 6,142 sample households were members of the *kye*. That percentage declined to 35% in the 1976 survey, however.

13. Before the establishment of the IFCs in 1972, there were no open markets where business firms could sell their promissory notes and other commercial papers within the RFM.

14. Commercial bills eligible for rediscount are not commercial papers (either industrial or finance papers). They are real bills, similar to bankers' acceptances.

15. KDFC, *Money and Capital Markets*, p. 11.

16. The monthly interest rate on 30-day notes issued and resold by these companies is currently 1.725%. See BOK, *Monthly Economic Statistics* (February 1979).

17. According to a newspaper article, this type of operation has become more widespread in recent periods of tight monetary policy; *Dong-A Ilbo* (daily newspaper), Seoul (March 14, 1979).

18. "The Curb Market, Its Mechanics of Transactions," *Chosŏn Ilbo,* (daily newspaper), Seoul (July 20, 1971).

19. A newspaper article from 1971 indicates that they were powerful enough to ruin large business firms, and had, in fact, done so on several occasions, by cutting off the supply of credit or by downgrading their credit worthiness; ibid.

20. Ibid. The branch manager would normally receive a commission for this arrangement, but one must point out that he was not likely to have been so much attracted by the pecuniary return as the subsequent increase in deposits at his branch. Most branch managers were, in fact, drawn into these transactions as a means of expanding their deposits and meeting the deposit quotas or targets often assigned to them.

21. Certified checks are the major instrument of credit transaction in this market.

22. There is an indication that several of the nation's largest conglomerates and wholesale traders were actively involved in this market both as borrowers and lenders up to the mid-1960s. Some of the foreign loans were also diverted into this market. Ibid., and also "Structure of the Curb Market," *Chosŏn Ilbo,* March 12, 1968.

23. *Chosŏn Ilbo,* March 24, 1979.

24. *Dong-A Ilbo,* March 13, 1979.

25. *Dong-A Ilbo,* April 12, 1979.

26. There were in fact two types of *mujin.* The first were *mujin* in the narrow sense, where a number of accounts were organized into a group contract and the precedence in loans was determined by auction. This business was mostly handled by the *mujin* companies and some of the PFs. The second was mutual installment contract or pseudo *mujin,* where no group contracts were organized and loans were not dependent upon chance factors. Account-holders who had paid installments for a certain period could borrow the money, or might have the use of it whenever they wanted. This was the major business of the PFs.

27. On the basis of this ordinance, the Ministry of Finance could and, in fact, did regulate their financial activities until 1961. *Mujin* were declared illegal with the enactment of the Citizens' National Bank Act in 1961, but, because the government did not enforce the law vigorously, they could be established under the commercial code and grew rapidly. See below, pp. 123–125.

28. Central Federation of Fisheries Cooperatives, *Report on Fishing Household Credit Survey* (August, 1975), pp. 45, 63.

29. Bureau of Finance, Ministry of Finance, *Sŏmin kŭmyung mit mujin hyŏnhwang*, Finance Research Report No. 10 (June 1972). This report will henceforth be referred to as *MOF Report*.

30. In a typical group contract that consists of 25 members with a lump-sum *mujin* remuneration of 100,000 wŏn, each member contributes a monthly deposit of 4,400 wŏn prior to receiving the *mujin* loan, thereby pooling a lump sum fund of 110,000 wŏn. Out of this sum, only 100,000 wŏn or less is paid out to the winning member each month, and the remainder is distributed among other members as interest payments. After receiving the *mujin* remuneration, each member contributes 5,900 wŏn up to the 14th month, 5,800 wŏn up to the 21st month, and 5,700 wŏn thereafter. The first-position winner will therefore pay, in addition to his monthly installment deposits, 34,500 wŏn altogether during the contract period. The difference between the fixed monthly contribution (4,400 wŏn) and the installment deposit after receiving the *mujin* loan accrues to the *mujin* company as the organizing and administration fees. In our example, the total of such fees amounts to 419,500 wŏn at the expiration of the group contract. This means that the *mujin* can earn 16,780 wŏn per month (or 17% of the *mujin* loan) by organizing a single 25-member *mujin* contract.

The rate of interest on *mujin* loans, assuming that each member receives 100,000 wŏn, was relatively low as compared with the interest rates in the UFM in 1971. In a typical contract with 25 members, the loan rate was 28.4% per annum up to the 12th winning positions, 27.2% from the 13th to 22nd positions, and 26% thereafter. The interest rate on installment deposits was much higher; the 24th position winner could earn 30% per annum on his installments; the last position, 42%. Often the first-position winner reloaned his *mujin* remuneration to the company at the interest rate of 3.5% to 4% per month. In this case the rate of return on his savings would rise to 80% per annum. See BOK, *Mujin ŭi hŏnhwang kwa munje chŏm* (Seoul, 1972), pp. 26–29.

31. Bank of Japan, Economic Research Dept., *Money and Banking in Japan,* trans. S. Nishimura, ed. L. S. Pressnell (New York, 1973), p. 21.

32. Ibid.

33. Campbell and Ahn, p. 65.

34. Ibid.

35. BOK, *Flow of Funds Accounts in Korea,* 1963–1977 (1978).

36. J. G. Gurley, H. T. Patrick, and E. S. Shaw, "The Financial Structure of Korea" (United States Operations Mission to Korea, July 1965), p. 81.

37. Sogang University Research Institute for Economics and Business,

"Study of Money Market and Industrial Investment Financing in Korea" (mimeo, November 1970), pp. 46–52.

38. B. K. Shim et al., *A Study of Preferential Interest Rate Structure– The Korean Experience, 1963–1971* (October 1972), pp. 95–97.

39. W. S. Choi and H. J. Paik, "Sach'ae sijang ŭi naemak," *Chungang wŏlgan* (December 1972), pp. 226–239.

40. Y. C. Park, *The Unorganized Financial Sector in Korea, 1945–75*, Studies in Domestic Finance No. 28, Public and Private Finance Division, IBRD (November 1976), Chapter 4.

FIVE   *Interactions of the Regulated and Unregulated Financial Markets*

1. Shaw, *Financial Deepening*, p. 92.

2. Palais, Chapter 7.

3. Bloomfield, "A Report on Monetary Policy."

4. Ibid.

5. See, for example, W. Arthur Lewis, *The Theory of Economic Growth* (Homewood, 1955).

6. Foreign credit has been an important source of business financing. However, since the payment of the principal and interest of foreign loans is guaranteed by commercial banks, there is no point in differentiating this source of credit from the domestic banking source.

7. Wontack Hong, *Trade, Distortions, and Employment Growth in Korea* (Seoul, 1979), pp. 188–189; B. K. Shim et al., *Preferential Interest Rate Structure*, p. 28; see Table 30, pp. 131–132.

8. It should be pointed out that the distinction between short-term and long-term commercial loans on the basis of maturity is less clear, both conceptually and practically, than the definition might indicate. Nor is the automatic renewal and roll-over feature of commercial loans unique to Korea. Even in advanced countries with sophisticated financial structures, commercial banks are in general reluctant to deny a request from a customer for an extension of a commercial loan beyond the original maturity. The denial of such a request from a financially sound firm would jeopardize the bank's customer relationships and, even in the case of potential bankruptcy, the large costs of collection also make it expeditious for the bank to extend the loan in hope of obtaining full payment in future. D. M. Jaffee, *Credit Rationing and the Commercial Loan Market* (New York, 1971), p. 3. What we are emphasizing here is that the automatic loan renewal tendency has been more conspicuous in Korea because of the gov-

ernment development strategy and the institutional characteristics of the financial system, as will be explained below, in Chapter 6.

9. One possible reason for the lack of the demand for term loans is the relative high cost of credit associated with the installment payment, but the major reason seems to be the inexperience of businesses in the cash-flow management in Korea.

10. Bloomfield, "Monetary and Financial Development."

11. BOK, *Financial System in Korea* (1974), p. 81.

12. BOK, *Ilban ŭnhaeng ŭi kyŏngyŏng kaesŏn ŭi wihan kaepyŏn pangan* (1970), p. 9.

13. H. Myint, *Economic Theory and the Underdeveloped Countries* (London, 1971), p. 328. For the vital role of working capital as an input into productive process, see R. I. McKinnon, *Money and Capital in Economic Development* (Washington, 1973), pp. 80–88.

14. See McKinnon, *Money and Capital,* pp. 105–111; Shaw, *Financial Deepening,* pp. 135–138; Brown, *Korean Pricing Policies,* pp. 197–205.

15. Jaffee, *Credit Rationing* pp. 124–125.

16. The financing of net trade credit and net liquid assets other than inventories is, for the moment, ignored.

17. It is certainly possible that firms rationed by commercial banks may also be rationed in their attempt to obtain UFM financing. This possibility is, for the moment, ignored.

18. For the derivations, see Jaffee, Chapter 5.

19. For the theories and empirical studies of fixed inventory investment behavior, see M. K. Evans, *Macroeconomic Activity: Theory, Forecasting, and Control* (New York, 1969), Chapters 4 and 8.

20. Most of the empirical studies show no significant relationships between inventory investment and the cost and availability of funds. As Evans points out, there are several theoretical reasons for this. A large percentage of the total cost of fixed business investment represents interest payments; this is never true for inventories. The internal risk factor on fixed investment is virtually absent for inventory investment, because firms are not committed to any long-term debt service. There is more of a short-term technical relationship between inventories and sales than between fixed investment and production. See Evans, pp. 213–214.

21. In the United States, it is shown empirically that inventory investment and trade credit are the main determinants of the demand for short-term commercial loans, and fixed capital investment may also be financed by commercial loans, but only in the short run when commercial banks are buffering the adjustment of long-term liabilities. See Jaffee, p. 145. It should be noted that, even in a competitive financial environment, firms

do divide their financing between different financial markets on the basis of the nature of the assets. Such a division would be more pronounced when borrowers of commercial loans are subsidized and rationed, as in Korea.

22. The issue concerning the firms' financing behavior in the UFM can only be resolved through empirical examination. Because of the absence of reliable data, we can present only indirect evidence supporting our view. The surveys by the BOK, Chamber of Commerce, Medium Industry Bank, and the Federation of Korean Industries suggest that business firms enter the UFM primarily to acquire short-term working capital.

23. Throughout the analysis, rigid prices will be assumed.

24. Firms may now channel some of their funds made available due to the inventory decumulation into financing fixed capital investment. Investment demand is then further increased, causing more unintended inventory decumulation, which allows more of funds for fixed investment, and so on. The initial relaxation of rationing will have a multiplied effect on fixed capital investment. This is the central notion of Tucker's credit contraction multiplier; D. P. Tucker, "Credit Rationing, Interest Lags, and Monetary Speed Lag." *Quarterly Journal of Economics,* (February 1968), p. 78. In the Korean context, such a transmission process of credit rationing is not likely, as firms finance only a small percentage of their fixed capital through the UFM.

25. S. Kanesa-Thason, "Stabilizing an Economy: The Korean Experience," in I. Adelman, ed., *Practical Approaches to Development Planning: Korea's Second Five-Year Plan* (Baltimore, 1969), p. 266.

26. BOK, *Report on the Results of the August 3, 1972 Presidential Emergency Decree* (August 1973), pp. 19–21.

27. Choi and Paik, pp. 226–239.

28. BOK, *Financial Statement Analysis, 1975* (August 1976).

29. R. J. Bhatia and D. R. Khatkhate, "Financial Intermediation, Saving Mobilization and Entrepreneurial Development: The African Experience," *IMF Staff Papers* (March 1975).

SIX   *Policies to Influence Resource Allocation*

1. Shaw, *Financial Deepening.*
2. McKinnon, *Money and Capital.*
3. Wontack Hong, *Trade, Distortions, and Employment*, pp. 110–145.
4. Ibid., pp. 168–169.
5. Ibid., p. 169.
6. There are numerous unsubstantiated but widely believed reports of

credit diversion by the financial institutions. In the 1960s, one could qualify himself as a poultry farmer and for a preferential loan at NACF if he raised more than 11 chickens. No one seems to be able to explain why the NACF set the minimum at 11 chickens, but the minimum would have no doubt allowed for an enormous range of poultry farmers to choose from.

7. Hong, *Trade, Distortions, and Employment,* Tables 7.23 and 7.24, pp. 202–203.

8. Wontack Hong, *Factor Supply and Factor Intensity of Trade in Korea* (Seoul, 1976), pp. 18–35.

9. Ibid., pp. 230–243.

10. Interest-rate subsidies on export credits amounted to 2–3% per dollar exported between 1970–1978; see Chong Hyun Nam, "Trade and Industrial Policies and the Structure of Protection in Korea," in Wontack Hong and Lawrence B. Krause, eds., *Trade and Growth of the Advanced Developing Countries in the Pacific Basin* (Seoul, 1981), p. 194. Wontack Hong, in *Trade, Distortions, and Employment,* p. 278, uses the real rate of return to capital in his estimates of interest-rate subsidies, whereas Nam uses the curb-market interest rates. As a result, Hong's estimates are higher by a couple of percentage points.

SEVEN *Policies to Influence Resource Mobilization: The Monetary Reform of 1965*

1. On average, however, the bank lending rates were lower than deposit rates, and the negative margin incurred by lending operations was supported by the BOK.

2. McKinnon, *Money and Capital,* Chapter 8.

3. Chang-Nyol Lee, *Mobilization of Domestic Capital,* pp. 16–17.

4. Gurley, Patrick, and Shaw, "Financial Structure of Korea."

5. R. I. McKinnon, "Money, Growth, and the Propensity to Save: An Iconoclastic View."

6. N. H. Leff and K. Sato, "A Simultaneous-Equations Model of Savings in Developing Countries," *Journal of Political Economy* (December 1975).

7. McKinnon, *Money and Capital,* Chapters 6 and 7, and "Money, Growth, and the Propensity to Save," pp. 487–502. See also Shaw, *Financial Deepening,* Chapter 3.

8. For the economic rationale for the complementarity between the two assets, see McKinnon, *Money and Capital,* Chapter 6. The nominal rate of return on money is approximated by the average nominal interest rate on deposit and currency, set and controlled by the government

authorities. The real assets are a composite of such diverse assets as capital goods, precious metals, inventories, consumer durables, and even livestock and foodstuffs. The real rate of return on these assets cannot be easily defined, but is assumed to be non-negative in real terms.

9. This existence of the UFM may not upset the complementarity between money and capital. Our point is that UFM securities are substitutes for both money and capital.

10. McKinnon concedes that the direct impact of higher interest rates on savings is subject to an ambiguous income effect that makes it unclear theoretically as to whether current saving would actually increase. However, the experiences of Taiwan, Korea, and Japan, he argues, strongly suggest that the stock of money can be expected to increase when the rate of return on it rises. See "Money, Growth and Propensity to Save." Our point is that the increase in desired stock of money, to the extent that it is at the expense of other assets, such as the UFM securities, does not imply that real savings will increase by the same amount.

11. McKinnon points out that this relationship is likely to be significant when monetization in the form of owned cash balances is limited as when the real return to holders of money is negative. Once, however, the real return on money is raised to the best marginal and intramarginal returns to be earned on other assets, the substitution effect becomes dominant. See *Money and Capital*, p. 61.

12. B. K. Min, "Financial Reconstruction in Korea, 1965–74" (PhD dissertation, University of Hawaii, 1976), Chapter 2; Maxwell J. Fry, "Money and Capital or Financial Deepening in Economic Development?" *Journal of Money, Credit and Banking* 10.4:464–475 (November 1978).

13. See Shaw, *Financial Deepening*.

14. M. J. Bailey, *National Income and the Price Level* (2nd ed., New York, 1971); R. Mundell, *Monetary Theory* (Pacific Palisades, 1971); Stanley Fischer, "Money and Production Function," *Economic Inquiry* (December 1974).

15. E. M. Claassen, "On the Indirect Productivity of Money," *Journal of Political Economy* (April 1975), pp. 431–436.

16. A. Sinai and H. H. Stokes, "Real Money Balances: An Omitted Variable from the Production Function," *Review of Economics and Statistics* (August 1972), pp. 290–296.

EIGHT *Price-Stabilization Problems and Policies*

1. Palais, Chapter 7.
2. Sang-Chul Suh; Kim and Roemer.

3. Bloomfield and Jensen, p. 33.

4. Ibid., p. 32.

5. Bloomfield and Jensen discuss the matter as follows: "Inasmuch as the budget deficit (and the net expansion in bank loans) ran well ahead of current collections from the sales of ECA supplies, with the result that those collections were already, in effect, being fully utilized, and in view of the grave inflationary situation, the United States refused to permit any formal withdrawals from the Counterpart Fund (or the 'collections account'). Since, however, the Korean Government was able without difficulty to finance its budget deficits by borrowing from the Bank of Chosun, it did not press for any such withdrawals; in fact, it apparently preferred to finance its deficit in that way since the consent of the United States was not required. In May 1950, however, authorization was finally given by the United States for the release of a small sum (9.8 billion wŏn) from the Counterpart Fund to finance necessary maintenance work and construction projects in process, and to initiate preparatory work on specific recovery projects." Ibid., p. 37.

6. Ibid., p. 35.

7. Ibid., p. 37.

8. The Pusan retail price index is used as an indicator of price movements from 1950 to 1953, because Seoul was occupied by the Communists in the 3rd quarter of 1950 and 1st quarter of 1951. The capital was moved to Pusan, and entry into Seoul was restricted through 1952.

9. For a description of the disagreements between the U.S. and Korean governments over the issue of wŏn advanced to the UN forces, see Gene M. Lyons, *Military Policy and Economic Aid, the Korean Case, 1950–1953* (Columbus, 1961), pp. 88ff.

10. The U.S. government introduced the MPCs in both Korea and Japan after World War II as a means of controlling the flow of U.S. currency into these countries and possibly on into the Communist countries. The MPCs were converted several times into new issues to discourage the demand for them as financial assets. Nevertheless, both Koreans and Japanese held large amounts of MPCs, which traded at a discount relative to U.S. dollars because of risk of conversion. See C. R. Frank, K. S. Kim, and L. Westphal, *Foreign Trade Regimes and Economic Development: South Korea* (New York, 1975), pp. 32–33, for a table of effective exchange rates from 1945 to 1970. The official rate of exchange between local currency and MPCs was consistently below the free-market rate, so most military personnel used the MPCs directly for local expenditures.

11. B. K. Kim, pp. 34–40.

12. Ranis.

13. There have been numerous studies of the Korean post-war inflation,

such as B. K. Kim, *Central Banking Experiment,* Clark Joel, "Korea: A Case Study in Inflation (PhD dissertation, University of Wisconsin, 1961), and Hyung Kon Kim, "Korean Monetary and Credit Policy: A Study of Financial Policy in an Underdeveloped Country" (PhD dissertation, University of Washington, 1967). Most of them emphasize the role of monetary policy, the ineffectiveness of conventional monetary policy instruments, and the interrelations between foreign aid and domestic monetary changes.

14. Commercial bank loans increased by 60% between the end of 1957 and 1959. With negative overall price change for these two years, the real increase was slightly larger.

15. Wontack Hong and Anne O. Krueger, eds., *Trade and Development in Korea* (Seoul, 1975); Frank, Kim, and Westphal, *Foreign Trade Regimes;* Cole and Lyman, *Korean Development;* Wontack Hong, *Factor Supply;* Brown, *Korean Pricing Policies;* Anne O. Krueger, *The Developmental Role of the Foreign Sector and Aid* (Cambridge, Mass., 1979).

16. Jones, "Korean Financial Problems."

17. Hyman P. Minsky, *John Maynard Keynes* (New York, 1975).

18. EPB, *Major Statistics of the Korean Economy* (1976).

19. BOK, "The Role of Money in the Korean Economy," *Staff Papers* (June 1977).

20. S. W. Nam, "Dynamics of Inflation in Korea," KDI working paper 7813 (November 1978).

21. I. Otani and Y. C. Park, "A Monetary Model of the Korean Economy," *IMF Staff Papers* (March 1976).

22. BOK, *Han'guk ŭi kŭmyung chŏngch'aek* (December 1977), pp. 227–243.

23. This observation is based on the movements of some of major economic indicators used to calculate the BOK diffusion indices. See Table IV-1-4, BOK, *Financial Policy in Korea,* p. 232.

24. This statement requires qualification in that no one knows the features of the business cycles in the absence of any monetary policy actions.

25. Kim and Roemer, *Growth and Structural Transformation.*

NINE   *Financial Development and Economic Development*

1. See the quotation from Bloomfield, p. 139.

2. Wontack Hong, *Factor Supply,* pp. 79–80.

3. Mahn Je Kim, "Possibilities for Readjustment of the Interest Rates" (Korea Development Institute, June 1971).

4. Leroy P. Jones and Il SaKong, *Government, Business, and Entre-*

preneurship in Economic Development: The Korean Case (Cambridge, Mass., 1980), Chapter 8.

5. For a further discussion of the Japanese trading company, see L. B. Krause and S. Sekiguchi, "Japan and the World Economy," Chapter 6 in H. Patrick and H. Rosovsky, eds., *Asia's New Giant: How the Japanese Economy Works* (Washington, 1976), pp. 389–394.

TEN   *Lessons from the Korean Experience*

1. Wallich and Wallich characterize the Japanese financial system in the post-war period as a disequilibrium system. See H. C. Wallich and M. I. Wallich, "Banking and Finance," Chapter 5 in Patrick and Rosovsky, *Asia's New Giant*, p. 314.

2. Jones and SaKong, *Government, Business, and Entrepreneurship*, pp. 282–285.

Epilogue

1. See the articles by Mike Tharp and Shim Jae Hoon in the *Far Eastern Economic Review*, May 28, 1982.

2. *The Asian Wall Street Journal* carried almost daily articles on the development of and reactions to the scandal from late May through June 1982.

3. *The Asian Wall Street Journal*, June 17, 1982.

4. Ibid.

5. Article by Shim Jae Hoon in the *Far Eastern Economic Review*, July 9, 1982.

6. Ibid.

Bibliography

Asian Wall Street Journal, May and June 1982.

Ayre, P. C. I., ed. *Finance in Developing Countries.* London, Frank Cass, 1977.

Bailey, M. J. *National Income and the Price Level.* 2nd ed. New York, McGraw Hill, 1971.

Balassa, B. *Industrial Policies in Taiwan and Korea.* World Bank Working Paper no. 68. Washington, 1970.

Ban, Sung Hwan, Pal Yong Moon, and Dwight H. Perkins. *Rural Development.* Studies in the Modernization of the Republic of Korea: 1945–1975. Cambridge, Council on East Asian Studies, Harvard University, 1979.

Bank of Japan. *Money and Banking in Japan.* Trans. S. Nishimura. Ed. L. S. Pressnell. New York, St. Martin's Press, 1973.

Bank of Korea. *Annual Economic Review.* Various issues.

——. *Economics Statistics Yearbook.* Various issues.

——. *Financial Statement Analysis, 1975.* Seoul, August 1976.

——. *Financial System in Korea.* Seoul, 1974 and 1978.

——. *Flow of Funds Accounts in Korea, 1963-1977.* Seoul, 1978.

——. *General Review on Savings in Korea.* Seoul, 1978.

——. *Monetary Statistics of Korea.* 1963-1973.

——. *Monthly Economic Statistics.* February 1979.

——. *National Income in Korea.* Seoul, 1978.

——. *Report on the Results of the August 3, 1972 Presidential Emergency Decree.* Seoul, August 1973.

——. *Review on Price Index.* Seoul, 1949.

——. "The Role of Money in the Korean Economy," *Staff Papers* (June 1977).

——. *Survey of the Savings Behavior.* Seoul, 1967, 1969, 1971, 1973, 1976.

Han'guk Ŭnhaeng (Bank of Korea). *Chosa wŏlbo* (Monthly research review), Nobember 1972.

——. *Han'guk ŭi kŭmyung chŏngch'aek* (Financial policy in Korea). Seoul, December 1977.

——. *Ilban ŭnhaeng ŭi kyŏngyŏng kaesŏn ŭi wihan kaepyŏn pangan* (Suggestions for the improvement of commercial bank management). Seoul, 1970.

——. *Kiŏp kŭmyung mit sagŭmyung silt'ae chosa* (Survey of business financing and unregulated money markets). Quarterly report. Various issues since 1963.

——. *Mujin ŭi hŏnhwang kwa munje chŏm* (Current status and problems of *mujin*). Seoul, January 1972.

Bennett, R. L. *The Financial Sector and Economic Development: The Mexican Case*. Baltimore, Johns Hopkins University Press, 1965, 1966.

Bhatia, R. J., and D. R. Khatkhate. "Financial Intermediation, Saving Mobilization and Entrepreneurial Development: The African Experience," *International Monetary Fund Staff Papers* (March 1975).

Bloomfield, Arthur I. "Monetary and Financial Development in Korea." Mimeographed. 1952.

——. "A Report on Monetary Policy and Banking in Korea: Report submitted to the United Nations Command Economic Coordinator and to the Governor, Bank of Korea, 30 November 1956.

——. "Central Banking in Underdeveloped Countries," *Journal of Finance* (May 1957).

—— and J. P. Jensen. *Banking Reform in South Korea*. New York, Federal Reserve Bank, 1951.

Boskey, S. *Problems and Practices of Development Banks*. Baltimore, Johns Hopkins University Press, 1959.

Brown, Gilbert T. *Korean Pricing Policies and Economic Development in the 1960s*. Baltimore and London, Johns Hopkins University Press, 1973.

Cameron, Rondo, with the collaboration of O. Crisp, H. T. Patrick, and R. Tilly. *Banking in the Early Stages of Development: A Study in Comparative Economic History*. New York, Oxford University Press, 1967.

——, ed. *Banking and Economic Development: Some Lessons of History*. New York, Oxford University Press, 1972.

Campbell, D. C., and C. S. Ahn. "Kyes and Mujins—Financial Intermediaries in South Korea," *Economic Development and Cultural Change* (October 1962).

Central Federation of Fisheries Cooperatives. *Report on Fishing Household Credit Survey*. Seoul, August 1975.

Chandavarkar, A. D. "Some Aspects of Interest Rate Policies in Less Developed Economies: The Experience of Selected Asian Countries." *International Monetary Fund Staff Papers* (March 1971).

Chandler, L. V. *Central Banking and Economic Development.* Bombay, University of Bombay Studies in Monetary and International Economics No. 3, 1962.

Choi W. S., and H. J. Paik. "Sach'ae sijang ŭi naemak" (The inside story of the curb market), *Chungang wŏlgan* (December 1972).

Chosŏn Ilbo. Seoul daily newspaper.

Claassen, E. M. "On the Indirect Productivity of Money," *Journal of Political Economy* (April 1975).

Cline, William R., and Sidney Weintraub, eds. *Economic Stabilization in Developing Countries.* Washington, Brookings Institution, 1981.

Cole, David C. "Concepts, Causes and Cures of Instability in Less Developed Countries," in Ronald McKinnon, ed., *Money and Finance in Economic Growth and Development.* New York, Marcel Dekker, 1976.

—— and Princeton N. Lyman. *Korean Development: The Interplay of Politics and Economics.* Cambridge, Harvard University Press, 1971.

Diamond W. *Development Banks.* Baltimore, Johns Hopkins University Press, 1957.

——. *Development Finance Companies.* Baltimore, Johns Hopkins University Press, 1968.

Dong-A Ilbo. Seoul daily newspaper.

Dorrance, G. S. "The Instruments of Monetary Policy in Countries Without Highly Developed Capital Markets," *International Monetary Fund Staff Papers* (July 1965).

Drake, P. J. *Financial Development in Malaya and Singapore.* Canberra, Australian National University, 1969.

Economic Planning Board. *Major Statistics of the Korean Economy.* Seoul, 1976.

Evans, M. K. *Macroeconomic Activity: Theory, Forecasting, and Control.* New York, Harper and Row, 1969.

Far Eastern Economic Review, May 28, 1982, and July 9, 1982.

Firth, Raymond, and B. S. Yamey, eds., *Capital, Saving and Credit in Peasant Societies.* Chicago, Aldine, 1964.

Fischer, Stanley. "Money and Production Function," *Economic Inquiry* (December 1974).

Fousek, P. G. *Foreign Central Banking: The Instruments of Monetary Control.* New York, The Federal Reserve Bank, 1957.

Frank, C. R., K. S. Kim, and L. Westphal. *Foreign Trade Regimes and*

Economic Development: South Korea. New York, National Bureau of Economic Reserach, 1975.

Fry, Maxwell J. "Money and Capital or Financial Deepening in Economic Development?" *Journal of Money, Credit and Banking* 10.4 (November 1978).

Galbis, Vicente. "Financial Intermediation and Economic Growth in Less-developed Countries: A Theoretical Approach," *Journal of Development Studies* (January 1977).

Geertz, C. "The Rotating Credit Association: A 'Middle Rung' in Development," *Economic Development and Cultural Change* (April 1962).

Goldsmith, Raymond W. *Financial Institutions.* New York, Random House, 1968.

——. *Financial Structure and Development.* New Haven, Yale University Press, 1969.

Government General of Korea. *Korea Statistics Yearbook.*

Gurley, John G. "Financial Structure in Developing Countries," in D. Krivine, ed., *Fiscal and Monetary Problems in Developing States.* New York, Praeger, 1967.

—— and Edward S. Shaw. "Financial Aspects of Economic Development," *American Economic Review* (September 1955).

——. *Money in a Theory of Finance.* Washington, Brookings Institution, 1960.

——. "Financial Structure and Development," *Economic Development and Cultural Change* (April 1967).

Gurley, John G., Hugh T. Patrick, and Edward S. Shaw. "The Financial Structure of Korea." United States Operations Mission to Korea, July 1965.

Hasan, P. and D. C. Rao. *Korea: Policy Issues for Long-Term Development.* Baltimore, Johns Hopkins University Press for the World Bank, 1979.

Hong, Wontack. *Factor Supply and Factor Intensity of Trade in Korea.* Seoul, Korea Development Institute, 1976.

——. *Trade, Distortions, and Employment Growth in Korea.* Seoul, Korea Development Institute, 1979.

—— and Anne O. Krueger, eds. *Trade and Development in Korea.* Seoul, Korea Development Institute, 1975.

Jaffee, D. M. *Credit Rationing and the Commercial Loan Market.* New York, John Wiley, 1971.

Joel, Clark. "Korea: A Case Study in Inflation." PhD dissertation, University of Wisconsin, 1961.

Jones, Homer. "Korean Financial Problems." Report prepared for the United States Operations Mission to Korea. June 1968.

Jones, Leroy P., and Il SaKong. *Government, Business, and Entrepreneurship in Economic Development: The Korean Case.* Studies in the Modernization of the Republic of Korea: 1945-1975. Cambridge, Council on East Asian Studies, Harvard University, 1980.

Kanesa-Thason, S. "Stabilizing an Economy: The Korean Experience," in I. Adelman, ed., *Practical Approaches to Development Planning: Korea's Second Five-Year Plan.* Baltimore, Johns Hopkins University Press, 1969.

Kim, B. K. *Central Banking Experiment in a Developing Economy: Case Study of Korea.* The Korean Studies Series, Vol. 12. Seoul, The Korean Research Center, 1965.

Kim, Hyung Kon. "Korean Monetary and Credit Policy: A Study of Financial Policy in an Underdeveloped Country." PhD dissertation, University of Washington, 1967.

Kim, Kwang Suk, and Michael Roemer. *Growth and Structural Transformation.* Studies in the Modernization of the Republic of Korea: 1945-1975. Cambridge, Council on East Asian Studies, Harvard University, 1979.

Kim, Mahn Je. "Possibilities for Readjustment of the Interest Rates." Seoul, Korea Development Institute. June 1971.

Korea Development Finance Corporation. *Money and Capital Markets in Korea and the Potential for Their Improvement: A Proposal.* Seoul, September 1970.

Korea Development Institute. *Korea's Economy: Past and Present.* Seoul, May 1975.

———. *Long-Term Prospects for Economic and Social Development 1977-91.* Seoul, 1978.

Korea Stock Exchange. *Stock.* Seoul, February 1979.

Krause, L. B., and S. Sekiguchi. "Japan and the World Economy," in H. Patrick and H. Rosovsky, eds., *Asia's New Giant: How the Japanese Economy Works.* Washington, The Brookings Institution, 1976.

Krueger, Anne O. *The Developmental Role of the Foreign Sector and Aid.* Studies in the Modernization of the Republic of Korea: 1945-1975. Cambridge, Council on East Asian Studies, Harvard University, 1979.

Kuznets, Paul W. *Economic Growth and Structure in the Republic of Korea.* New Haven, Yale University Press, 1977.

Lee, Chang-Nyol. *Mobilization of Domestic Capital.* Seoul, Korea University Press, 1965.

Lee, Chang-Nyol. "The Unorganized Money Market and Interest Rates in Korea." Unpublished manuscript. 1965.

Lee, H. B. *Time, Change, and Administration: Korea's Search for Modernization.* Honolulu, University Press of Hawaii, 1968.

Leff, N. H., and K. Sato. "A Simultaneous-Equations Model of Savings in Developing Countries," *Journal of Political Economy* (December 1975).

Lewis, W. Arthur. *The Theory of Economy Growth.* Homewood, R. D. Irwin, 1955.

Light, J. O., and William L. White. *The Financial System.* New York, John Wiley, 1979.

Lyons, Gene M. *Military Policy and Economic Aid, the Korean Case, 1950-1953.* Columbus, Ohio State University Press, 1961.

Marquez, J. "Financial Institutions and Economic Development," in H. S. Ellis, ed., *Economic Development for Latin America.* New York, St. Martin's Press, 1961.

Mason, Edward S., Mahn Je Kim, Dwight H. Perkins, Kwang Suk Kim, David C. Cole. *The Economic and Social Modernization of the Republic of Korea.* Studies in the Modernization of the Republic of Korea: 1945-1975. Cambridge, Council on East Asian Studies, Harvard University, 1980.

McGinn, Noel F., Donald R. Snodgrass, Yung Bong Kim, Shin-Bok Kim, Quee-Young Kim. *Education and Development in Korea.* Studies in the Modernization of the Republic of Korea: 1945-1975. Cambridge, Council on East Asian Studies, Harvard University, 1979.

McKinnon, Ronald I. *Money and Capital in Economic Development.* Washington, The Brookings Institution, 1973.

———. "Money, Growth, and the Propensity to Save: An Iconoclastic View." Stanford University, Research Center in Economic Growth, Research Memoranda Series, Memorandum #135. 1973.

———, ed. *Money and Finance in Economic Growth and Development.* New York, Marcel Dekker, 1976.

Mills, Edwin S., and Byung-Nak Song. *Urbanization and Urban Problems.* Studies in the Modernization of the Republic of Korea: 1945-1975. Cambridge, Council on East Asian Studies, Harvard University, 1979.

Min, B. K. "Financial Reconstruction in Korea 1965-74." PhD dissertation, University of Hawaii, 1976.

Ministry of Finance. *Uri nara kŭmyung chedo mit chŏngch'aek kaegwan* (Outline of banking system and policy in Korea). Seoul, August 1966.

———. *Sŏmin kŭmyung mit mujin hyŏnhwang* (Current status of popular funds and *mujin*). Finance Research Report No. 10. June 1972.

Ministry of Justice. *Taehanmin'guk hyŏnhaeng pŏmnyŏngjip* (Laws and decrees of the Republic of Korea).

Minsky, Hyman P. *John Maynard Keynes.* Essays on the Great Economists. New York, Columbia University Press, 1975.

Moskowitz, Karl. "Current Assets: The Employees of Japanese Banks in Colonial Korea." PhD dissertation, Harvard University, 1979.

Mundell, R. *Monetary Theory.* Pacific Palisades, Goodyear, 1971.

Myint, H. *Economic Theory and the Underdeveloped Countries.* London, Oxford University Press, 1971.

Nam, Chong Hyun. "Trade and Industrial Policies and the Structure of Protection in Korea," in Wontack Hong and Lawrence B. Krause, eds., *Trade and Growth of the Advanced Developing Countries in the Pacific Basin.* Seoul, Korea Development Institute, 1981.

Nam, S. W. "Dynamics of Inflation in Korea." Korea Development Institute working paper 7813. November 1978.

Nevin, Edward. *Capital Funds in Underdeveloped Countries.* London, Macmillan, 1961.

Newlyn, W. T. *The Financing of Economic Development.* London, Oxford University Press, 1977.

Oh, K. C. "The Economics of Kye: An Informal Association of Individuals for Savings and Loans." PhD dissertation, Vanderbilt University, 1972.

Otani, I., and Y. C. Park. "A Monetary Model of the Korean Economy," *International Monetary Fund Staff Papers* (March 1976).

Palais, James B. *Politics and Policy in Traditional Korea.* Cambridge, Harvard University Press, 1975.

Park, Y. C. *The Unorganized Financial Sector in Korea, 1945–75.* Studies in Domestic Finance No. 28. Washington, International Bank for Reconstruction and Development, November 1976.

Patrick, H. T. "Financial Development and Economic Growth in Underdeveloped Countries," *Economic Developmen and Cultural Change* (January 1972).

Psilos, D. D. *Capital Market in Greece.* Athens, Center of Economic Research, 1964.

Ranis, Gustav. "Economic Development and Financial Institutions," in Bela Balassa and Richard Nelson, eds., *Economic Progress, Private Values and Public Policy: Essays in Honor of William Fellner.* Amsterdam, North Holland Publishing Co., 1977.

SaKong, Il. "An Overview of Corporate Finance and the Long-term Securities Market," in C. K. Kim, ed., *Planning Model and Macroeconomic Policy Issues*. Essays in the Korean Economy, Vol. 1. Seoul, Korea Development Institute, 1977.

Sayers, R. S. "Central Banking in Under-Developed Countries," in *Central Banking after Bagehot*. London, Oxford University Press, 1957.

Securities Supervisory Board. *Chŭnggwŏn chosa wŏlbo* (Monthly review). Various issues.

Sen, S. N. *Central Banking in Under-Developed Money Markets*. 3rd ed. Calcutta, Bookland Limited, 1961.

Shaw, Edward S. *Financial Deepening in Economic Development*. New York, Oxford University Press, 1973.

Shim, B. K., et al. *A Study of Preferential Interest Rate Structure—The Korean Experience, 1963-1971*. Seoul, October 1972.

Sinai, A., and H. H. Stokes. "Real Money Balances: An Omitted Variable from the Production Function," *Review of Economics and Statistics* (August 1972).

Sogang University Research Institute for Economics and Business. "Study of Money Market and Industrial Investment Financing in Korea." Mimeographed. November 1970.

Suh, Sang-Chul. *Growth and Structural Changes in the Korean Economy, 1910-1940*. Cambridge, Council on East Asian Studies, Harvard University, 1978.

Tucker, D. P. "Credit Rationing, Interest Lags, and Monetary Speed Lag," *Quarterly Journal of Economics* (February 1968).

Wai, U Tun. "Interest Rates in the Organized Money Markets of Underdeveloped Countries," *International Monetary Fund Staff Papers* 5.2 (August 1956).

——. "Interest Rates Outside the Organized Money Markets of Underdeveloped Countries," *International Monetary Fund Staff Papers* 6.1 (November 1957).

——. *Financial Intermediaries and National Savings in Developing Countries*. New York, Praeger, 1972.

—— and Hugh T. Patrick. "Stock and Bond Issues and Capital Markets in Less Developed Countries," *International Monetary Fund Staff Papers* (July 1973).

Wallich, H. C., and M. I. Wallich. "Banking and Finance," in H. Patrick and H. Rosovsky, eds., *Asia's New Giant: How the Japanese Economy Works*. Washington, The Brookings Institution, 1976.

Westphal, Larry E., and Kwang Suk Kim, "The Inter-Industrial Structure of Policy and Development in Korea." Development Research Center, International Bank for Reconstruction and Development," Washington, 1974.

———. "Industrial Policy and Development in Korea." International Bank for Reconstruction and Development Staff Working Paper No. 263. Washington, August 1977.

Williamson, J. F. "Why Do Koreans Save 'So Little'?" *Journal of Development Economics* 6 (1979).

Yi Yun-sŏk. "Sŏmin kŭmyung ŭi silche wa tayanghwa" (Small loans business for consumers and small enterprises), *Kŭmyung* (November 1972).

Index

Government intervention *(continued)*
186, 195, 211, 283, 289; and price
stabilization, 212-259, 287; and import-substitution policy, 263-264; and
industrialization, 276, 287; and balance
of power, 292-293. *See also* Credit, allocation of; Exports
Great Depression, 5, 215
Growth: and inflation, 9, 12, 213, 223,
227-231, 233, 259; periods of, 13-14,
35, 165, 277; and rate of investment,
138-139; and reform of 1965, 211,
266; as prime objective, 245, 253-259.
See also Development, economic; Presidential Emergency Decree of August
3, 1972
Gurley, John G., 3-4, 10, 14, 25, 201,
242, 282

Harrod-Domar growth model, 138
Hong, Wontack, 191, 193, 194
Households: loans to, 59, 111, 112, 128,
170; savings of, 30, 34, 192-193, 237,
290

Import-substitution, policy of, 11-12,
174-175, 180, 263-264, 267, 268; and
control over credit allocation, 275,
277-278
Imports: financing of, 188-189, 234,
236, 268-269; increase in, 204, 223;
liberalization policy on, 208; and inflation, 213, 226, 229; and foreign aid,
249; and growth, 259, 266, 292. *See
also* Exports; Import-substitution, policy of
Inch'ŏn, 44
Industrial Bank, 49, 52
Industrial Development Corporation, 58
Industry, chemical, 77, 78, 276, 278
Industry, construction, 176, 184, 195
Industry, petrochemical, 176, 197, 234,
277
Industry, public utility, 174, 182, 195
Industry, steel, 176, 197, 277
Inflation: and interest rates, 8-9, 139,
140, 161, 162, 200, 204, 206; and
economic growth, 9, 12, 214; history
of, 13, 48-49, 51, 52, 58, 59, 212-
239; during colonial period, 135, 137,

214-215; effect of 1965 reform on,
159, 203; suppressed (1976-1978),
235-239; average rate of, 245; and export drive, 268-269; as result of oil
crisis, 271. *See also* Money supply;
Prices
Interest rates, 8-10, 49, 77-78, 81, 89,
285; reform of (1965), 30, 34, 64, 89,
102, 180, 198-211, 265, 267, 268; in
credit associations *(kye)*, 114; government policy on, 137-148, 248, 275,
282; in unregulated financial markets,
143-148, 159, 160, 161; in LDCs, 150,
172; disparity of in financial markets,
170, 189; subsidized, 189-197, 202,
208, 286; and savings, 204-206, 271,
285; and scandal of 1982, 296. *See
also* Deposit money banks (DMBs);
Presidential Emergency Decree of August 3, 1972
Interest Rates Restriction Act, 139
Intermediation, 3, 4, 29-38, 42, 71, 171,
266; in traditional sector, 134-135,
136; and credit allocation policies, 184;
and trading companies, 279; financial
institutions for, 282, 290
International Monetary Fund (IMF), 214,
231, 258, 286
Investment: government allocation of,
10, 86-87, 96, 161-162, 236, 286,
291; types of companies, 42, 81-83;
and interest rates, 138; debt financing
of, 160-161, 233; fixed, of business,
168, 236; and growth, 292. *See also*
Savings

Japan: as model, 11, 25, 35, 57, 125,
276, 282, 288; colonial rule of, 13, 18,
20, 21, 105, 134-135, 136, 138; Korean relations with, 43-50, 60; treaty
settlement with, 203; exports to, 234
Jensen, J. P., 48, 49, 50-51, 58, 66; on
inflation, 215-219; on causes of monetary expansion, 220
Jones, Homer, 8, 66
Jones, Leroy, 284

kaekchu (informal lenders for fisheries
industry), 121, 122-123
Kanghwa Agreement (1876), 43

Harvard East Asian Monographs

46. W. P. J. Hall, *A Bibliographical Guide to Japanese Research on the Chinese Economy, 1958–1970*

47. Jack J. Gerson, *Horatio Nelson Lay and Sino-British Relations, 1854–1864*

48. Paul Richard Bohr, *Famine and the Missionary: Timothy Richard as Relief Administrator and Advocate of National Reform*

49. Endymion Wilkinson, *The History of Imperial China: A Research Guide*

50. Britten Dean, *China and Great Britain: The Diplomacy of Commerical Relations, 1860–1864*

51. Ellsworth C. Carlson, *The Foochow Missionaries, 1847–1880*

52. Yeh-chien Wang, *An Estimate of the Land-Tax Collection in China, 1753 and 1908*

53. Richard M. Pfeffer, *Understanding Business Contracts in China, 1949–1963*

54. Han-sheng Chuan and Richard Kraus, *Mid-Ch'ing Rice Markets and Trade, An Essay in Price History*

55. Ranbir Vohra, *Lao She and the Chinese Revolution*

56. Liang-lin Hsiao, *China's Foreign Trade Statistics, 1864–1949*

57. Lee-hsia Hsu Ting, *Government Control of the Press in Modern China, 1900–1949*

58. Edward W. Wagner, *The Literati Purges: Political Conflict in Early Yi Korea*

59. Joungwon A. Kim, *Divided Korea: The Politics of Development, 1945–1972*

60. Noriko Kamachi, John K. Fairbank, and Chūzō Ichiko, *Japanese Studies of Modern China Since 1953: A Bibliographical Guide to Historical and Social-Science Research on the Nineteenth and Twentieth Centuries, Supplementary Volume for 1953–1969*

61. Donald A. Gibbs and Yun-chen Li, *A Bibliography of Studies and Translations of Modern Chinese Literature, 1918–1942*

62. Robert H. Silin, *Leadership and Values: The Organization of Large-Scale Taiwanese Enterprises*

63. David Pong, *A Critical Guide to the Kwangtung Provincial Archives Deposited at the Public Record Office of London*

64. Fred W. Drake, *China Charts the World: Hsu Chi-yü and His Geography of 1848*

65. William A. Brown and Urgunge Onon, translators and annotators, *History of the Mongolian People's Republic*

66. Edward L. Farmer, *Early Ming Government: The Evolution of Dual Capitals*

67. Ralph C. Croizier, *Koxinga and Chinese Nationalism: History, Myth, and the Hero*

68. William J. Tyler, tr., *The Psychological World of Natsumi Sōseki*, by Doi Takeo

STUDIES IN THE MODERNIZATION OF THE REPUBLIC OF KOREA: 1945–1975